8|q5

Two
LIVES

The Political and Business Careers of
EDWARD DU CANN

For JENIFER

One day, I pray,
we shall be together again

Two LIVES

The Political and Business Careers of
EDWARD DU CANN

IMAGES
PUBLISHING

First published in Great Britain 1995 by
Images Publishing (Malvern) Ltd
Upton upon Severn
Worcestershire

British Library Cataloguing in Publication Data

A catalogue record for this book is available
from the British Library

ISBN 1 897817 60 6

Designed and Produced by Images Publishing (Malvern) Ltd.
Printed and Bound in Great Britain by Bookcraft, Bath, Avon.

CONTENTS

Note

---

*The majority of the political cartoons in this book have been
reproduced from Sir Edward's private collection of originals.
Some have been created by the publisher's artist, Chris Redman.*

There are so many people I wish to thank.

Those who helped me with this book: the publisher, my agent, editors, designers, typists – a legion of enthusiasts who patiently and enthusiastically guided this novice author along correct paths.

In my two lives in business and in politics, over three score years and ten, I have been fortunate indeed to enjoy the support, camaraderie and friendship of so many good people; not least from the worthy and independent electors (as the old phrase correctly has it) in Taunton and Somerset.

Now, life for me these last few years has been, in the Old Testament mode, a proper Job's journey. Without the constant and generous encouragement of so many old, good friends the journey could not have been attempted, let alone made.

I am so deeply grateful to them all.

Out of loyalty to the Conservative Party, I have kept silent for almost four years since the Government sanctioned civil proceedings against me and I retired. I have been in purdah long enough. The more I contemplate the events in which I was involved the surer I have become that it is right that my experiences should be told, recommendations made for the future, scandals and mistakes revealed. Maybe that will help to ensure that the trust which the Tories enjoyed in my years in Parliament is recovered. For certain, it has been lost. If some lessons can be learned by those who govern, and the mistakes are not repeated, I shall be wholly content. For clearly, this will be in the general interest.

Edward du Cann
Alderney – May 1995

A NOVICE
in the HOUSE

It was the highest point my life had reached. A brand-new MP, entering the House of Commons for the first time, I was being led into the Chamber amid a bedlam of noise, cheers from my fellow Tories and counter-cheers from the Labour benches. The House was pretty full. The two established Members who were introducing me marched on either side; on my right Edward Heath, then Government Chief Whip, on my left John Peyton, MP for Yeovil, the neighbouring seat to Taunton where I had just won the February 1956 by-election to become, at the age of thirty-one, the constituency's youngest ever MP.

The ritual for these occasions is rigidly prescribed. We had rehearsed it several times: stand shoulder to shoulder at the Bar of the House, bow together when the Speaker calls, march five paces, bow again, another five paces and then you're on your own with uproar going on all round you. Despite the rehearsals, when the Clerk at the Despatch Box presented the Register for me to sign after I had taken the oath of allegiance my hand was trembling so badly it was hard to write my name.

It continued to be a disconcerting morning. After I had shaken hands with the Speaker I left the Chamber in accordance with custom. There's public life in Britain for you: one moment you're the centre of attention among a crowd, a hero perhaps to some; the next you're alone and a nobody again. The calm of an empty corridor was eerie after the row in the Chamber. Unsteadily, I found my way to the Smoke Room. Although it was only eleven o'clock I ordered myself a drink. I thought I deserved it. I was alone and feeling good. I picked up a newspaper. Was there anything about Taunton's new MP in it? I wondered.

A giant of a man sat down in a chair uncomfortably close to mine. I had no idea who he was. Every other chair in the room was empty. Why didn't he sit somewhere else?

He glared at me. 'I suppose you think me an utter bastard,' he said.

I stuttered a reply. 'No, no, not at all.'

Who on earth was this madman? I looked about for help if it should be needed. Luckily there was a steward nearby.

'Don't lie to me, boy,' said the man. 'I had to be a bastard. That was my job.'

I thought he seemed angry. It was time to get reinforcement. I waved at the steward, who came over. The man ordered a drink too, and it was not until then that he introduced himself as the former Chief Whip, Ted Heath's predecessor, Patrick Buchan-Hepburn, now Lord Hailes, the disciplinarian who kept the Government's small majority intact in a difficult Parliament between Churchill's re-election in 1951 and the general election in 1955. Telling me about this, his manner changed abruptly. He became friendly and affable and gave me a lot of good advice which I never forgot.

It was an odd beginning to a Parliamentary career. I suppose I was all the more taken aback because I knew even on my first day that I was being frowned on as something of a maverick. That was not my intention at all, but the truth was that I had already disobeyed orders. I should have taken my seat the previous day and the Government whips had been pressing me hard to do so. Their reason, as I found out later, was to avoid giving the Labour Party the chance for a demonstration in the Chamber over the arrival of a new Member just when Harold Macmillan, then Chancellor of the Exchequer, was due to make an unwelcome announcement of economic retrenchment. (He was in fact doing so, and being loudly shouted at by Labour MPs, while I was sitting in the Smoke Room.)

The Opposition had been given an easy line of attack: the new restrictive measures came only nine months after the Conservative Government had been elected to carry out a programme of economic expansion. At such a vulnerable moment the Party managers felt that a new boy should do as he was told, take his seat on the day before the Chancellor made his statement and not make their life any harder. But I had another priority. I had earlier arranged to tour my constituency to thank the supporters whose hard work .and enthusiasm had made my narrow victory possible, and I would not break my promise. I owed everything to my friends in Taunton. It would be a poor show if my first act as an MP was to demonstrate a careless ingratitude.

It was typical of the Conservative Party's attitude at that time that nobody had thought to tell me why I should enter the House on the earlier day. Too often the feeling at the top of the organisation was that backbench MPs (and, still more, constituency workers) were like the troops in the First World War. Their business was to go over the top when the whistle blew and not ask questions; theirs to do and die while the generals got the credit and the medals. All through my political life I fought against that approach, and it was this more than anything that separated my views from Edward Heath's when we had to work together during his leadership of the Tory Party. It was not the only difference we had but to me it was the most important.

A democracy is a state whose rulers have won an open competition for power. Anyone with experience of that competition knows how often it can be bruising, tedious and bitterly disappointing. To persist in the struggle until one reaches the top demands strong motivation. To adapt a wise saying from another field, if you ask a hundred politicians whether they enjoy the exercise of power ninety will say they do and the other ten will be lying.

I would never pretend that I myself felt a saintly indifference to the seductions of power. I have always enjoyed being in charge. What I do claim is that I understood and sympathised with the democratic roots from which that power should grow. One of the things of which I am most proud in a political career that lasted for more than three decades is that when I was Chairman of the Conservative Party I developed a structure and style of working that allowed the ordinary Party members and constituency workers to feel that they mattered, that the hard work they did would be appreciated and used effectively, and that they could, and should, contribute ideas which the Party leaders had to take seriously. The result of this was that ideas did indeed flow and when we came to fight the general election of 1970 we did so on the basis of a whole new platform of radical and exciting policies, and with a Party machine that worked vigorously and efficiently. Later, when I came to chair the 1922 Committee, it was my job to represent the backbench Members of the Tory Party and to see that their voices were heard. Since they re-elected me as Chairman for a record number of years I suppose they must have felt that I did the job satisfactorily.

It is a sad theme of this book that in recent years much of what my fellow workers and I achieved in democratising the Party has been apparently neglected and allowed to decay. The result is discontent and disaffection to an extent that threatens the Party's unity, along with a dearth of new ideas and a sense among the electorate that apart from a slavish adherence to Thatcherite dogma the Tories have run out of steam.

The same intention of shifting power towards the bottom of the pyramid has been at work in my business career. What I am most proud of there is that I inaugurated the modern British unit trust industry, through which ordinary people could invest their money in British and overseas businesses – often in quite modest amounts – giving them remarkable opportunities in consequence for the accumulation of capital.

To me, the thing that makes a free market socially just and also gives it stability and staying-power, is that the ownership of commercial enterprises should be spread as widely as possible. A 'share-owning democracy' is not a mere political slogan. It is the only viable alternative to the twin evils of oligarchy (domination by a small rich elite) and socialism (domination by a small political elite). It is also worth noticing a point which was made unmistakably clear to me during the struggle between Lonrho and the Fayeds over the ownership of the House of Fraser and Harrods: the small shareholder (and Lonrho had many small shareholders) can sometimes have a shrewder insight into the situation than the financiers, accountants and lawyers who claim such professional expertise and charge so heavily for it.

This philosophy of practical Conservatism was already quite clearly formed in my mind by the time I found myself sitting in the Smoke Room of the House of Commons that February morning in 1956. Of course I didn't know then what roads it was going to lead me down in the future, but if I had known I suppose I would have felt a mixture of pleasure and exhilaration at the journey ahead, tinged with sadness at the way things were to turn out. One thing, though, was perhaps already predictable: I was never going to find it easy to practise docile conformity. I was my own man, I hope. Incomplete, not always right, but true to my principles and my friends. And on the whole I must admit I'm pleased rather than sorry that there have always been some people who have taken the same view of my later self as the Party managers did of that young man who disregarded their orders in 1956: That fellow du Cann – a bit of an awkward blighter.

10

CHAPTER 1

FAMILY
AFFAIRS

When I was ten or eleven my family became seasonal migrants. For most of the year our home was in a seaside village near Worthing, but each summer, for several years, we moved to a place in Gloucestershire, a wooden shack with a corrugated iron roof, no electricity, no bathroom and no indoor sanitation. A little stream, a tributary of the Windrush, flowed by the back door; on sunny days my brother and I took a cake of soap and scrubbed ourselves in its cold waters.

The summers I remember most clearly were 1938 and 1939, just before the War. A new RAF airfield was being built nearby by Irish labourers who got drunk at the weekends. The wireless played 'Red Sails in the Sunset' incessantly and my mother, my brother and I went everywhere by bicycle. I played cricket for the nearby village of Little Rissington. Some evenings we lowered nets baited with rotten meat into the river and pulled up crayfish which hid in the weed and came out to feed on this foul attraction. How could they possibly smell the bait under water? I wondered. Mother cooked the crayfish in a rice kedgeree on the oil stove. Used as we were to a fairly restricted diet, these delicacies became our favourite food.

Those were happy days, but I have to say that it was not a romantic love of the simple life that took us to our summer home. It was shortage of money. Mother could sub-let our Sussex house for more than she paid to rent the Gloucestershire shack and she badly needed the difference. We were what would now be called a one-parent family, my parents having divorced when I was nine and my younger brother five. My father remarried but my mother did not. Her life was devoted to her children and to the financial struggle to keep the little family going.

Divorce in those days was not taken lightly. It spoiled my father's career and my mother never got over the hurt of it. It was all the more

11

sad because their early life together had been so full of happiness and promise. She used to tell me how they would go to the theatre and she would long for the interval to come so that she could listen to my father talk: he was so much more interesting than any play.

My parents had met without benefit of formal introduction. Mother, a pharmacist, was working in a chemist's shop in Holborn. Father was not long out of the army at the end of the 1914-1918 War. He came into the shop wearing a blue suit and brown boots. Mother thought this perfectly extraordinary: no gentleman in those days would wear brown shoes with a blue suit. While Mother was dispensing some concoction for him she asked him how he came to be dressed so unconservatively. Father gave the simple explanation that they were the boots he had become used to wearing in the army. They were comfortable and he really didn't mind what other people thought. One thing led to another and they ran away to Devon to be married in a church that was not registered for marriages, Saint Michael's, Honiton.

By the time I arrived in the world my father was a barrister and they were living in a flat in Gray's Inn. As a young child I loved the place. The flat had four rooms but only one gas fire; father would stand with his back to it and scorch his trousers. We got the hot water in the bathroom from a monstrous geyser. I always expected, half in terror, half in pleasurable anticipation, that one day it would blow up. The floors on the Gray's Inn Road side of the old building sloped abominably; that was also the noisy side, since there was a tram terminus outside our windows and at five-thirty every morning the trams started up with a clatter that went on all day. The other side was quiet and peaceful, overlooking the Inn gardens where I used to bicycle round and round with the only other child living in the Inn apart from my brother and myself. I don't think that the staid Benchers of the Inn approved of that, or indeed of children being there at all. When my younger brother committed the impertinence of actually getting himself born there my father was accosted by the Under Treasurer, a Mr Doughty. In a voice that thrilled with anger Doughty said to him: 'I hear you have a son born in the Inn.'

'Yes,' said my father with some pride, 'my second son, you know.'

'Damn it,' said Doughty, 'that's illegal. No children have been allowed to be born in the Inn since the days of Queen Elizabeth.'

I myself had not been guilty of the same indiscretion. Either my mother had miscalculated or I was so fearful of coming into this wicked and troubled world that I delayed my entrance as long as I could. At any rate I was late arriving. Both my parents got bored waiting for me and my mother went off to stay with her parents in Beckenham, where I finally emerged. It was a good house in which to be born. My mother's father was a Scotsman whose family came from the Isle of Arran. He was a splendid man, an engineer by profession, and had made his living in the Far East acting as an agent for British manufacturers of machinery. My grandmother, who came from farming stock in Shropshire, had courageously voyaged out alone to Singapore to marry him, and if ever it was truly written of a couple that they lived happily ever after it was true of this lovely pair. Grandfather, for all his strength, was modest and retiring. Grandmother more than made up for that. She was tough, formidable and indomitable. I was devoted to them both.

Grandfather had come back from the Far East to retire early, as was the habit in those days. He set up an export-import business in Victoria, which gave him an occupation and an excuse to travel up and down to London each day. When I stayed in the house in Beckenham as a small boy he always brought me home a present in the evening. A stick of rock was my favourite: I got that if I kept quiet while my hair was cut. I never let on how much I enjoyed both things.

13

My grandparents on my father's side were very different. His mother, May Lott, came from an old and respected family in Honiton which had once owned fine houses and land in the district and had provided it with a Port Reeve (the equivalent of a mayor today) and a Member of Parliament. The family had, however, fallen victim to tragic bad luck, typified by the fate of my great grandfather, Herman James Lott, who died in prison in Exeter. Visiting that town one day he suffered a heart attack in the street. The ignorant people who found him lying on the pavement did not realise he was ill. They threw him in the drunkards' cell and there he expired before his family could rescue him. I have always held a grudge against Exeter.

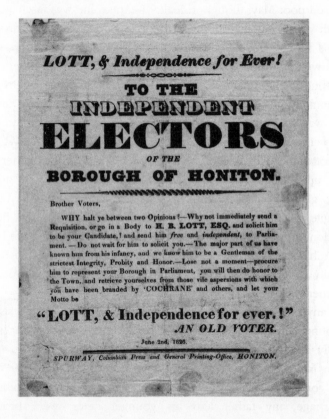

The Lott family was ruined when it turned to banking, in partnership with another family, the Floods. They lent money to their friends and neighbours, as local banks did, mostly on the security of their property, and when a run on the bank came, engineered so it is said by rivals in Exeter, they had the assets but not the liquid resources to meet it. This ending of the bank's life was felt by our family to be shameful, though there was nothing improper in their conduct of affairs. Many banks at the beginning of the nineteenth century faced runs on their deposits, often engineered by rivals, and failed in consequence. Before going out of business the Flood and Lott partnership managed to meet its liabilities in full, but all the family property had to be sold, and when May Lott ran off with Mr du Cann she was a poor spinster.

Impoverished or not, the family did not like the marriage and thoroughly disapproved of my grandfather. He was supposedly an American professor of science but he earned his living as a lecturer (which was quite fashionable in those days) and he gave readings. He was besides something of a public entertainer, a conjuror of sorts and even a hypnotist. The Lott family unkindly supposed that he must have hypnotised poor May, though in reality I expect she was fascinated by his way with words, his man-of-the-world manner and his air of mystery. He made his money travelling round the West Country villages and town halls, as well as further afield, and many years ago a constituent of mine showed me a cutting from a West Somerset newspaper referring to an 'entertainment' given by a Mr du Cann in the Town Hall at Dulverton. I guess it was my grandfather. The name du Cann is unusual and indeed I have never met any other du Canns in England, though it may be an old Huguenot name. However, I have wondered if my grandfather did not make it up; Cann is a West Country name and perhaps he added the prefix to give a certain glamour to his stage appearances. It would have been quite in character for a man who certainly did not feel bound by conventional rules. My father used to excuse his odd way of life by telling me that Charles Dickens too earned his living by giving readings and this was really a very respectable occupation. I think the reality is that my grandfather was probably a bit of a bounder.

At any rate it is said that he died when my father and his sister were very young, my father just three years old. Though father searched devotedly all his life he never found my grandfather's grave. I suspect the man just went off – but who is to tell? Alas, poor May du Cann died of consumption, then a common disease, and the two children of the marriage, my father and his younger sister, were brought up charitably in a Protestant convent in Derbyshire. They were shown affection and solicitude, but for all that they were lonely and had no resources.

The convent education gave my father two interests which remained with him all his life. One was religion, the other was writing. As a boy he won prizes for essays on religious subjects: later in life he used to contribute articles to the atheistic magazine *The Freethinker*, though he kept the habit of regular churchgoing. It was his skill in writing that first provided him with a career. He left school when he was eleven and quite soon afterwards began to earn his living as a teacher. Not surprisingly, such an immature schoolmaster found it hard to keep discipline but he stuck at it for several years and all the time he never stopped writing. This earned him some badly needed money and it also introduced him to some influential people. After his death I found among his papers letters that he had exchanged over the years with distinguished authors, among them Arthur Quiller Couch, Bernard Shaw and Arnold Bennett. When he turned to journalism as the chief source of his income he wrote to Lord Northcliffe, the newspaper tycoon. Northcliffe agreed to see him, was impressed by his portfolio of writings and offered him employment. Father was lucky enough to overhear Northcliffe on the telephone instructing the editor of the *Evening News* to give him a job so when he went for his interview with the editor he knew he was safe. (At that time father was so unsophisticated a country bumpkin that he had never previously seen a telephone, let alone used one.) The editor of the *Evening News* refused to make it easy for him but eventually a deal was struck, as father knew it had to be, and he was put on the staff. He was paid five golden sovereigns a week and his digs in Saint James's Square cost him only thirty shillings with full board. 'I lived like a fighting cock,' he used to say. His bank was a pocket in an unused jacket in his wardrobe: he enjoyed feeling its growing weight as he saved money each week.

Then in August 1914 came the War. Father immediately volunteered for the army and was accepted. Northcliffe congratulated him warmly: 'You are just the stuff, my boy, of which England is or ought to be made.' He went on, 'Don't worry, I'll speak to Kitchener and see you have a commission, and you'll be back again working for me within four weeks.' It was generally believed that what turned out to be a filthy four-year struggle would last for a glorious month or two at most.

Father drilled for a few days on the barrack square with a broomstick. Then his commission came through and within a short time he was in France and in the trenches. In those days most officers had sources of income other than their pay, which was not enough to allow them to settle all their bills. Father was one of a few volunteer, non-regular officers and the army's arrangements at the beginning of the War were not designed to accommodate a vast civilian influx. He had a bad time in France. He endured not only the horror of it – the death, the mud, the filth and the agony – but also the appalling financial embarrassment of not being able to pay his mess bills. He decided to earn money writing short articles and selling them to newspapers in England, notably the *Daily Mirror*. It was hardly the thing for a serving officer to be at the same time a journalist and it was certainly frowned on, if not despised, by his fellow officers.

It was during the War that my father decided to become a barrister. He obtained some law books and kept them with him in the trenches. I possess them still. Some pages are spoiled by candle grease where he had pored over them during the night watches or in the dugouts which would be dark when the sun was shining brightly outside. He took his bar exams while he was in France, obtaining leave for a day or two at a time in order to do so. It was an astonishing performance.

I remember him telling me once how he had been faced with a question on one of his papers that he could not answer, and indeed the whole paper seemed a mystery. He had had no one to teach him and obviously he had prepared the wrong material. He wrote in one of his answers, 'I have been in the trenches in France, where such things as this are not understood.' He was passed by an examiner whom I can only assume to have been patriotically sympathetic.

The day when he was scheduled to go to England to take his Bar Final his Colonel refused him leave. It was just before a 'push' – an attack. 'I can't let you go, du Cann. If you go now everyone will think it's cowardice.' father protested that he had not fixed the date of the examination and had never made any secret of his intention to ask for leave to take it. The Colonel still refused. Father appealed to the General. The General said, 'If that young man thinks he'll still be alive in a fortnight's time he's welcome to go to London on a port-to-port leave of forty-eight hours.' father went to London, took his examination and passed. Though he took part in other pushes he proved the General wrong; he survived not just the fortnight but the whole War.

After the War father became a successful barrister and he also continued to write indefatigably. He turned out a multitude of articles and no less than seventeen books. The most successful one, *The Secret Hand*, was the tale of a murder committed by an ape: it went into a paperback edition and made him a good deal of money. The time for writing had to be found in what was already a busy life, but father was a tireless worker. He was developing his criminal practice at the Bar and was highly thought of among his contemporaries. He was eccentric, there is no doubt about that, and he was known as 'The Duke'. Like all the best barristers who work before juries (and like the best politicians) he was to an extent an actor. He was a brilliant advocate, a better advocate than a lawyer, and he had a busy practice. He was in court almost every day and used to work far into the night on his briefs for the following day's appearances. Among my best memories are the days I spent with him in court, taking a note. When I was a boy I thought the Bar was the most splendid profession in the World.

He was an ambitious man. He stood twice as a Parliamentary candidate, unsuccessfully. Those were the days when cash bought a safe Tory seat, a practice which was not outlawed by the Party until after World War Two. He was baffled in a third attempt when the local Conservatives withdrew their invitation on hearing of his divorce.

That divorce was the pivotal point of my childhood and I am sorry to say that the whole business showed my father in his worst light. For years he had been consistently unfaithful to my mother and in 1933 she felt she could endure it no longer. Taking me and my brother with her she left my father and our home in Gray's Inn. Many of her friends criticised her, believing that she should have stuck to her husband through every circumstance, however humiliating, and some were not so willing to help her in her distress as they might have been. In my view she was entirely right to leave my father. I just wish she had not been so unhappy. She was a sweet, kind, generous, trusting person and she deserved better of life. Father married again and happily, and his second wife was a fine and loyal companion for him. Father and I quarrelled later over something he said about my mother: I regret that now, though not my loyalty to her. However old the children may be the divorce of their parents invariably brings great unhappiness to them.

When my mother left home she had no money and nowhere to live, but her younger sister, who had two children of her own, took us in. One of my father's first actions was to write to Colet Court, the preparatory school where I was a weekly boarder, saying that he would no longer pay the fees. Mother was told by the school to take me away and she had no alternative. Later I was entered for Christ's Hospital. Mother had to submit to a means test and then I took the entrance examination. We both passed. Father again made a fuss: I believe his pride was hurt by the thought of his elder son attending a school for poor boys, even if he would not pay the fees at a more expensive one. The upshot was that Christ's Hospital also refused to take me.

Poor Mother must have been in despair. She had a friend who recommended Woodbridge School in Suffolk because she thought highly of the headmaster, so that is where I went, as a boarder. I made a wretched start. I was sent up to Woodbridge by train, alone and, by accident, a day early. Worse, I was equipped with combinations for my underclothes. All the other boys wore pants and vests. I was mercilessly teased.

Woodbridge was an old Grammar school, founded three hundred years ago. It was a tough, uncompromising place. The masters used the boys as their agents for the maintenance of discipline, and the cane was in frequent use by both. In my time at Woodbridge I received a total of 135 strokes from masters alone. There was a considerable amount of bullying and great emphasis was put on physical prowess. In bad weather the place could be ferociously cold: we often woke on winter mornings to find the washing water in the jugs frozen over.

I hated Woodbridge in those early days. I don't suppose I was bullied any more than any other small boy but mine was a pretty miserable existence. Two aspects of our communal life I remember with particular loathing. The first was an unpleasant ritual in the junior boarding house for boys up to the age of fourteen. Every night we attended Chapel, which meant a trip of eight hundred yards across the playing fields. All the boys in the house, about thirty of us, were made by the head boy and his two prefect assistants to form ourselves up into an elongated rugby scrum formation: three boys in the front row standing upright and two boys scrummaging down behind them, then another three boys scrummaging down behind them, then another two boys and so on. This human juggernaut was called the Loch Ness Monster. The head boy and his two assistants would ride on top of us between the junior house and the Chapel. It was an horrific experience in the winter in the dark to be part of this scrum, especially if you had to carry any part of the weight of one of the three larger boys. It collapsed often and we fell in the wet and the mud.

The second experience I remember with detestation was that of the courts that used to take place on Sunday mornings in the dormitory at about six a.m. before we went down to breakfast. These invariably involved the trying of one or more small boys for alleged offences, usually insolence. The prosecution, an older boy or boys, merely had to allege the offences, not to prove them. The wretch who was accused defended himself as best he could. He never succeeded. He was always found guilty. The penalty was invariable – a beating from all hands. When in later life I was in the Navy I occasionally reflected that had I been captured by the Nazis I would have known exactly how to conduct myself under interrogation.

What I do not regret is that we boys were made to work extremely hard. In summer we were at our lessons by seven a.m. and at night, winter or summer, we would do homework until nine p.m. The masters were erudite, cultured and devoted – I can only remember one who was a poor teacher – and we learned willingly. Few of us escaped the clutches of the school without a reasonable education, though we were an extraordinary mixture of boys – the sons of farm labourers, the sons of professional men in Woodbridge and a few odd characters like myself who were boarders at school for reasons which were frankly eccentric.

I was never very proficient at sports but I did play rugby, cricket and hockey for the first teams and represented the school at Eton Fives, a game I much enjoyed. I also sat for and obtained a scholarship which reduced the fees somewhat for my poor mother.

Six years after I went to Woodbridge, on the morning of 3 September 1939, my grandmother, my mother, my brother and I sat together at home in Sussex to hear Neville Chamberlain's broadcast, telling us that Britain was at war. 'Thank God the boys are too young to be involved,' my mother said. She was wrong. All the family were to be heavily involved before the War's end. Grandmother was blitzed when the bombing started, my brother and I both did military service and Mother was to see more enemy action than all of us put together. For many days and nights she was on duty in civil defence in the Red Cross in London when the city was being bombarded from the air. Although I have four medals to mark my war service and she had only one, I guess she had by far the tougher time in the War.

France, Belgium and Holland fell in the early summer of 1940. The day its formation was announced by Eden, I enrolled in the Local Defence Volunteers, as the Home Guard was originally called. In the south of England we waited for the German invasion we were sure would come sooner rather than later. We read manuals telling us how to disable tanks with petrol bombs. I sewed a carving knife and five rounds of .303 rifle ammunition into the lining of my mackintosh. We had no uniforms and no weapons of any kind. My family had moved from the seaside but our home in Partridge Green was only ten miles from the Sussex coast. Every night I went to bed expecting to be wakened by church bells announcing parachute and glider landings by German troops. Thank God it never happened. We would have done our best but it would have been a pitiful affair. Against seasoned and well armed troops we would have been slaughtered. We never gave a thought to the odds against us. We mounted guard at night, built pill boxes and feeble anti-tank obstacles and our morale was sky-high. In September came the climax of the Battle of Britain, when the few brilliant fighter pilots of the Royal Air Force held at bay a numerically vastly superior enemy. We watched the vapour trails in the sky; we cycled to the fields in which enemy planes fell; we prayed for success and we hung on every word of Churchill's speeches. Now, fifty-five years later, the nation hawks with laughter at the repeats of 'Dad's Army'. It is all a huge joke. At the time, it was deadly serious.

The War wreaked havoc at the already under-staffed Woodbridge school. We lost two masters at once, one to the Air Force and the other to the Army. They were both killed within a few months of joining up. Three more were struck at the same time by illness, and that meant that I had to do much of my work for the Higher School Certificate on my own. I can't regret it. I learned the habit of working alone without any form of discipline and for that I have always been grateful.

I passed my Higher School Certificate tolerably well and the headmaster arranged for me to be accepted at the absurdly young age of sixteen for St John's College, Oxford. Oxford in 1941 was an empty place. Apart from very young men like myself and slightly older young men awaiting their call up, the only undergraduates were those who had been declared unfit for service in the armed forces or those who were in reserved occupations: trainee scientists, doctors and the like. As soon as I could, I put my name down for the Navy, the flying branch. I started my studies not knowing how many university terms I would be able to complete before I went off to sea.

There was a remarkable mixture of talent at St John's in those days. Kingsley Amis, Philip Larkin and Bruce Montgomery (who later wrote under the name of Edmund Crispin) were contemporaries and friends of mine. Larkin and I and one other undergraduate published a magazine. I myself wrote – and even had published – a little poetry. I was reading Law with the intention of following in my father's footsteps and practising at the Bar, but I am sorry to say I did less academic work than I should. At such a time it seemed to be of little importance. No one could foresee what the future held for any of us.

Politics played no part in my life in University. Most of my friends were frankly contemptuous of fellow students who took the political clubs or the Oxford Union seriously. The activists of Left and Right were equally unattractive: those on the left struck us as dogmatic lunatics, those on the right were snobbishly irrelevant. Those in the Liberal centre were not much better, living in a fantasy world, dreaming of the glories of Lloyd George and utterly incapable of formulating realistic programmes suited to the contemporary world. My friends and I did join political clubs, but we only went to meetings addressed by speakers who interested us. We were equally selective over our lectures, only attending when we thought we would be excited or entertained by what we were likely to hear.

I learnt to drink beer – when it was possible to buy it. Often, because of shortages, the pubs were shut. I played rugby and cricket for my college and in my first term was offered a rugby trial for Oxford. Like an idiot I turned the invitation down because I was not as fit as I reckoned I needed to be. That was a bad mistake: even if I had only played in that one trial I would like now to be able to boast about it. In life, opportunity usually knocks once. I was not asked again.

Our tastes were catholic. We were regular attendees at the Oxford University Rhythm Club where we listened to performances by many who became celebrated in later years, such as George Shearing, the blind pianist. Amis and Larkin were most knowledgeable on the subject of jazz.

One regular piece of fun was the 'Suggestion Book' kept in the St John's Junior Common Room. Despite its name, the entries in this book were by no means confined to practical suggestions. It was a place for undergraduates to display their wit, and Larkin, Amis and others were indefatigable scribblers of letters in it. Kingsley's style was exactly that of his novels to be. To read his earlier novels today is to read again the letters in the JCR book of all those years ago. He was invariably very funny and his observation was as acute as it is now. I became Secretary of the JCR with the right of reply. I have always liked answering back.

Although we were not politically active, the atmosphere in the University was to the left of centre and quite strongly so. No propaganda was offered by the Conservatives: it was as if the Party was asleep. But the Labour Party's propagandists were active and the seeds were being sown for Labour to win the first post-War general election in 1945. There was always Communist literature available, and eulogies of Mother Russia, for by this time Russia had entered the War and was playing an heroic part – in contrast to her earlier friendliness with the Nazis and the consequent unpatriotic and discreditable lack of support by British Communists for the British War effort.

We followed the War news closely. We had all been involved already to a greater or lesser degree – in the bombing, in training, through family or friends – and military training was obligatory for every student at the universities during the War, unless one was unfit. Happily I was not unprepared. At school I had been a member of the Officers

22

Training Corps and had risen to the dizzy rank of Sergeant. I earned a marksman's badge shooting with a short Lee Enfield .303 calibre rifle and learned to play the bugle: in later life I found the first qualification more useful than the second. Perhaps I should have tried the trumpet.

There was no separate naval training organisation at Oxford. Most of those intending to go into the Navy joined the army-based Training Corps and hated every minute of it. Those like myself who intended to go into the Navy's Air Arm joined the Air Squadron. We were taught drill (which I already knew), how to handle the rifle (which, again, I already knew) and esoteric skills such as the use of a morse sender and receiver, aerial navigation, meteorology, engineering, aerodynamics and the like (which I knew nothing about). Sadly, we were taught nothing about the sea or ships (which I wanted to learn about most of all).

I went through my examinations steadily, taking a different exam at the end of every term: Roman law, Torts, Contract, International law and so on. I passed them all. Although I had volunteered some time earlier, the Navy seemed not to want my services as promptly as I would have liked. I made enquiries. I was told that I would receive my call when the Navy was well and truly ready. In consequence I was able to complete the five terms' work which would qualify me for my degree as a Bachelor of Arts, provided that I subsequently carried out two full years of service in the armed forces. So by the time that I was told to report myself at HMS *Daedalus* at Lee-on-Solent in April 1943 at the age of eighteen I was qualified as a BA (Oxon).

Once in the Navy I received a few months' preliminary training in the UK. At the gunnery school at Whale Island in Portsmouth I learned how to shoot a six-inch monster of a gun firing a 56-pound projectile under a legend which told me to 'Engage the enemy more closely'. It is a good rule, always practised by HM ships in wartime. It is a good rule of personal conduct in peacetime too, I have found.

I also put in some sea time on HMS *Activity*, one of the so-called Woolworth aircraft carriers, a merchant ship with a flat steel deck built on her and one of her holds used as hangar for half a dozen fighters. She was a splendid ship, inexpensive and effective, allowing British and Allied convoys to achieve air cover many miles from land in a way which previously had not been possible. Before this the enemy had too often had his own way far out to sea. British merchant ship convoys were shadowed in mid-Atlantic for days on end by long-range German aircraft operating with impunity from the French Atlantic coast and directing the U-boat attacks, often with devastating results. After I left her, *Activity* was sunk in Northern waters on Russian convoy duty. One lesson I learned from her stayed with me long after the War was over. She was an uncomplicated, functional man of war, comparatively cheap to fit out for her role, and she taught me that the excellent is often the enemy of the good. Subsequently, when Chairman of the Public Accounts Committee in Parliament, I watched and criticised the designers of aircraft, ships and tanks working at the frontiers of technology (which, it is true, invariably pose fearful problems of cost and choice) aspiring to produce the ultimate in design when something less complex would be almost as effective and certainly cheaper and easier to produce, and one could get more of them for the same money. Committee men invariably over-design our military hardware for fear that they will be blamed for having left something out. So defence costs mount inexorably and to an extent unnecessarily. There never seem to be the same financial constraints on military expenditure in peacetime as there are in war.

After my few months of training in Britain I went to Canada and the US to learn to fly, and I failed. Of the sixty of us who started out on my particular course, only four won their wings and a commission. It seemed to me that there was something wrong with the selection process – or maybe the standard required for a Fleet Air Arm pilot was especially high. I had been unpleasantly ill in Canada, thanks to the incompetence of a service doctor, but though that affected me at a critical moment, the truth is that I would not have made a good pilot. The irony was that I had volunteered to be an observer but the doctors said my eyes were good enough only to be a pilot! Ever since then I have been somewhat sceptical about the opinions of naval doctors, whom sailors unfairly but invariably call 'quacks'.

So I returned to England in the winter of 1943, feeling miserable. I was asked if I wanted to leave the Navy and join the Army as a foot soldier or join the RAF as an air gunner, as many did, but any alternative to the Navy was unthinkable. I did time in Portsmouth barracks, a squalid experience. There were too few plates for us all in our mess, so some of us ate off the oilcloth; there were too few utensils, so that sometimes we ate with our fingers. My messmates said that the Navy had changed little since Nelson's day. Conditions were so bad that I complained formally to the Commander.

'You'd be worse off at sea,' he said.

'Perhaps that's true,' I replied, 'but it's not the fault of any of us that we're not. We've all volunteered to go to sea; it's the system that delays us.'

He got his own back. He made me lecture to the assembled ratings one Saturday morning, the whole ship's company in Pompey barracks, on the subject of the English judicial system. It was quite an ordeal addressing a thousand cynical matelots, but somehow I got through it.

'You used too many swear words,' the Commander said afterwards.

'I wanted them to feel at home,' I replied.

In the Navy the word 'bastard' is a term of endearment.

Perhaps I got to sea quicker than I would have done if I had not complained. It was only training cruiser, HMS *Dauntless*, but it was better than nothing. We were based on Rosyth, where Russian sailors were taking over the old British capital ship HMS *Royal Sovereign*. They seemed not to be allowed to fraternise with us, an odd state of affairs, we thought. The accommodation on *Dauntless* was wholly inadequate for a wartime complement of men. There were about a dozen washbasins for more than a hundred and fifty of us. Condensation in the washroom was fearful. The blue dye from our serge uniforms came off on our skin. On the rare occasions we were allowed to go on shore it was a struggle to get ourselves clean beforehand. To evacuate your bowels at sea you sat on a hole and put your backside out over the ocean. In really cold or stormy weather it was a hazardous proceeding. It shocked me that such conditions were tolerated and nobody did much to improve them. The wags said it was more comfortable than boarding school, and it is true that the public schoolboys on board were often better apprenticed for this sort of communal living than the working-class boys. My idea of bliss in those days was to get a night off when we came in from sea, take the bus into Dunfermline and visit the public bathhouse where for one shilling and sixpence (half a day's pay) you could get a Turkish bath, a cup of tea and a biscuit, a massage afterwards from the horny handed attendant and an hour's kip on a clean bed with clean sheets. Sheets! After a hammock and rough blankets, sheets were Nirvana.

I was glad to get off *Dauntless* when I was recommended for a commission and found myself at HMS *King Alfred*, a collection of buildings on different sites in the Brighton area. This was the Navy's officer training centre for the seaman's branch of the Royal Naval Volunteer Reserve. When I arrived there I made immediate friends with David Wickins who, although English, was serving in the South African Navy. He was an accountant working in South Africa when War began, and had enlisted out there. By that time I had been promoted from Ordinary Seaman to Able Seaman which meant that my pay went up from three shillings a day to three shillings and three pence: Wickins earned three times that amount, a veritable fortune. He led me, a willing participant, into endless mischief, and he became the dear friend of a lifetime. Neither of us was altogether in sympathy with the disciplines in HMS *King Alfred* but as aspirants for a commission we needed to be on our best behaviour: the penalty for receiving low marks for ability or keenness would be to be thrown off the course and sent back to the lower deck.

The divisional officer in charge of our course was a Commander Kirkwood, a destroyer captain. He had been awarded two Distinguished Service Crosses for gallantry and the all-white and rare Polar Medal. He was a god-like figure to us. In our half-term examinations Wickins and I came either first or second in most of our subjects, navigation, meteorology, gunnery, seamanship and the like. Kirkwood sent for me and told me he was dissatisfied with my achievement. My heart sank. I grumbled that to have come in one of the two top places in almost every subject didn't seem to me to be a bad performance.

'You have a university degree,' he said, 'you should be first in everything.'

'Aye, aye, Sir,' I replied. It was all I could think of to say.

'Watch it,' I said to David Wickins as I came out and he went in. He got a similar telling off from Kirkwood, who had a disconcerting habit of closing his eyes when he spoke.

'Sir,' said Wickins, 'why are your eyes shut?'

'Because I can't stand the bloody sight of you.'

'Aye, aye, Sir,' said Wickins. Kirkwood was a difficult man to argue with.

I am afraid that Wickins and I were less amenable to restriction than we should have been. The dance halls in Brighton were out of bounds to officer cadets from HMS *King Alfred*. We just took off the white cap bands that marked us out and substituted the standard blue ribbons so as to look like ordinary sailors. The dog track was also out of bounds and naturally we visited that too. Wickins said he had an infallible system, something to do with forecasts and doubling up, I forget what exactly (if it had been any good I would have remembered it). He lost every penny we had and we walked all the way back to Hove and our bunks that night.

We were asked to say what branch of the service we wished to join if we received our commissions and to list three choices in order of priority. Wickins put down Motor Torpedo Boats first, second and third. I did the same and added a p.s. for submarines. I cannot now remember why I did that. I must have had a rush of blood to the head.

By now British and Allied troops were landing in France and the Navy was suddenly afraid it would suffer heavy casualties on the beaches. 'Let there be more young officers,' someone in the Admiralty probably commanded, and one day to our delight and infinite relief Wickins and I found ourselves in receipt of our commissions. I was now a Temporary Acting Sub-Lieutenant, Royal Naval Volunteer Reserve. I was just twenty years old. My pay went up to ten shillings a day – 50p in today's money. Wickins wore a straight stripe on his arm as a Sub-Lieutenant in the South African Navy, not a wavy one like mine, and again his pay was more than three times as much. He has always had a knack of turning every situation to his advantage. We felt very self-conscious in our made-to-measure uniforms. We longed to be at sea again and yet I confess to some apprehension. On the lower deck we had been quick to identify an officer who was not fully the master of his responsibilities: I hoped I would be up to the test when it came.

The Navy knew what it was doing. Impatient as we all were to get to sea we were given time to become accustomed to our new status. There was not long to wait. A week's course at Roedean, the famous girls' public school, another at St Dunstans (both taken over by the Navy for the duration) and finally at the Royal Naval College at Greenwich, where Wren's magnificent painted hall was a considerable remove from the lower-deck surroundings I was more accustomed to. Then my posting came.

I reported myself to the Commander at HMS *Midge* at Great Yarmouth, the name for a shore establishment servicing several flotillas of MTBs. I found to my delight that David Wickins had the same posting. We were allocated to boats in the same flotilla as spare officers. Wickins joined the MTB commanded by the senior officer in the flotilla (he would); I was the spare officer aboard HM MTB 730. Within twenty-four hours I was at sea. I have never been more excited at any time in my life.

Our flotilla consisted of some twelve Motor Torpedo Boats of the Fairmile D type. They were 115 feet long with a crew of some 28 ratings and three or sometimes four officers. They were heavily armed with four 18-inch torpedoes in tubes, two six-pounder guns in power-operated turrets, four half-inch machine guns also in two power-operated turrets, and twin Oerlikon rapid-fire guns. In addition, they carried anti-submarine depth charges. Their original design displacement was less than 100 tons, with a top speed of nearly 30 knots and a range of about five hundred miles, but constant redesign and the addition of extra and heavier armament increased the displacement to about 120 tons, with a consequent fall-off in speed and range. They were powered by four Merlin engines each of 1,250 HP fuelled by high-octane petrol. On long trips, for instance across the North Sea, they carried additional fuel drums on deck and sometimes long range tanks. They were built of two layers of five-ply mahogany, on wooden frames; hard chine boats, partly prefabricated, and assembled and finished at some thirty small shipyards all round the country. They were formidable fighting machines but their design left much to be desired. They were extremely noisy so that over protracted periods our crews became noise-drunk and less alert for combat than they should have been. In really heavy weather the boats flexed and were prone to suffer damage. Worst of all, the use of high-octane petrol made them floating fire bombs.

The German equivalent, the *schnellboote* (which we called E-boats) were less heavily armed but they were markedly superior in several respects. They were a third faster than our Fairmile boats, being capable of 40 knots. They had diesel motors and so suffered vastly less fire risk. They were well designed round-bilged boats, capable not only of travelling faster than our Fairmiles but able to maintain high speeds in heavy seas which our slower, hard chine boats could not. Their function was to attack British shipping with torpedoes or guns or both and then to retire at high speed. They were well commanded and fought with skill and courage.

Our MTBs were part of the Navy's 'light coastal forces' and we attacked enemy shipping, raided harbours and even landed agents on the enemy coast; President Mitterand was one such. In the early stages of the War, fighting in the Channel and in the southern North Sea was a hard and bitter business; control of these waters was vital to the defence of the United Kingdom against a powerful enemy who commanded the Continental land mass. It was important also to interrupt the enemy's ability to supply his own operations. So successful were coastal forces in this aggressive endeavour that before the invasion of France by Allied forces in 1944 there was little or nothing in the way of German coastal traffic operating in the Channel. In all, British and Allied coastal forces sank some 600 enemy warships and merchant ships in the Channel, the North Sea and the Mediterranean. We engaged the enemy more closely. We lost perhaps 150 ships. Also, as the War progressed, British coastal forces and our other naval and air defences permitted a reasonable amount of traffic to take place on our side of the Channel and the North Sea without serious interference. Every week two or more convoys of twenty or thirty ships sailed each way between the Thames and the Forth and half that number along the Channel.

By the time David Wickins and I arrived at HMS *Midge* in the second half of 1944, coastal forces' duties in the bases on the East Coast of Britain were mostly defensive, to lie with engines cut outside the convoy routes waiting to intercept and destroy the enemy when he dared to come. These routes, like a trunk road, ran north-south five or ten miles off the coast the whole length of the UK through a channel swept clear of mines twice daily. We waited some miles outside these lanes, ready to repel surface attacks from E-boats based in Holland or dispose of mine laying submarines, especially the midget variety. Sometimes, however, our duties were aggressive: we would sail over to the enemy-occupied coast to interfere with his shipping. These operations, for obvious reasons, were known as 'bangers'.

One of the strangest and most memorable operations I took part in occurred just after the end of the War in Europe, by which time I was navigator of HM MTB 758. My friend of a lifetime, Owen Fisher, was First Lieutenant. The surrender of the German forces taken by the British and Allied commanders in Germany was not immediately acknowledged by the enemy in Norway and there was talk of the fight continuing in that country. Accordingly, our flotilla of MTBs, plus several commanded and crewed by free Norwegians, sailed across the North Sea from Lerwick in three groups. The weather was foul. Our destinations were Bergen, Christiansand South and Alesund. Our mission was to test the German coastal defences, in case it should be necessary to mount an invasion of Norway by sea. It was thought that if we were fired upon, our MTBs would have the speed and manoeuvrability to gather the intelligence and escape unharmed. We were instructed not to go ashore.

It was a barking idea. In the first place, if the heavy coastal batteries had opened fire we should have certainly been blown to bits; in the second place, once our Norwegian friends came within a mile or two of their homeland nothing on earth could stop them from landing. Fortunately we were not fired upon, I think probably because our boldness took the Germans by surprise. We just sailed straight in. My boat was in the most northerly group of our flotilla, and with another British boat and three Norwegian MTBs we went alongside at the town of Alesund. Our welcome was ecstatic. Aisher took an armed party ashore to the Gestapo headquarters to flush out the filth but the birds had flown. One of the Norwegian midshipmen with us – later a distinguished Vice Admiral in the Royal Norwegian Navy – by an amazing coincidence found his father on the quay among the welcoming crowd at Alesund, on the run from the Gestapo. It must have been an emotional reunion.

That was to be my last naval action. I asked to be transferred to the Far East, where the War was expected to continue for some considerable time, and no doubt would have done but for the surrender of the Japanese after the two atomic bombs were dropped by the Americans at Hiroshima and Nagasaki. It is hard to contemplate that action even now, fifty years later, without horror and revulsion. Nonetheless, in my view it was the correct decision. It shortened the War and so saved many British, American, Australian and Allied lives: Allied prisoners of war in Japan would assuredly have been slaughtered the day the first Allied soldier landed on Japanese soil. The Japanese had forecast this. The atomic bombs involved heavy Japanese casualties in those two cities but they were nothing by comparison with what Japanese suffering might otherwise have been in many more cities if the War had not ended when it did – probably ten times that number, in the estimate of American commanders at the time. It should also be remembered that for every person who died at Hiroshima or Nagasaki as a result of American action, several hundreds had died in the preceding six years of conventional warfare which Japanese aggression had begun.

After the War's end the youngest in the British armed Services were, quite rightly, the last to be demobilised. David Wickins, of course, escaped early from the South African Navy and was set up in the Motor Auction business before you could say 'sold to the gentleman at the back of the hall.' He was brilliantly successful and developed his business into the biggest of its kind in the world. I had the fun of attending his first auction in Chichester and a gang of us pushed the cars into place for sale. I left the Navy in the autumn of 1946. I was just twenty-two years old. My last appointment was in command of a D Class Fairmile MTB, all 115 feet of her, though I retired with the rank in which I was originally commissioned in 1944, Temporary Acting Sub Lieutenant in the Royal Naval Volunteer Reserve.

I look back on my time in the Navy with gratitude. Life was often hard and uncomfortable, sometimes foul. There were occasions when I was afraid, many when I was cold and tired and miserable, and I was always seasick during the first few days at sea after a period ashore. But it was deeply rewarding and there was always a sense of achievement – a landfall after a passage, a target hit, a convoy safe, and eventual victory at the War's end. When finally I had command of my own MTB, I was the happiest and proudest man in England.

CHAPTER 2

POLITICAL
BEGINNER

Once out of the Navy I was eager to make a start on my civilian life – soon to become my two lives, in business and in politics. The first thing, of course, was to secure myself an income: a penniless and unemployed young man is not in a strong position to launch himself into a political career. I advertised in *The Times*. I got one offer: of course, I took it.

That first job was rather an odd one. I became Secretary, at a salary of £250 a year, of a small company which owned a derelict London hotel, the Mostyn, just off Portman Square. During the War half of it had been severely damaged by a bomb and the undamaged remainder had been requisitioned by the Government. After the War it was bought by a private investor who formed a company into which he brought some friends from a City institution headed by a man who was to become important in my life, Denys Lowson. The hotel was a shambles. My task was to make it habitable and get it back into operation. I was not merely Secretary of the company that owned it: I was its only employee.

To start with I set myself to learn everything I could about the hotel business, which included doing a spell at the Dorchester as a clerk in the bill office. Working at the Mostyn, negotiating with architects, builders and authorities of various sorts, I got to know and like many people who later became prominent figures in the hotel industry. Max Joseph was one. Many years later, just before his death, he told me that he knew even in those days that we would both of us succeed in something, though he did not know what.

The entrepreneur who began the Mostyn Hotel project had wildly underestimated its cost. Lowson's institutional interests, who owned the majority of the company, were canvassed for further financial support; they gave some but in the end lost patience and instructed me to sell the company. This was a tall order but I set about it with enthusiasm and was lucky to interest a neighbouring hotel owner in a purchase. Lowson told me he was impressed with what I had done and offered me a position as assistant secretary to a group of investment companies under his control at a salary of £500 a year, a rise of £150. He also promised me a commission on the sale: he never paid it, but I felt my prospects were looking up. I was able to buy myself a new suit and a new pair of shoes.

The time had come to make a serious start on my political career by finding a parliamentary seat to fight. Strictly speaking it was not quite the start because I had already become involved in local politics. It happened in rather a curious way, not so much parish pump politics as the politics of the parish cricket pitch.

In 1949 I was living in the Sussex village of Partridge Green. This was one of three villages represented by the West Grinstead Parish Council, the others being West Grinstead itself and Dial Post. The number of voters in Partridge Green was around twice the total for the other two villages put together – they were tiny places – but we had a smaller number of representatives at the Council than either of them. This became a source of considerable irritation because the Parish Council administered the splendid playing field on which the Partridge Green Cricket Club and the Partridge Green Ladies Stoolball Team played their matches. (Stoolball, for those who have never heard of it, is an ancestor of cricket, played by two teams of eleven women. The wickets resemble small notice boards on stilts, the bats look like half-size tennis rackets.) In the years after the War I played cricket regularly for the Partridge Green club. It was a pleasant, carefree, friendly group, but there were growing mutters of complaint that the affairs of our clubs were so much in the hands of a parish council on which our village was under-represented. What, we asked ourselves, did the people of Dial Post and West Grinstead know about either cricket or stoolball? They didn't have the population, let alone the skills, to have teams of their own. Local patriotism was mounting in Partridge Green.

Then someone told us that there was to be an election of parish councillors. This was our chance. Led by John Kidd, a retired bank manager who was the nearest thing to a squire we had, we put together a list of eight candidates, including myself, who could be trusted to uphold the Partridge Green view. We printed their names on a postcard, with a message urging everyone to vote for them and only them. We mobilised the members of the Cricket Club – the officers, batsmen, bowlers, umpires, spectators and tea ladies. The stoolball ladies and their supporters joined in with enthusiasm. That made almost half the village. A

32

few days before polling we distributed that card by hand to every house in Partridge Green. Our tactics were brilliantly successful. People who had never bothered to vote in a parish election turned out and voted for our men and for nobody else. The complacent candidates from Dial Post and West Grinstead never knew what hit them: they were bottom of the poll. Partridge Green candidates filled all the top places.

It was a good early lesson in how to run a successful election campaign. We had a cause, we had an organisation and we knew what to do. It also taught me the most important political lesson of all: almost everyone judges politics and policies by the way their daily lives are affected. The great concepts are all very well, but votes depend as much or more on the issues that are relevant to the man in the street: the price of bread, the state of the pavements, how much he has in his pocket, the frequency of the bus service, or even the administration of the cricket ground. A candidate forgets that simple truth at his peril.

A year before I became a Parish Councillor I had become involved in politics in another way. In 1948 our constituency MP, Earl Winterton, an elderly Irish peer first elected in 1904 at the age of 21 and an archetypal Tory of his generation, had come down to address a meeting in the village hall. The place was packed; it seemed that the entire population of Partridge Green had turned up. We were to be furiously disappointed. Lord Winterton had nothing at all to say about the contemporary scene; he gave us a lecture on the repeal of the Corn Laws in 1846. When it was over there was a complete silence. The Chairman of the meeting called for questions. Again there was silence. I was sitting at the back of the hall, as disappointed as anybody. My neighbour gave me a nudge and I got to my feet. 'That was a splendid lecture,' I said, 'but we would all be very grateful if the Member of Parliament would kindly tell us something about what policies for the future are on offer by the Conservative Party.'

Lord Winterton went scarlet in the face. He took my question to be an attack and he was blisteringly rude in reply. My friends in the village were as astonished at his rudeness to me as they had been by the subject of his speech. The Chairman called for other questions. There were none, and the meeting broke up with a less than effusive vote of thanks.

The Chairman came up to me. 'Edward,' he said, 'I had no idea you were a Socialist.'

I was not a Socialist. It is true that, like many young men and women of my generation, I had hoped to see a brave new world built by the Attlee Government – and was in due course disappointed – but I would have voted for Churchill in 1945 if it had not been for the fact that, although I was old enough, my name was not yet included in the electoral register. So now, in the Partridge Green village hall, I said to our Chairman, 'Heavens, I'm not a Socialist. It's just that our MP's performance was enough to turn one to drink, let alone to Socialism.'

'Oh,' he replied, 'Well if you're not a Socialist then you must come and join our committee.'

So I found myself a member of the West Grinstead, Partridge Green and Dial Post Conservative Committee. I attended my first meeting a week or so later. The Chairman resigned before any other business was taken and on his proposal I was elected Chairman in his stead. It happened almost before I had time to get comfortable in my seat.

The committee members were kind and respectful to their new Chairman, and if they were doubtful at being led by an inexperienced young man they were too polite to show it. I learned much from working with them. I learned about chairmanship and I also learned how to organise a political unit at grassroots level, how to canvass support for our Party and how to manage a branch programme and to prepare for an eventual general election. All this preparation paid off when that election came, in February 1950. To me the campaign was wildly exciting. I was flattered to be included in the team of speakers who would address Lord Winterton's eve of poll meetings in Horsham, Pulborough, Petworth and Midhurst. I was cast in a subsidiary role but I was thrilled to bits to be included at all. Then, two days before the eve of the poll, one of our local stalwarts fell ill. I was told that I must be the principal and only supporting speaker in Horsham, the first of the candidate's meeting places and the largest of the four towns. I would have to open the meeting and speak until the candidate arrived.

It was a great opportunity and a frightening one. No soldier ever polished his buttons or shone his boots more carefully than I burnished the notes for my speech. I sat up half the night, I worked in the train going to and from London, and for two days I am sorry to say that I did almost no office work. The meeting took place in the open air in the Carfax which was then the centre of the town and the bus terminus. It was a mild night for February but it was dark. I climbed up onto the bandstand, having had to push my way through a crowd of two thousand or more, so many that the buses and the traffic were stopped. I had never seen so many people at a meeting. It should have been nerve-racking but it wasn't. There was no time to get anxious. No sooner was I up on the bandstand than the Chairman for the evening introduced me and I was off.

It was as well that I had rehearsed so carefully and memorised exactly the headings of what I wanted to say. It is difficult, if not impossible, to hold a microphone and a wad of notes, to gesticulate and to keep an eye on a large crowd all at once. There was some heckling and a good deal of shouting from time to time. To a practised speaker, such interruptions can be a help, giving him a chance to score and please his supporters. I was not experienced enough to do that well, but as the meeting progressed I found to my surprise that I was enjoying it. All the same, when I finished I was wet with sweat and my hands were trembling so that I had to hide them.

The Conservative candidate, Lord Winterton, arrived and made the first of his four speeches of the evening. He was well received, and then he was off to the next place and it was all over.

The next week I had my leg pulled by the cricket team. There was a story that I had been pelted with vegetables at the meeting, including a whole cabbage. It was said that I caught it one-handed and held it up to the crowd, claiming that someone in the audience had lost his head. Loud cheers followed. The cricket team told me they knew very well the story couldn't be true: I would never have caught the cabbage.

A more serious comment came from my father who had been standing by the bandstand. 'That wasn't bad,' he said. 'You have a lot to learn, but there's only one way to learn about politics and that's to practise it. You've no business to be speaking for someone else. You should be speaking for yourself.'

Even though I was puffed up with excitement and probably more than a little vain in consequence, that seemed to me a ridiculous

35

proposition. But my father would have none of this modesty. 'Talk to Winterton,' he said. 'You've done a good deal for him. Ask him if he'll back your candidacy. He'll probably be pleased to do so.'

Again, I thought this a ridiculous idea, though it was true that when the result of the election was announced Winterton – who had no doubt quite forgotten his annoyance at my question after his Corn Law Speech – had every reason to feel pleased with our efforts. His proportion of the vote increased and our local Conservative West Grinstead Branch had played its modest part in his success. Nationally, Labour remained in office but with a much reduced majority. Their number of Parliamentary seats fell from 384 to 315 while that of the Conservatives and their allies rose from 193 to 298. It was clear that the new Government's position was too precarious for it to last a full term. There had to be another election in a year or two, and I decided that when it came I wanted to take part in it on my own account. I plucked up my courage, followed my father's advice and wrote to Lord Winterton asking if he would recommend me to Conservative Central Office for a canditature.

In those days, as today, those selected as Parliamentary candidates had to have the endorsement of the Party organisation, and a Vice-Chairman of the Party was responsible for vetting them. It was an informal process, very different from today's procedures. In my case it was all done very simply. I had a letter from Lord Winterton telling me that he had 'had a word with Mr J. P. L. Thomas one evening on the front bench.' Mr Thomas was the MP who then had responsibility for selecting candidates and on Winterton's recommendation he was apparently happy to approve me, without fuss and without even a personal interview.

All I needed now was a seat to fight. I scoured the small print in the newspapers looking for one that lacked a Conservative candidate and I found two, Wood Green and Walthamstow, both on the north-eastern edge of London. I wrote to them. Both asked me to come for an interview with their selection committees. Both asked me for the same evening. Like an idiot I agreed to go, feeling rather pleased with myself at being asked to attend the two of them and not appreciating that the lists of applicants for both seats were short enough to mean that my two invitations were not so great a triumph.

The urgent question was, how was I going to appear in both places on the same evening? Fortunately I had a good friend who came to the rescue. The directors of the Mostyn Hotel had by then appointed a manager for our hotel project, now nearing its unhappy end. He was a Frenchman with the name of Georges Celestin Elie Dertu, a pupil of Boulestin, and he owned a 1938 Austin 10 which he drove with a rapture and panache only a Frenchman could achieve. To drive with him made one want to go out and quadruple one's life insurance. The timing of the two selection meetings meant that I could just reach Wood Green in time if Walthamstow did not run late – and if I was being driven by Georges Dertu.

I met the Walthamstow selection Committee in a converted shop rented by the Conservative Association in the Markhouse Road. The name Markhouse, they told me, was a corruption of Marx House since Karl Marx had lived in that area for a period. When I heard this I fancied myself truly in the front line of the anti-Socialist political struggle.

Walthamstow was a typical East End area, filled with the kindest and most steadfast people. They traditionally voted Labour out of an old loyalty, but the local Tories, who were perhaps the most courageous supporters of our Party you could find anywhere in the United Kingdom, believed with an unassailable optimism that given a good candidate at the next general election a miracle might well be achieved. I remember the friendliness with which I was received, tinged with disappointment that I was not yet married so that if they selected me they would not get two workers for the price of one. I was asked if my mother would be willing to canvass four nights a week. I thought that was a bit hot and said so: I added that she was a working woman, as she was. They all roared with laughter.

I left Walthamstow after my interview not knowing whether I was selected, but elated by the experience. We set off for Wood Green, Georges driving like Jehu son of Nimshi through the North London streets. We were lucky to avoid being arrested several times, luckier still to arrive in one piece. I was a bit twitchy when I entered the Conservative Party's premises in Wood Green: I was also rather miffed to find that the selection process was running late, so that we need not have taken such appalling risks.

The people at Wood Green had been told that I had been at Walthamstow previously. I was slightly surprised to find that they were not impressed. Anyway, they much preferred one of the other candidates and told me so without much ado. Curiously enough I was not really disappointed. It is true that Wood Green had been my first choice when I was weighing up the two constituencies in advance, for the reason that the sitting Labour MP there had had the smaller majority at the last election. But I now saw that I had been neglecting a much more important fact. The MP for Wood Green was a Mr W. J. Irving; the Member for Walthamstow was Clement Attlee. There would be far more kudos in losing to the Prime Minister than in fighting a little-known trade unionist.

Two days later I had a letter from the Walthamstow committee inviting me to be their candidate at the next general election and asking me to meet the Chairman of the Conservative Association within the next few days to discuss plans. It meant the start of a new life for me. From now on my evenings and weekends would be devoted to the streets and the committee rooms. It was goodbye to the rugby games, goodbye to the cricket field. I looked forward to the new experience: I had no idea how it was to dominate my life for the next thirty-five years and more.

My candidature at West Walthamstow was hard work. I would visit the constituency on two or three evenings a week after a full working day in the City office, mostly calling on the electors in their homes. It cost a bob or two besides, as the phrase went in those days. I was lucky to find a room in London for only £1.50 a week (it was over a furniture shop in Lower Sloane Street) but I had precious little change left out of my small salary when all my expenses were paid. It was fortunate I was a bachelor.

My reception in the constituency was almost always polite. I can only recall a few times when doors were slammed in my face. Some people expressed surprise that they were being called on by a Conservative; some wanted to argue on the doorstep and waste my time; most were Labour Party supporters out of loyalty, as they saw it, to their class; but a few people were warmly appreciative and glad to have their faith in the Conservative Party renewed by a personal call from the prospective candidate.

There were some extraordinary incidents. At one house on which I called, introducing myself by name as the prospective Conservative candidate, the lady of the house rebuffed me firmly. 'No thank you,' she said, 'we do Littlewoods Pools here.'

On another occasion I had lost my voice after a bout of open air speaking: I could only whisper. I knocked on one door and as it opened a smell of boiled cabbage hit me in a gust. 'Are you Mrs Jones?' I whispered to the lady on the doorstep. She was overralled, plimsolled and clothcapped – and short of teeth.

'Yes,' she whispered back.

'I hope you'll support me,' I hissed.

'Oh yes.'

I was keen to gather every possible vote and the electoral register showed that there was a Mr Jones at that address. 'Is your husband in?' I whispered.

'Not for an hour at least,' she whispered back. She seized my hand eagerly. 'Why don't you come in for a bit?'

There are some sacrifices for the cause that the Conservative Party should not expect of even its most devoted servants.

We did everything we could to attract publicity, especially in the local newspapers, to which we sent accounts of my activities and digests of my speeches. I visited the social clubs, I drank beer in the local public houses, I ate my meals in the local cafés, and I did my best to meet as many opinion formers as possible, the doctors, the parsons, the shopkeepers. We had few Conservative councillors in West Walthamstow but we had a good liaison with them and discussed tactics at regular intervals. We challenged our opponents to debates. Sensible people that they were, they ignored us.

Best of all, we took our politics to the people in a programme of outdoor meetings. In Walthamstow there is a particular street where a market of a hundred or more stalls traditionally takes place on Saturdays. There we did our best to make a noise and get ourselves noticed. Early in the morning we would park two motor-cars in a side street outside a public house, reserving a pitch. Just before two-thirty in the afternoon we would move the cars and set up our speaker's stand in the vacant space. We had a team of speakers: each did a quarter of an hour, so the man actually talking was always fresh and full of go. We began these meetings at the moment the pubs turned out in the hope that there would be a drunk or two willing to pass the time in argument. The moment you got a member of the public standing below the rostrum shouting and arguing it was possible to gather a crowd, and we were rarely disappointed. There was always a drunk or two, there was often an argument, and we frequently had a good crowd in consequence. Saturday afternoon after Saturday afternoon for hours on end we would hold forth. I don't say that we made many conversions to the Conservative cause but we did make people aware that we existed.

All this time we were, of course, waiting eagerly to know when a general election would be called. Our eyes were on the Attlee Government, as we wondered how long it could hold out. During this period I met Mr Attlee only once. We attended a church service together.

39

He and his wife greeted me like a friend and we were photographed together. It was a characteristic generosity on his part which made a great impression on his young opponent. He must have found it an irritant to have a busy if small band of opponents in his constituency, always working away, their voices and activities often reported in the local newspaper; but when we met, his welcome was as warm as if I had been a political ally.

I remember one episode in particular. Some Labour Party speakers – without Mr Attlee's knowledge, obviously – began to make speeches suggesting that the Tories were warmongers. Perhaps those who made the charge genuinely believed it: I guess they certainly supposed that Labour was more of a pacifist Party than the Conservatives, and that was probably true. What concerned me was that my name was always mentioned by those who were making these warmongering allegations in West Walthamstow. It was interesting to me that my name was being mentioned at all by Labour Party speakers in the Constituency. My supporters reported this to me with glee, and cited it as evidence that we were beginning to make a mark. I daresay this was true. Rule Number One in any election campaign is to avoid giving your opponents publicity of any sort.

But the warmonger jibe hurt. It was a monstrous thing to say. I have always identified myself with what I believe Lord Nelson said in his maiden speech in the House of Lords: 'I am a man of peace. I am a man of peace because I know the horrors of war. But if any man impugns our nation's honour then I shall know where my duty lies.' I do not doubt that Mr Attlee shared the same sentiment. My supporters were disturbed at this line of attack by some of our political opponents. Memories of the War were fresh in everyone's minds a mere five years after its end: bomb damage was still to be seen everywhere in London and Walthamstow. I wrote a private letter bringing Mr Attlee's attention to what was happening and asking him if he did not think it should stop.

He replied in most friendly terms, a page and a half of foolscap in his own hand. He absolutely understood my point of view and sympathised with it. He also made the point – a kindly lesson to a younger man – that sometimes in politics people get a little carried away by what they are saying and say more than they really mean. Anyway, he would use his influence to see that suggestions of that sort would not be made again, especially in Walthamstow. Of course, he kept his word.

As Prime Minister Mr Attlee had the cares of our country and the world on his shoulders, and he must have known by then that the days of his Government were numbered. He had to deal with its feuding members, the constant bickering between right and left that is the habitual characteristic of the Labour Party, and to cope with the personal jealousies between the giants who were members of his Cabinet. One can only guess how these anxieties affected him personally. Yet he could find time to write in his own hand to an insignificant opponent, to write at length, to pay serious attention to a sincere complaint and to deal with it. He was a gracious and good man, and he exemplified a truth that should never be forgotten: the best men in public life may be fundamentally divided about policies but they can work together in our democratic society because they share common aspirations for it. It has shocked me when, on occasion, I have heard some bigoted Conservatives accuse their Labour opponents of a lack of patriotism. That is ridiculous, unfair and wrong. It is not love of our country and her way of life that divides our main political parties. The argument is about how we can improve the state of our society and the methods to be adopted to do so.

Shortly before the general election campaign began I purchased an old London taxi for the (to me) huge sum of £80. It was what was called a landaulette, which meant that it had a fabric roof which we used to let down so that I could stand on the rear seat with a microphone in my hand and a loudspeaker in front of me on the roof-rack. We plastered the sides of the taxi with posters urging the electors to vote for du Cann.

The crowds we met were never tiresome. True, we had a few vegetables thrown at us; true, I also saw bricks thrown; but by and large people acted in the best English way, pleasant, sometimes interested but mostly not, sometimes amused, sometimes abusive, but almost always tolerant. Politics forty-five years ago lacked the organised, extremist, slogan-chanting, missile-throwing, groups that one sometimes encounters today, democracy's vicious enemies, unwilling to tolerate any opinion but their own.

I did political work outside Walthamstow and became Chairman of the City of London Young Conservatives. Our most important activity was open-air meetings. We conducted these on bombed sites and other open spaces in the City where we could attract lunch-time crowds, particularly on Tower Hill, a more traditional spot for speakers even than Hyde Park. I also accepted speaking invitations elsewhere all over the country, but especially in the north eastern area of London.

During this time I came in touch with leading figures in our Party, all of whom treated me with kindness and encouragement. Notable among them were Iain Macleod and his friend and contemporary Enoch Powell, but I have to admit that they were the two with whom I felt least at home. I should have been their unqualified admirer but they always gave me a feeling of slight discomfort, if not distaste. I was ashamed of this reservation at the time: now in the light of subsequent events I understand it better. Enoch was often unpredictable in his opinions, apparently brilliant but often eccentric. Iain, for all his cleverness, struck me as simply untrustworthy.

There was one man I met in those days whom I came especially and deeply to respect. John Harvey was the prospective Conservative candidate in Walthamstow East, the constituency next to mine. This seat was also held by Labour but on a small enough majority to give the Conservatives a good chance of taking it. We decided that once our campaign was up and running in Walthamstow West we would draft some of our supporters into John's constituency where there was a better chance of victory, and in the event that was what we did. Meanwhile we continued to wait impatiently for the announcement of a general election. It surely could not be long. Mr Attlee was beleaguered. Abroad, there were tensions; at home, economic stringency. The Government lacked cohesion. Ill health had forced the resignation of the Chancellor of the Exchequer, Sir Stafford Cripps. The greatly respected Ernest Bevin, Foreign Secretary throughout the six years of Labour's administration, had died. Aneurin Bevan, Minister of Labour, Harold Wilson, President of the Board of Trade, and John Freeman, a junior Minister at Supply, had resigned as Ministers in protest at the introduction of charges in the Health Service. Since the 1950 general election Labour's majority over the Conservatives in the House of Commons had been only 17, with an overall majority of 6. Twice votes were tied, with the Chairman's vote given in the Government's favour; once its majority was only one. The Labour Government was walking a tightrope and being relentlessly harried by the Conservatives, especially over its dogmatic proposal to nationalise the steel industry.

In a radio broadcast after the nine o'clock news on 19 September 1951, Mr Attlee announced that the general election would take place on 25 October. At last the time had come and we could start our campaign in the two Walthamstow seats, East and West. We worked and we worked. It was canvassing all day and meetings all evening. John Harvey had a certain amount of outside help, as he deserved in his marginal seat. Churchill came to make an outdoor speech for him. He made it standing on the running board of my London taxi. It was thrilling to be introduced to the great man, to shake him by the hand and have his good wishes, and to stand at his side as he spoke to the huge crowd which pressed around us.

The weeks flew by – and then came the moment of truth. For John and me, as for Attlee, our fate was to be settled – life in Government or death in opposition. The poll closed at nine p.m. The sealed ballot boxes, thirty or forty of them, were brought under police supervision to the Walthamstow Town Hall, where the counts for both Walthamstow seats took place together in one room.

Imagine the scene. A huge room filled with trestle tables in four lines, each a hundred feet long, two hundred local officials sitting on either side to count the votes. Some hundreds of the most partisan supporters of each Parliamentary candidate are also present, a number sitting at the tables opposite the officials checking the counting process, the majority in the large gallery watching the scene. The Mayor and other officials are walking about, supervising and looking important. The atmosphere is curiously hushed and there is an air of expectancy. First the counters and the returning officer check that the number of votes in each box corresponds with the returns from each polling station of the numbers actually voting. Then all the votes are counted and totalled. That done, it is time to total each candidate's share – and now the excitement begins.

Mr Attlee did not appear until the count was well advanced. He greeted his principal supporters, the civic dignitaries, the returning officer and the other candidates, then he came to me. He spoke to me like an old friend and ally, and we talked together of literature and politics for a full half hour without interruption. He spoke of his experiences in Government in peace and war. I was mesmerised. I later learned that his kindness to me had been the subject of some criticism among his supporters. He smoked his pipe and was quite relaxed. You would not have thought he had a care in the world, certainly not that he had been fighting in the general election for his political life and that in the next hour the fate of the Government he led was to be decided. Whenever things have gone badly for me later in life I have thought of that patriotic and modest Englishman's example of calmness at a time of crisis.

Half an hour later the count in the borough of Walthamstow was almost complete. First the candidates and their agents were called to an adjudication of the spoiled ballot papers. Filling in a simple ballot paper is apparently beyond some people's competence, even in these days of universal education. There were fifty or sixty spoiled papers, some mutilated, some with crosses in the wrong place, one or two with

43

obscene messages and a dozen with the word 'socialism' written across them.

'What does that mean?' I asked Mr Attlee.

'They think I'm not socialist enough,' he replied. 'I know them of old.'

The adjudication complete, the result was ready to be announced. The hall was feverish with excitement. We went up onto the stage, the candidates, the agents, the returning officer and a few others. The candidates and the agents wore huge rosettes. I was trembling a bit.

Walthamstow West was the first result to be declared. 'As returning officer for the Parliamentary constituency of Walthamstow West,' intoned the returning officer in that extraordinary tone of voice only returning officers and masters of ceremonies at boxing matches affect, 'I declare that the votes for each candidate at the Election were as follows: Attlee, Clement Richard.' He paused. '23,021 votes.'

There were loud cheers, and the returning officer had to pause for quite some time.

'Du Cann, Edward Dillon Lott.'

('What funny Christian names,' I heard someone remark.)

'11,447 votes.'

I felt deflated. The result in West Walthamstow was a crushing defeat for us, but of course it inevitably had to be. It was not until later that I came to realise that we had done pretty well. True, the Labour vote had increased by 2,000 votes but ours was up by 2,450. We had polled the highest Tory vote in Walthamstow West since the landslide general election of 1931, a twenty years' record, and I could truthfully say that I had reduced a Labour Prime Minister's majority. Anyway, the campaign had been a marvellous experience and I had enjoyed every minute of it.

John Harvey was narrowly defeated at Walthamstow East. His re-elected Labour opponent gave the Communist clenched-fist salute and his supporters sang 'The Red Flag'. The Tories did their best with 'Land of Hope and Glory'. 'Reminds me of the Eatonswill election,' Attlee said to me in an aside, 'where each one sang the song that best he knew.'

Nationally, things went well for the Conservatives. The Parliamentary stalemate was over and Labour was defeated, its overall majority of six replaced by an overall majority of seventeen for the Conservatives. Winston Churchill was again Prime Minister. For me it was a return from the excitement and prominence of the hustings to a workaday and private existence; back to earning my daily bread. I was twenty-six years old. What next? I wondered.

The question was answered for me. If I wanted to keep my job in Denys Lowson's company, I was told by my superiors, I had to give up active politics. He was now Sir Denys, first Baronet, Lord Mayor of London, and he took his civic duties seriously. He never refused an invitation and the office buzzed with stories of his eating two dinners on several evenings: once, it was whispered, he ate three. He could not, he said, have a young man on his staff opposing the Prime Minister while he was prominent in civic affairs. As Lord Mayor he was expected to be politically neutral. I bore him no ill will. He was entitled to employ whoever he wanted and to make his own terms. I resigned my candidature in Walthamstow with the full agreement of the local Tories. I needed the wages. They understood.

So for the next four years I concentrated on my own career and by 1955 I was earning enough money to buy my first new car, a small open-top Morris. I parked it at night in Kensington outside my new digs and drove to the City every morning. There I left it on a bombed site. There were still plenty to choose from. One sunny evening in mid-April 1955 I walked to the car after my day's work and switched on the radio. The new Prime Minister, Anthony Eden, Churchill's successor, was to broadcast in a few minutes. I put down the hood and sat waiting in the sunshine. He announced the forthcoming general election. I felt sick. I would be out of it.

The next day I was at a lunch attended by Sir Denys Lowson. 'What seat are you fighting?' he asked.

'I don't have a candidature,' I replied. 'You made it clear that you wanted me to give up active politics while I worked for you.'

But by now he had changed his mind and to my delight he told me I ought to fight in the general election if I could find a seat. It was the eleventh hour and I telephoned Conservative Central Office that afternoon. What candidatures remained unfilled? Out of the 630 constituencies in the United Kingdom, I was told, there were only two, Ebbw Vale in South Wales and Barrow in Furness in Lancashire. Ebbw Vale had Aneurin Bevan as its sitting Member. What fun, I thought, to have opposed Attlee in 1951 and Bevan in 1955. But the Welsh Conservative Area Office in Cardiff told me they were sure that the Conservative candidate who had fought the seat in 1951 would be selected again, so I turned to Barrow.

I looked up the result of the 1951 general election there and found that there had been a straight fight between Labour and Conservative, ending in a Labour majority of 6,484, some 12 per cent of the electorate.

45

That was substantial, but not impregnable. To put it at its best, it was only half as bad from the Conservative point of view as West Walthamstow.

I rang up the Conservative office in Barrow. No, they said, they had no candidate yet. Did I want to be the candidate?

'Yes,' I said, 'very much.'

'Well,' they said, 'we have a public meeting next Saturday and we don't yet have a speaker; why don't you come up?'

I had never been to Barrow, but I did some careful researches. Most of the employed men worked in heavy engineering, in Vickers' shipyards. There was little light industry and the number of women employed locally was well below the national average. It was virtually a one-industry town.

Barrow's situation was magnificent. The town, with its wide streets, was well laid out and it had many attractions – beaches, parks and, nearby, the glorious Lake District. However, it was an isolated community, remote from the main body of the County of Lancashire in which it was then included. Its people had bitter memories of unemployment between the wars, and even in the late 1950s, in a period of national full employment, there was, I thought, substantial under-employment of both sexes and of women especially, and too little choice of work for both men and women.

I was struck by the neatness and tidiness of the town, as I was also by the friendliness of everyone I met. They were warmer than London people, less reserved, more ready to give friendship a short apprenticeship. When I went up to address the public meeting I had a crowd of about a hundred; all Conservative supporters. The Chairman was a foreman in the shipyard, a small man, dark, thin, an engineer. He was wearing a blue suit, a white shirt and shoes that were polished like those of a sergeant major. I thought he seemed wary of me, but when the meeting was over he shook my hand and would not let it go. 'We've got a meeting of the committee now,' he said. 'You'd better come.'

'Give me a minute,' I said.

I went to the exit of the hall and shook hands with everyone who was leaving. All were working people, most from the shipyard. Their handclasps were ferocious, like vices, even the women. I've never had my hand shaken so hard. I moved on to the committee meeting, in a little room in the club. They all stood up and applauded.

'Well,' I said, 'thank you very much.'

'Are you going to be the candidate?' the Chairman asked.

'Do you really want me?' I asked. (That was a foolish error, I reflected: I should have said yes at once and with emphasis.)

'Do you want us?' he said.

'Oh,' I said, 'with all my heart I do.' I felt some tears pricking at the back of my eyeballs. This won't do, I thought.

'That's settled then,' said the Chairman.

'Thank you very much,' I said. 'I'll do my best.' They applauded again. They were all grinning.

'We could have a meeting soon, to plan the campaign perhaps,' I said.

'You're the gaffer now,' said the Chairman. 'You say what you want and we'll do it.'

We all had a drink in the Conservative Club. Most of the people there had come to have a drink in congenial surroundings – the price of a pint was less than in the pubs – or they were there to play snooker or darts, or just to gossip with friends. Few were in the club primarily to support the Conservative Party, though all were professed Party members. From the political point of view, the club had been asleep since the last general election. Now the members were ready to be woken up. I spoke to every one of them and shook them all by hand – again those vicelike grips. To all of them I gave the same message: Barrow had been a Labour seat since 1945. It was time for a change.

I returned to the office in London to get time off to campaign. My superiors wanted to refuse me but they had heard Sir Denys Lowson encourage me to find a candidature so they were not able to. Bang went my summer holidays for the year. I started to mobilise support. The Conservative area office in Manchester was helpful. We were promised a little cash and an agent for the campaign's duration. I spoke to everyone I could find who could tell me about Barrow and I learned a great deal. In a week I was back there with a team of friends from the City of London Young Conservatives, all of whom similarly gave up their holidays and spent their savings on this adventure. We all came up squeezed into the open-top Morris and we found inexpensive digs easily. Barrow was well accustomed to accommodating sailors waiting to commission ships.

We planned our campaign: outdoor canvassing all day and indoor meetings at night. We wrote leaflets, each with a local message. We stuck up 'Wanted' posters with my picture on them and the text 'Sentence this man to five years hard labour at Westminster.' We appointed team leaders, one for preparing the envelopes to take the election address, one for organising leaflet deliveries, one for the evening meetings, one for press relations, one for canvassing returns, one to oversee polling day tellers at the polling stations. We were backed by the local Party members but we badly needed more workers. The bandwagon was beginning to roll; but it had long lain unused in the garage. Too long, perhaps?

As I trudged the streets all my original views were confirmed: Barrow, it was clear, was a one-industry town, dominated by the Vickers shipyards with its proud record of naval shipbuilding. Unemployment was obvious, at a time when the rest of Britain enjoyed full employment. It was not difficult to decide what I would do if I were elected MP for Barrow – work hard to bring new industries to the town. It could be done and it should have been attempted by the Labour Council and the sitting Labour MP years before: they had failed those who had elected them. The theme for my campaign was obvious and I set to work with a will. It was a good message, simple, clear, unanswerable. It went home and we made progress, but we were starting very late.

We got ourselves in the local newspaper every day and we made ourselves as conspicuous as we could in every part of the constituency. We bought a van from a scrap yard for £10, painted it bright blue, put a loudspeaker on it and drove it around the constituency from early in the morning to late at night, advertising our meetings, our candidate and our views. Because of his oft-reiterated broadcast message, the driver became known as 'Peace and Prosperity'. We made ourselves heard and we got ourselves noticed. I particularly enjoyed our daily lunch-time outdoor meetings at the shipyard gates. Every day we spoke to crowds of workers, sometimes a thousand or more, and they were always polite and attentive while I was speaking – though once, when I left, they pushed one of my supporters' cars over.

We could not have done more. The agent, my friend of many years, Jack Ashworth, was superb. Polling day came. We knew we were close but we could not tell how close. We did not have a comprehensive organisation in spite of its reinforcement, so our intelligence was inadequate. Our canvass was incomplete and in spite of all our efforts we had failed to reach many of the electors, even with leaflets.

The count began sensationally. When half the votes had been counted we Conservatives were a thousand votes ahead. I could hardly believe my good fortune: by the law of averages we should be two thousand votes ahead at the end. But, alas, it was too good to be true. The boxes of uncounted votes were from areas in the constituency less well inclined to our cause than those that had been opened first. In the final result Labour retained the seat with a majority of 2,759 votes. It was something that we had reduced Labour's majority of 6,484 by more than half; but the aim in an election contest is to win. There are no consolation prizes for coming second. Robert Rhodes James tells the story of Mo Udall, the US Congressman who was defeated by Jimmy Carter in his campaign to become the Democratic Party's Presidential Candidate. His concession speech was short and to the point. 'The people have spoken,' he said. 'The bastards.' It is reasonable to assume, as he did not serve in the Royal Navy, that he did not mean the word as a term of endearment.

It was in the Parliament of 1955 that regional policy first came to be introduced as an integral part of Government activity. The purpose was excellent. Financial aid was provided to help the less prosperous areas of our country and to cushion the impact on local communities of the decline of certain of Britain's basic industries. Substantial grants were awarded as of right to new industries setting up in these areas. I would have worked hard to exploit that policy in the interests of the good people of Barrow in Furness, but I did not have the chance.

I left a not inconsiderable part of my heart in Barrow: the people there may well have forgotten me – why indeed should they recall my short excursion there? – but I shall never forget them. Nor shall I forget the campaigning lesson that Barrow taught me, the vital importance of a good constituency organisation that is prepared to work hard not just in the run-up to an election but for years beforehand, recruiting, organising, broadening the base of support in every area of the constituency through local functions and activities, establishing trade union branches, Young Conservative groups, women's organisations and the like, especially a strong local government presence. This lesson was to be of the greatest importance to me later when I became Chairman of the Party.

But at the time I thought, what is the good of learning lessons if you are not going to have the chance to apply them? It seemed like bad news for me personally that the Conservative Party had done well nationally, winning an overall majority of sixty seats. It was a good working margin and it would be unrealistic to expect another general election for at least four years. I would not have another chance to get myself elected to Parliament until I was thirty-five, unless there was a by-election and I could get myself selected as a candidate. What were the odds? On average there were at that time twelve by-elections each year. About six would probably take place in seats that were comparatively safe for one Party or the other: the remainder would be marginal. That meant only three or four chances a year, and competition for the Conservative nominations would be fierce indeed; hundreds would apply in any seat where there was a chance of election. I resigned myself to waiting. There was nothing else to do.

In the office I had been promoted to Secretary of Sir Denys Lowson's unit trust management companies. I had put through a reorganisation of their constitutions. I had extended the lives of those that were about to mature, adopted more modern trust deeds, and developed a number of modest marketing procedures. My legal training stood me in good stead. My salary, more than adequate for a bachelor, had reached over £3,000 a year. I had bought my first house, our home in Partridge Green that Mother was renting, for £1,060. I was proud to have done that.

Financially I was doing well enough, but in other ways I was far from content with my job and found myself increasingly opposed to the management of the business. I had put forward a series of ideas to develop it but they were all rejected with little serious consideration. More important, I disliked the way in which the investment policies were sometimes conducted. Too often they seemed to me to put the interests of management ahead of the investor. Again I proposed changes; again they were turned down. Finally, my immediate superiors made it clear that they disliked my political activities. In their view I was too big for my boots.

I decided to leave and set up a company of my own. Once I had made the decision I felt greatly relieved and started to look forward eagerly to this new enterprise. But my plans had to be unexpectedly deferred: the news came that there was to be a by-election in the Somerset constituency of Taunton (the neighbouring one to Honiton, where my great great uncle had twice been the MP). I wrote at once offering myself as a candidate – and so, I later found out, did more than a hundred others.

The constituency included the county town of Taunton, the smaller town of Wellington (from which the great duke took his name) and a large area of some of the most beautiful countryside in England, quite sparsely populated. Disraeli had been a candidate for election there in 1835 and enjoyed his celebrated row with O'Connell, leader of the Irish Catholics. Before the 1939-45 War Taunton had sent either Liberal or Conservative members to Parliament, but in the general election of 1945 it had elected its first Labour MP. The Conservatives were determined to win back the seat and in the 1950 general election they did. Henry Hopkinson, a former diplomat and friend of Anthony Eden, was elected with a slender majority of 1,372 votes, which in 1951 he increased to 3,981 and in 1955 to over 5,000. But he made a blunder, a surprising one for an ex-diplomat. He had been appointed Minister of State for Colonial

Affairs and one day in the House of Commons he was unwise enough to say that the island of Cyprus could never expect to be fully independent. (A good politician's rule: never say never.) He was given a rough time in the House and his words continued to be quoted against him. In the end they probably cost him his job. At the end of 1955 he resigned from the Government and chose to go to the Lords rather than continue on the back benches.

The Conservative Party in Taunton was shocked and angry but it set to work to find a candidate. The list of a hundred aspirants was reduced to ten and that number included every person living locally who had sent in his name. I was one of the lucky ones to be interviewed by a selection committee, meeting in a small room in the Castle Hotel in Taunton. My name was included largely by accident. Faced with over a hundred names, most of them quite unknown to the committee, its members were anxious to recognise any they could. Smith, Jones, Brown and Robinson are all excellent names but they do not stand out. Du Cann does stand out, like a sore thumb. When my name was mentioned a young Conservative present said he had heard me speak well and amusingly at a weekend school in Torquay, so I was pulled out of the scrum and included in the short list.

Several days later I was delighted to learn that, the short list having been further reduced to four, I was still among them. A few days after that there was to be a meeting of representatives of every branch of the Taunton Conservative Association which each of us would be invited to address and a final selection would be made that same night.

The day came, and with it the fog, like a shroud. The four of us were in the Castle Hotel waiting to be summoned when Edgar Betts, the agent, came to tell us that the meeting was cancelled as the representatives could not get into Taunton from the country branches. A week later we were summoned back and this time there was no fog. Each of us addressed the meeting and I spoke first, not the easiest position. (I believe now that the agent had placed me badly in the list on purpose. I may be wrong, but I guess he wanted a rich man as his candidate.) My speech was only modestly applauded, I felt. Clive Bossom, one of my friendly rivals that night, told me later that they were all laughing as I left the room but I don't remember that at all. I waited in the outer office while the others had their turn. They all seemed to get more applause than I had.

At last it was over. The agent appeared. 'Will you come in?' he said to me. He did not even tell me the reason why I was wanted back in the hall, nor did he say why the others were apparently unwanted. I realised it only when I was standing on the platform like an idiot while the Chairman and officers shook my hand and waited for me to say a few gracious words. I could have kissed everyone in the room, I was so elated. I don't remember what I said. The legend goes that I promised three things. First that I would make my home in the constituency – which I did , even though I may not have made the promise at the time. Second that I would always do my damnedest for the Conservative Party – I hope that I have done that too. And third, that I would get married. That I am sure I did not undertake, though I might have become engaged to almost any one of the members of the Women's Advisory Committee that night, I was so carelessly rapturous.

Clive Bossom said I had concluded my original speech with the declaration: 'Ladies and gentlemen, those are my principles, but if you don't like them I am perfectly willing to change them.' That I know I have not done, though both he and I have known many who might have done so and one or two who probably did. I was told later that I received more votes from those attending the meeting than the other three candidates put together. Not that I minded: a majority of one would have sufficed.

I returned to London to make plans. The news that I had been selected as the candidate was grudgingly received by my superiors in the office, but they agreed that provided I did not take any holiday for the rest of the year I could go down to Taunton for the whole period of the campaign. That made the second year running I had no holiday. Who cared? The date of the by-election was fixed for 14 February, Saint Valentine's day, and the sooner I got into the hard work, the better. Luckily I had the experience of two previous campaigns behind me, but I knew Taunton and its people not at all and they didn't know me from Adam. I was a countryman at heart but I knew little in a practical sense about the constituency's principal interest, agriculture. Unlike my predecessor, I was no horseman either: I hadn't even been astride a donkey in Weston-Super-Mare.

There were other demerits in the scene which I began to learn about. In early 1956 the Government was vastly less popular than it had been at the time of the general election of 1955, a mere eight months before. I found, to my growing anxiety, that there were divisions among the Conservatives in Taunton, and these soon took overt form. Two brothers, prominent in business affairs in the town of Taunton, Bert and Jim Wilson, later to become firm friends of mine, were protesting publicly about the policies of Eden's Government, one in a letter published in *The*

Times. This glaring disagreement in the Conservative camp was being gleefully exploited by our opponents and other national newspapers were taking up the story. The spotlight of national attention and publicity concentrated on a single constituency always makes a by-election campaign harder for the candidates to manage than a general election campaign. The chief skill is to avoid mistakes which the press will feature and your opponents exploit. Looking back on the campaign I find that on the whole we received good publicity in the national press, but the political correspondents' scepticism about Conservative chances was plain – 'Fickle Taunton,' they wrote in eager anticipation of an upset. Nor was the reason for the by-election completely understood or sympathised with. There were many Taunton Conservatives who thought that Henry Hopkinson should not have accepted a peerage but should have remained on the back benches; others resented Eden's dismissal of a loyal Minister; and there were few of my supporters who relished the work involved in organising a by-election in mid-winter with snow and ice on the ground, especially on Exmoor.

As the campaign developed Harold Wilson came down to Taunton to take personal command of his Party's effort. It was an ominous sign of confidence in the Labour camp: he was too careful and cunning a campaigner to risk his reputation unless there was a good chance of enhancing it. I began to realise that I would have a hard fight. Hopkinson's majority of 5,542 was by no means as secure as the numbers indicated. Nothing could be left to chance. I visited as many Conservative branches and functions as possible in the week before the campaign proper started with my formal adoption as the candidate. Getting myself known was the most constructive thing I could possibly do. I shook innumerable hands. Everyone was friendly enough: I thanked Heaven for past canvassing experience which made me at home in such situations, and for past speaking experience too. It is important when you talk to make your audience feel relaxed. In open-air speeches this is crucial. You will lose all your audience in seconds if you fail at this. Those weeks and months and years of work up and down the country were paying off.

Then I had a stroke of luck. The *Somerset County Gazette*, our local weekly newspaper, taken by and read in eighty per cent of the households in the Taunton area, printed a picture on its front page of the new Conservative Parliamentary candidate surrounded by a group of supporters one sunny afternoon. It was a happy photograph, but what made it really telling was that on the same evening I appeared on television – and in those days a TV appearance marked one out as a celebrity. The programme was 'This is Your Life', and the life in question was that of my friend the late Donald Campbell, sometime holder of the world's water and land speed records. I knew him because his first wife was a girl who had lived in Partridge Green: she and I had grown up together. In 1948 my late brother Dick and I went with the Campbells by small motor boat, a converted naval torpedo recovery vessel, to Lisbon. We had filled the boat with samples of British manufactured goods hoping to bring home enough orders to pay our expenses and make some cash besides. The trip was not a success. We got fewer orders than we hoped for, and after I had left to come home the boat sank in Lisbon; calor gas in the bilges had caused an explosion. My brother and Donald were lucky not to lose their lives.

I was instantly recognised in Taunton by many who heard my unusual name on the programme and who on the same day had become aware of my connection with the constituency through the *Gazette* photograph. It was indeed a happy coincidence. By accident I achieved any new candidate's chief campaign objective: I became known. The advantage enjoyed by my Labour opponent, that having fought the seat once before he was better known than me, was nullified. He had never been on television.

Edgar Betts, the Conservative agent, was a superb organiser. He set up our election programme with precision and thoroughness. Every part of the constituency was canvassed. Evening meetings took place in every ward in the towns of Taunton and Wellington and in every village, never less than four meetings each night during the campaign. There were supporting speakers at them all including Derick Heathcoat Amory, MP for neighbouring Tiverton and then Minister of Agriculture. The meetings were all well attended and the mood was serious.

But the battle was a tough one: there was an absence of enthusiasm among our supporters while the Labour people were growing unusually confident. Many Labour posters were in evidence and not so many of ours. I plugged away, canvassing all day, doing my best to awaken and develop enthusiasm, on the doorstep, in the committee rooms and at evening meetings. It was exhausting, but hard work was the only recipe for success.

John Harvey, my old friend from Walthamstow, was one of the visiting speakers. He dined out for years afterwards on the story of his experience. He arrived, he said, at the back of nowhere at some village hall five minutes before his meeting was due to start to find the hall in darkness, the electricity apparently cut off and not a soul other than his driver and guide in sight. Four minutes before time, a lady appeared. She announced that she was the secretary of the local Conservative branch and asked him to give her a shilling for the electricity meter. John obliged. She found the key to the hall under a mat and opened it up. A minute later and she had put a Union flag, a green baize cloth, a jug of water and two glasses on the table at one end of the hall and five people were present. The Chairman arrived one minute after that, and at one minute past the start time there were seventy-five people present, one third of the electorate in that village. The hall was packed to suffocation. 'Just as well,' said John, 'it was cold as charity outside. Body warmth was the only heat available – apart,' he added modestly, 'from my heart-warming speech. It was too bad I had to pay to deliver it.'

The votes were counted on 15 February, the day after polling day, and the result of the election was announced to a large crowd outside the Municipal Hall in Taunton at about lunch-time: du Cann, E. D. L. (Conservative) 19,820; Pestell R. (Labour) 19,163; Conservative majority 657.

There were gasps all round at the small size of the majority, but much relief among our supporters. John Harvey remarked that the result was very creditable to me: to reduce an apparently safe Conservative seat to the status of a marginal one was a prodigious achievement.

The newspapers had a field day. Three other by-elections took place that week – a miniature general election, the papers said, the first test of popular opinion as to the Government's standing since the general election nine months earlier. In the four by-elections, at Taunton, Gainsborough, Hereford and Leeds (where Sir Keith Joseph was elected for the first time) the Conservative candidates were returned, but all with sharply reduced majorities and the Conservative majority at Taunton fell the most.

The truth is that we might easily have lost. When Harold Wilson came down to take personal charge of the Labour Party's efforts towards the end of the campaign, he and the principal Labour workers in Taunton undoubtedly believed they were about to repeat their triumph of 1945. Cunning he certainly was. His visit, though well known locally, went unnoticed nationally. When the Tories won he kept his part in the campaign very quiet; had Labour taken the seat we should doubtless have heard his trumpeting from afar.

I believe we won because of the superiority of our organisation over that of our opponents. Our campaign was by far the more effective of the two. I can give one striking example of this. Through our ward and village organisations we gathered in no fewer than three thousand postal votes, substantially the greatest proportion of which were Conservative votes. Yet our majority was a mere 657. If we had been only half as efficient at ward and village level we would have lost the by-election by a thousand votes.

I do not claim to have been an ideal candidate, but my experience of two previous campaigns was invaluable. We made no mistakes; there were no tactless moves. We converted cynics into allies, made lifelong friends of our leading supporters, never forfeited goodwill and set an example of unrelenting effort. In eighteen days, I addressed almost a hundred meetings and I canvassed several thousand people in their homes; every day there were questionnaires and correspondence to answer, press handouts to issue, factories to visit, interest groups such as the farmers, the trades unions and the hospital workers with whom to conduct discussions – it was gruelling work but the adrenalin flowed. I was one member of a competent and loyal team. The Taunton Conservatives were well organised and that was why we won the day.

I spent the next two days touring the constituency (forty miles long and ten miles broad) to express my appreciation – another fifty speeches. By doing so, I made myself unpopular with the Party hierarchy in London, who had wanted me to be introduced into the House of Commons at once. But how could I let that even begin to spoil the delight I felt? For years I had worked and planned for this moment. As every young candidate does, I had faced hostility, discouragement and defeat. My father and I, between us, had fought four losing battles spanning thirty years. Now that was all past. I had fought a difficult election and won it. My Parliamentary career had begun.

CHAPTER 3

BIRTH
of a UNICORN

On the Monday morning after I had taken my seat in Parliament I went back to work in the office. I received a grudging welcome. My immediate superior promptly cut my salary by half and I was told that under no circumstances should I do any Parliamentary or constituency work in the office; no writing, no telephoning, nothing.

I asked for one last time if I might be allowed to develop the business. Again, I was refused. That put the lid on it as far as I was concerned. I got out my calculations for the establishment of a new unit trust management company, let a couple of months go by and then sent in my resignation. My immediate colleagues were, I regret to say, glad to see the back of me. It confirmed my feeling that they thought I had grown too big for my Company Secretary's boots. Even Sir Denys Lowson must have thought so: I was allowed to leave without a goodbye interview. I was not sorry; a discussion between us would only have led to my being critical of his management methods.

My income was now no more than my parliamentary salary of £1,250 a year, and my expenses were heavy. Rail travel to Taunton was free but I had to pay for a secretary, postage and telephones, as well as travel and other expenses in the constituency. Luckily, being still a bachelor, I had little by way of personal expenses to meet, except for my living costs in four places – London, Taunton, Partridge Green and the House of Commons. So it went on for months. No wonder the Taunton constituency agent had not been keen on me as Conservative candidate. All my predecessors had kept up a certain standard; comparatively, they were rich men; indeed, any one of my competitors would have been richer than me. Alas, I had to sell my Sussex house: my mother and I made a house together in Westminster.

I made my maiden speech in the House of Commons in the budget debate of that year. Re-reading it now, it seems to me pretty anodyne, but Mr Macmillan, then Chancellor of the Exchequer, described it in his winding up speech as one of the best he had heard. Perhaps he hadn't heard many, I thought; but I kept my opinion to myself and of course I was privately euphoric.

Those early days in the House were magic. I was asked to join a small group of Members which had its own research staff. We met each week to plan a joint approach to the issues of the moment and dined together monthly with an invited guest. It was a splendid experience as a young Member of Parliament to exchange ideas with such Parliamentary greats as Alan Lennox Boyd (who also had served in MTBs in the War), Derick Heathcoat Amory, Iain Macleod, Quintin Hailsham and R. A. Butler. Butler, I noted with amazement, found it impossible to express himself in straightforward language, even at a gathering of friends: all his ideas were retailed in convoluted terms.

Sitting opposite Harold Macmillan one night at a dinner I noticed he ate little. I asked him if he was unwell. 'It's not that,' he said. 'I just can't eat before making a speech.' That struck me as strange in someone who was such a master of public speaking, though as the years have gone by I too have found that I do not eat well before a speech. There is no demerit in nervousness: a total lack of it may come from insensitivity to the audience, the hallmark of the bore.

On the Conservative side of the House there are a number of dining clubs, each one made up of MPs who share much the same political outlook. The 92 Club, for example, has a right-wing stance; Nick's Diner is more to the left. Both have an exclusively Parliamentary membership. The Burke Club was different. On the right of the Party, its purpose was to effect a liaison between younger Conservative MPs and people active in the newspaper and literary world; its membership has included such literary figures as T. S. Eliot, Arthur Bryant, Kingsley Amis and many well known journalists. I was its Chairman for nine years.

These clubs, together with groups outside Parliament such as the Inns of Court Conservative Association (which was my father's original idea, and which David Maxwell Fyffe took up) do much original political work and have great value to the Party. When, later, I became Chairman of the Conservative Party I did my best – against some opposition – to encourage them.

Part of the magic of being in the House of Commons when I first entered it was to see the great Winston Churchill. Throughout question periods he would sit slumped in the end seat of the Treasury bench below the gangway and then, when they were over, would leave, assisted out of the Chamber by one of my senior colleagues. I never heard Churchill speak in the Chamber but we did talk one afternoon in the Smoke Room. He sat down next to Peter Rawlinson, the MP for Epsom, and myself. We were having tea, but Winston ordered brandy and smoked a cigar. During the War Peter, then in the Guards, had been sent to Chartwell with a message 'by hand of officer'. He was shown into a room which had several of Winston's paintings on the walls. Winston kept him waiting. When he came into the room, dressed in a siren suit, he said, 'Young man, you have been here some time. You have had a good opportunity to look at these paintings. Which do you like the best?'

It was a wretchedly difficult question for a young man to answer. One cannot offend a Prime Minister in wartime – or at any time – by saying the wrong thing. Should he say he liked them all? That would be tactful if cowardly. He must not dissemble. He pointed to a snow scene of Chartwell. 'I think this one, Prime Minister,' he said.

'Young man,' said Churchill, 'you show excellent' – he pronounced it 'egg-shell-unt' – 'judgement. It is my own favourite. Wait here please.' He left the room and reappeared a minute later, grinning, with a whisky decanter, a siphon, two glasses and a box of cigars. It was some time before Lieutenant Rawlinson could take his leave.

As we drank our tea and the old man puffed his cigar, Peter reminded him of the occasion. 'Hum,' said Churchill. 'Painting never did anyone any harm.'

1956, the year I was elected, was a remarkable year in the House of Commons. Within a few months I found myself trooping obediently through the lobbies in support of the Anglo-French invasion of Suez. I could not pretend to be comfortable in doing so. I did not like the bombing raids by the RAF, and the landings by Allied troops seemed to be lethargically executed. It was obvious that the nation was not being told the whole truth about the adventure, and some of the information we were given in private meetings of backbenchers turned out to be rubbish – for example that the Egyptians left to themselves would be incapable of operating pilotage in the Suez Canal. I had a private suspicion that the whole foray was an attempt to recapture an influence and a glory for our country that was already a thing of the past. The adventure was a profound misjudgement on the part of the Conservative Government. President Nasser was not Hitler and the Egyptians were not Nazis. The attitude of the Labour Party led by Mr Gaitskell was equally uneasy.

Appearing at first to be sympathetic to British action, Gaitskell soon reneged and became critical. The atmosphere in the House of Commons was charged and unhappy.

Having faithfully supported the invasion of Egypt we Conservative backbenchers were then commanded to support the evacuation. Both instructions couldn't be right: if it was appropriate to mount the invasion, it should have been prosecuted to the end; if it was right to come out early the invasion should never have been undertaken at all. But we trooped through the lobbies like sheep.

The failure of the Suez invasion was a profound shock; it soured my early years in the House. I felt I could not again wholly trust our leaders, and we would be wise not to trust our allies. I sensed in my bones that I had lived through a critical period in our country's fortunes which perhaps spotlighted something I had not been aware of previously, namely that after 1945 a period of serious decline in our world influence and authority had begun. Suez was a watershed.

If 1956 was a critical year in politics, 1957 was to prove a watershed year for me commercially. I took my careful and modest proposals for the establishment of a new unit trust management company, which Lowson had turned down, to a host of potential financial backers. All without exception gave the same discouraging two-part response. The first part was a flat statement that the idea was very unlikely to succeed. No one I spoke to had the least confidence in it. The second part of the response was in effect the *coup de grace*: 'If this is such a good idea, Mr du Cann, pray tell us, why has no one else thought of it before?'

All those I saw, merchant bankers, investment trust managers, entrepreneurs, the representatives of the UK's leading financial institutions, thirty or so in all, were plain sceptical; some were disdainful; a few were rude; all told me that my optimism was misplaced, if not foolish. Quite a number made it plain that had I not been a Member of Parliament they probably would not have bothered to give me an interview at all.

This was the reality of the City of London in 1957 as it represented itself to one eager seeker of capital. I was trying to get finance to launch an enterprise with a proud record of financial success in the United States, from where so many commercially successful ideas have been imported into the United Kingdom, and its purpose was to popularise the investment facilities provided by the City. Naïve as I was, I supposed that this objective would be immediately attractive to City leaders, especially if there was some cash to be made out of it. I was hopelessly wrong. The attitude of investment managers was complacent and unadventurous. My carefully typed prospectus grew increasingly dog-eared with repeated handling, but I would not give up. I was so sure I was right and everybody else was wrong.

I was utterly convinced that the man in the street would eagerly invest in unit trusts if only he could be made aware that they existed and if their advantages were demonstrated to him. The problem, as I saw it, was that Mr John Bull was thoroughly overawed by the City and its institutions. A stockbroker, he believed, existed only to serve the rich: even a banker's parlour was a forbidding place. At that time, the overwhelming majority of our fellow citizens did not have bank accounts, or even building society savings accounts, and for those who did push their way into the closed world of investment it was a hazardous business. If they put their money into only one or two companies they risked everything on the success of those companies. If they spread it among a greater number each investment became so small that the cost of making it could wipe out much of the profit. It is true that some unit trusts did already exist, but they attracted only a small number of investors and I believed I could see why. Their management style and investment practices were in my view unsatisfactory and obsolete. The enterprise I planned would offer improved protection for the investor and a better return on his or her money. If it had to be a Mini rather than a juggernaut to start with, at least it would be a huge improvement on the Model-T Ford that the older unit trusts resembled.

'Sliced bread' No, I'm afraid that would never catch on, Mr du Cann.

My aim was simple in essence: to popularise investment, and to give the man in the street a better deal in the savings market. Why should not ordinary people have the chance to invest in British industry? Equities, that is to say ordinary shares, historically gave a vastly better long-term return than fixed interest investments like bank or building society deposits. They provided potential growth of income and capital. They gave a chance to keep pace with, if not to beat, inflation. Why should not ordinary people have the opportunity to protect their savings in a way that rich people took for granted? Anthony Eden's dream of a property-owning democracy could be greatly assisted by the availability of unit trust investments for the masses. The more I considered the matter, the more enthusiastic and determined I became. I just could not understand why everyone I approached for financial backing was so unresponsive.

A few, however, did share my enthusiasm. Robert Vigars, a Conservative member of the Greater London Council and a partner in the leading City law firm of Simmons and Simmons was one. His backing was a splendid encouragement. At one moment, without previous reference to me, he put in an offer to the owners of the Allied company of Unit Trust Managers to buy them out for £48,000. I didn't have much more than 48,000 pence but Bob was wholly undeterred. Perhaps it was as well that they refused the offer.

The man who probably deserves most credit for getting me started is Peter Walker, now Lord Walker, and at that time prominent in the Young Conservatives. By profession an insurance broker, he introduced me to George Stewart, the Chairman of a firm of Lloyds brokers called Stewart Smith. Stewart Smith controlled a small general insurance company, the London and Edinburgh Insurance Co Ltd, and had ambitions to develop it by taking it into the life assurance field. Between us we thus had two ambitions: I wanted to start up a unit trust management company and George Stewart wanted to start a life assurance operation. We combined our forces, and we did both. It was as simple as that. After eighteen months when my income was less than my expenses I could at last start earning a living and saving again.

Thus, with Stewart Smith's capital and support I was to start a unit trust management company, but that was only half of the revolution we jointly achieved. We also launched a new life assurance endowment contract, one that invested a high proportion of the policyholder's premiums in a unit trust. This meant that anyone who took out one of our policies not only received life assurance in the usual way: he also embarked on a savings plan which paid him a lump sum when his policy came to its end. In this way he could handsomely increase his investment as the value of the shares held by the unit trust rose. There is, of course, always the chance of a temporary fall in the market, but all historical experience showed that over the whole life of a policy, usually ten years or more, prices would hold up to at least their original level. We felt so confident of this that we guaranteed the minimum sum assured. Heads, the investor won: tails, he could not lose.

Our competition was formidable for the orthodox life assurance companies. We gave a better bargain than they did. We invested a greater proportion of the policyholder's money for his eventual benefit. When he paid his hard earned cash over to us he could see exactly where his money was invested and what its value was: the price of our unit trust shares was quoted daily. Some existing life policies did pay out bonuses but they were at the whim of the directors of the life assurance companies which sponsored them. With our policies there was none of this disdainful patronage; an investor who bought our policies always knew exactly where he stood. There was also tax relief allowable on his premiums, so that in effect he could buy equities at a discount.

We launched our Unicorn Unit Trust in October 1957. Its principal aim was capital appreciation for investors over the years and the issue price was nine shillings and sixpence per share (less than 50p in today's money). We put display advertisements in all the main newspapers and it was an instant success.

The share capital of Unicorn's management company was a mere £13,000 – £10,000 in equity and £3,000 in loans – no great sum on the back of which to launch a revolution. The London and Edinburgh allowed me to subscribe for 24 per cent of the share capital but I thought it right to offer half of this to Peter Walker since he had found the finance. My share was therefore 12 per cent.

On the day we launched Unicorn in 1957 the *Financial Times* ordinary share index stood at 169. 'A bad time to start a new investment enterprise,' said the journalists when I gave a press conference. Four months later, the index stood lower still: in February 1958 it went down to 154. But our investment policy was sound and Unicorn Trust's offer price never fell below the level of the original issue. Later, when Stock Market prices were much higher, many said to us, 'You were lucky to start when you did.' And a few said, 'You were clever.' Both missed the point. The fact was we had a good idea, we believed in what we were doing and we were determined to succeed.

Amongst our earliest supporters were the police. Peter Walker's insurance broking firm introduced many policemen to Unicorn: numbers of them took to calling at our offices to pay their premiums or to make direct investments. This earned us, at first, suspicion ('What have you done so wrong that the police are always calling?' neighbours asked) and then a most healthy respect.

The arrival of Unicorn aroused the same hostility as the launch of equity-linked life assurance. Unbelievably, some people who saw our first advertisement tried to prevent us from starting at all. Sir Denys Lowson wrote me a letter threatening legal action. I replied as patiently as I could. I reminded him he owed me some commission on the sale of the Mostyn Hotel. Of course I heard no more. A meeting of the Institute of Actuaries heard several speakers criticising us: more than one said that what we were doing should not be countenanced. The Chief Actuary of the Legal and General Insurance Company wrote an article in *The Policy Holder*, an important and widely read journal of the insurance industry, describing our life policy as 'dishonest'. Writs for libel had to be issued. I am sure he was sincere, if misguided. Since then the Legal and General has paid us the sincerest form of flattery. It now manages a whole clutch of unit trusts.

These incidents illustrate the atmosphere of those times, almost universally antagonistic to us when we started. How things have changed! By 1970 unit-linked business represented almost a quarter of the total new life assurance business in the UK: by 1984 it was more than half.

Corporate advertising at that time was of the tombstone variety, a few lines from a chairman's speech at a company's annual general meeting and that was all. Unicorn splashed out with prominent display advertising and it was a sensation.

The police were not our only personal callers. Unicorn had an office off Cannon Street in the City, and the driver of a Number 6 bus used on occasion to pull up at the nearby stop, abandon his passengers and come into the office to deposit a few quid in his savings account. I was manning the counter one day and took his money.

'Mustn't stop, guv,' he said, 'I've a full load on.'

'You're taking a risk, aren't you?' I asked. 'What would an inspector say if he found your bus without a driver?'

'It's only a minute,' he said, 'but I get such pleasure out of it, you see.'

'Pleasure?'

'Yes,' he said. 'I drive my old bus down Oxford Street twice a day and I go past Boots and Marks and Spencer and Selfridges and see the people spending their cash and I look at those busy shops and I think – I own a little piece of you, you bastards.' He must have been an old sailor: unlike Mo Udall he used the word affectionately.

We even took in sums as low as ten shillings for our saving scheme (50p in today's money). There were many who prophesied our early failure in consequence. From our own point of view it was, I suppose, bad economics, since our maximum permitted charge for accepting every 50p and entering it in the books was 5 per cent or 2½p, and that did not pay the full costs involved in registering the transaction. Small sub-scriptions did the profit and loss account no good, but putting new share-holders on the register was what our business was all about. I was sure they would steadily add cash to their accounts and I was proved right.

As we succeeded, so the imitators came. Rothschild were the first, in partnership with Sir Denys Lowson (I savoured the irony) and Philip Hill, the old West End issuing house (later of course very City Establishment). This, I told myself, was an admission that we were very much on the right lines. And then the flood began. As the old City saying has it, one new business, alone in its field, is an aberration; two of the same kind constitute a trend; three or more is accepted practice. Nowadays there isn't a clearing bank, a merchant bank or a life assurance company without a clutch of unit trusts under its management. There are over 150 management companies in being, and around 1,500 unit trusts authorised by the Department of Trade and Industry to solicit subscriptions from the public. Total funds under management are about £90 billion in over 6 million accounts. The industry is big business: its progress is one in the eye for the city institutions who turned me down in 1956 and 1957.

Two years after launching Unicorn we started our second unit trust with investment objectives laying more stress on income than on capital growth. By this time Unicorn had doubled its share value and the income paid to shareholders had also increased, so we had a good record to advertise. In just one week we received subscriptions for that second unit trust totalling £7 million. It is a record which has since been beaten but at that early stage it was a lot of money.

We called our second unit trust Falcon – like Unicorn the name of one of the Queen's Beasts. We thought of establishing a family of unit trusts named after those mythical and real animals – the Greyhound, the White Hart, the Red Lion and so on – but we had to abandon the idea because the titles sounded too much like pubs. Later, when we started our own life assurance company, we named it after the only one that did not conjure up the idea of a saloon bar – Griffin.

There was another important way in which Unicorn was a pioneer: it set a standard of management practice which has become the norm. The trust deed establishing our first unit trust was written by Bob Vigars in accordance with clear views I had formed over the years. I daresay it has long been forgotten, but the provisions we incorporated into that original trust deed settled a number of controversies about technical matters which in the years before the War excited criticisms and on occasion passions. Above all, it was a matter of some pride to us in those early days that the high standards we set in management were followed precisely by all our successors and imitators.

I worked hard with Unicorn's rival firms to establish an association of unit trust managers in 1959 whose charter meant that it not only represented its members but also had a regulatory duty over them. Unicorn, of course, were founder members. I invited Sir Oscar Hobson, the doyen of Fleet Street's City Editors, to be our first Chairman. The leaders of the industry – such men as George Fletcher of Allied, Oliver Stutchbury and David Maitland of Save & Prosper, and Tim Simon of Target – all worked well together, and the growth of the industry over the years, with the public confidence that it enjoys, owes much to their selfless work and example. The Unit Trust Association was an early and effective example of self-regulation in the City. It celebrated its twenty-fifth anniversary in 1984: a deservedly happy affair.

The Society of Investment Analysts had not long been in existence when I was asked to lecture to them about unit trusts, in which there was now a growing professional interest. I accepted the invitation with pleasure. The lecture delivered, I thought I would expand my carefully prepared notes into a book, which I did. However, I could not find a publisher. No one believed the book would sell. My colleagues on the Board of Unicorn's Management Company decided that we should pay for its publication as an advertisement. I gave instructions that the print order suggested by the publishers should be doubled: it sold out within a year. To my mind, the story neatly illustrated two things: the lack of faith that sophisticated people still had in unit trusts and their future; and, on the contrary, the growing interest on the part of the general public.

One of the problems in the early days of unit trusts was that their charges were regulated by the Government and set at a low level. Unit trust management was therefore hardly a very profitable affair. In 1956, the year I was elected to Parliament, the Allied Unit Trust Management Company challenged in the courts the right of Government to regulate the service charges made by the managers on an initial investment and semi-annually thereafter. The general legislation which affected unit trusts did not mention service charges, and their control had not been mentioned by Ministers during the passage of the Bill through Parliament. It was obvious that the Government machine had assumed greater powers than had ever been intended by ministers or by Parliament, as the Government machine is often ready to do. Alas, Allied lost their case, with the court ruling that what mattered was what the Act as written in fact permitted, not what Parliament intended it to mean.

I went to see officials at the Board of Trade to argue the case for relaxation. I put to them and to Conservative Ministers the need to popularise share ownership and I argued as fiercely as I could. There was neither help nor encouragement from that quarter. My view was peremptorily rejected, an early lesson to me that too many Ministers have too little experience of the practical world outside their departments and that their civil service advisers have less. Now, some forty years later, officials have abandoned controls. Three cheers for that. It is better that competition rather than civil servants should settle charging levels, but why could the controls not be abandoned earlier and why were they ever imposed in the first place? I could not understand why hire purchase costs and the like were uncontrolled while the expenses involved in unit trust administration were maintained for so many years at a farcically low level. The controls imposed by Government were not even-handed and they were too rigid. If Governments think it right to control some aspects of the market place the mechanisms should be kept under review and adapted to changing circumstances. The market alters continually, but too often the civil servant's guiding principle is: 'If you change nothing, you can't be criticised.'

Launching and maintaining the revolution we had begun when we started Unicorn was an uphill battle. At the start we found ourselves under attack not only from the establishment in the life insurance world but also from many in the stockbroking fraternity, especially those outside London. 'You're taking the private investor's business away from us,' they complained. Of course, such attacks were just plain silly and in today's more favourable climate it seems incomprehensible they were ever made, but they were real enough to be hurtful at the time.

Not that Unicorn neglected the professional market. We received growing support from solicitors, accountants, branch bankers and insurance brokers all over the UK, and we hired a team of splendid men to liaise with them, mainly retired naval officers.

Over the years, I have heard many politicians and others pay lip service to the idea of a people's capitalism. Iain Macleod used to speak about its advantages with particular emphasis. Talk there has been in abundance, but though many Chancellors of the Exchequer have had the chance to assist the process in a practical way none did so except to a modest extent until Mrs Thatcher became Prime Minister. In that year it is estimated that there were some 3 million shareholders in the UK. By 1990 the figure had risen to 11 million. However, the percentage of UK ordinary shares held by the personal sector, as opposed to institutions such as insurance companies, pension funds and so on, has by now fallen from a third to a fifth. There is much more work to do to make a people's capitalism a reality; and much more work to do to make effective a shareholders' democracy.

I had one particular colleague in Unicorn on whom I relied completely to manage our day to day business. Arthur Fowler's friends called him Bill and I called him Uncle. He was an East End boy, a fanatical supporter of West Ham Football Club, by profession an expert in company registration work. He too had worked for Denys Lowson and when I left Lowson's employment in 1956 he came to see me to ask if we could continue to work together. I had nothing to offer and when we were contemplating starting Unicorn I didn't want to be open to an accusation that I was poaching staff from my old employers. Then, when I had at last obtained the promise of the finance I needed from George Stewart, I ran into Uncle again in a pub in the City. 'I've given in my notice and I'm coming to join you,' he said.

I did my best to dissuade him. I pointed out that he was a family man, which I was not, and that he couldn't afford to take the risk of a new venture, which I could; he would be saying good-bye to his prospect of a pension and so on.

'I've spoken to Alice,' he said (Alice was his 'good lady', as he used to describe her.) 'She says she'll stick with me even if I'm a bloody bus conductor.'

'That's a more honourable occupation than many,' I said '– playing football for West Ham, for example.'

That settled it. At the start he joined me for less money than Lowson was paying him but we soon made that up as Unicorn's business progressed. We worked together happily ever after. We did different things in the business and our skills complemented one another. I planned and organised and set the strategy and he did the day-to-day work.

And Unicorn's business grew all the time. We took over another ailing company. We continued to advertise: it was seemingly the best way of getting into direct touch with our customers, even if an expensive one, and it succeeded. Such was our confidence that on one occasion we offered shares for sale in one of our unit trusts and, for a small premium of 5 per cent, guaranteed investors against a fall in stock market values. The issue was a huge success.

We kept in close touch with the American scene, where the development of unit trust investment funds had been meteoric. There was much to learn from the American experience, especially in the field of investment management, but there were also a number of their practices which I found objectionable, mostly involving high-pressure sales-manship. For that reason in Unicorn we separated the functions of management and sales, concentrating the latter in a separate company. Although informed debate increasingly centres around the need to regulate sales practices in the UK and Government and the City of London together have now established a complex regulatory structure, Unicorn's earlier model has not been followed in the industry generally. Recent revelations in the life assurance industry and the fines imposed on many leading companies by the regulatory authority, especially in respect of sales practices, show that ours was a sensible arrangement. It is a pity it was not widely adopted. It would have made insistence on responsible selling practices more likely, not least in the field of endowment policies where there has recently been justified criticism.

We also made mistakes. Sir Mark Weinberg, early in his career, worked with Unicorn and wished to cooperate with us more closely. My friends in the London and Edinburgh regarded him as a competitor and were not keen on the association. It would have been better if they had invited him to take over the development of their company. In later years he was hugely successful and became, as his talents merited, a leader in the industry. With a little more imagination on the part of our parent company we might have been partners. This error apart, we had a splendidly supportive Board of Directors, including Admiral of the Fleet Lord Tovey, the man who sank the Bismark. George Stewart was our Chairman and there were two other directors from the London and Edinburgh. One was Sir William Charles Crocker, MC, the celebrated solicitor to Lloyds of London, the man who finally convicted the arch-arsonist Leopold Harris. On one occasion I put some material in front of Unicorn's Board for approval. I had taken a lot of trouble with it and must have shown some impatience when Crocker made a number of alterations. 'Dear boy,' he said, 'never forget that I am a lawyer. I cannot resist the temptation to redraft any document put before me. All lawyers are the same: give us the Lord's Prayer or the Ten Commandments and we would rewrite them.'

George Stewart was a marvellous friend and supporter. We had only one problem in developing Unicorn: our parent company's lack of financial strength. We were the first in the field with London and Edinburgh's equity-linked endowment policies and we had the market place virtually to ourselves; yet they held back from marketing the policy with any strength: the company's capital base was small and it simply could not afford the strains of a strongly expansionist programme. In consequence its sales activities were conservative in the extreme. We did not exploit our opportunity.

One day George Stewart was in a sombre mood. 'Edward,' he said, 'I've bad news for you. We can't go on supporting Unicorn. You've been too successful. The business has grown too big and we just can't take the financial risks involved.'

I could appreciate his point. By 1967 Unicorn was managing funds with a total value of some £48 million. It was a heavy responsibility for a small insurance company. I promised I would look for another parent company but my heart was heavy. Stewart Smith had been such good friends: without George Stewart's and his colleagues' vision and courage we should never have got started.

I opened discussions with the Westminster Bank and Martins Bank. Westminster had been a good friend, too. It had agreed to be Trustee of Unicorn's second unit trust, Falcon, the launch of which had been such a huge success. This had been Westminster's first venture into trusteeship in the unit trust world, at that time a great compliment to us. Martins Bank was, however, further advanced in its thinking, largely due to the remarkable foresight of one of its younger senior men, Derrick Hanson. Derrick had put to the senior management of the bank a proposal to concentrate all of Martins' non-banking activities into a separate organisation, a trust company, and to develop and expand its work, to act in effect as a launching pad for what we now describe as financial services. Hanson's thinking was years ahead of his time and so was the thinking of Martins Bank in consequence. His proposal had been agreed by the Board of Directors and the Martins Bank Trust Company Ltd had been established. In August 1967 it bought a controlling interest in the Unicorn management company while the London and Edinburgh Insurance Company remained as a minority shareholder with 25 per cent

70

of the equity. A new and happy era opened for us; it was quite a coup to have as our parent company a clearing bank, with its high standing and financial resources.We renamed our company Martins Unicorn: the name change was a prominent endorsement of our quality. From Unicorn's point of view the transfer of ownership was excellent in every way, and the London and Edinburgh Insurance Company could also be well pleased with its investment. Three quarters of its original shareholding in the Unicorn company, which in 1957 had cost £7,500 had been sold for £325,125 in 1967. It had received thousands of pounds in dividends in the intermediate years, paid out of Unicorn's hard won profits, and its sales of insurance policies linked to Unicorn must also have been profitable.

Unfortunately I myself did not gain financially from the sale. Five years earlier, as I shall be relating, my political life had taken off and I had become a Treasury Minister. Although the rules of conduct for Ministers would have allowed me to own shares in an investment management company, I thought it wrong to do so and I sold my holding to the London and Edinburgh for some £20,000, enough to buy me a slightly larger house in Lord North Street, Westminster. When I rejoined Unicorn after the Conservative Government lost the general election in 1964 and I was no longer a Minister, the London and Edinburgh would not agree to my repurchasing a shareholding. Friends of mine suggested that I should not rejoin Unicorn if I could not again acquire shares in the management company, and I was even offered finance to start a new company, but I felt a deep loyalty to my old colleagues and refused to do so. That loyalty was to cost me many thousands of pounds.

However, when Martins bought Unicorn I was asked to join the Board of its Trust Company and subsequently the Board of Martins Bank itself, which I was delighted to do. There was something special about Martins. With a tradition of four centuries of successful banking behind it, it had a deserved reputation for competence and friendliness. I travelled all over the country with some of my colleagues at Unicorn to talk to branch managers. Everywhere I went I was received with the greatest possible friendliness and enthusiasm.

But the days of Martins Bank as an independent entity were numbered. For many years, other, larger clearing banks had cast a covetous eye on the business. Martins was by some way smaller than the majors and so was an obvious target for a take-over bid. There were several suitors. Neither Martins' senior directors nor the bank's senior management apparently had the will to resist, and Martins' Chairman, Sir Cuthbert Clegg, and the Chief General Manager, Mr Maxwell, appeared positively to encourage and welcome these developments. Some of us on the Board argued for the continuation of the bank's independent existence, but we were not heard. It had at one time been suggested that Barclays, Lloyds and Martins should combine together to form one vast single banking entity, but out of the scramble Barclays Bank emerged as the successful bidder for Martins and became its new proprietor.

I remember that at our Board meetings the Chairman of Martins Bank invariably referred to Barclays' impending purchase of Martins as a merger. I ventured to correct him: 'There are no mergers of a larger company with a smaller,' I said. 'There are only takeovers.' The Chairman insisted that this was nonsense. He and the Chief General Manager of Martins had received categorical assurances from the Chairman and senior management of Barclays about the future; the staff of Martins Bank would keep their jobs, their pensions, and so on. Of course, I agreed. It would be astonishing if the Barclays Bank directors were not considerate and sympathetic to our staff. That is exactly what one would expect from people of high reputation and standing in the banking world and from good employers. But, I said, Martins will disappear.

And disappear it has. All that is left of four hundred years of its proud banking history is the symbol of the grasshopper, printed very small on just a few Barclays cheque books and perhaps a tiny notice outside a bank branch or two in the sticks.

The Chairman of Martins Bank and the two Vice Chairmen joined the Barclays Bank Board. Some of the rest of Martins' directors joined Barclays local boards in the provinces. Others retired. The rest of us joined a newly created Barclays local London Board which met each month in Martins' old Lombard Street offices, at the sign of the grasshopper. On the wall of the dining room was a picture of the destruction of the House of Commons by fire in 1834. Somehow, I always thought that appropriate.

At our first meeting it was made clear that the new London Board of Barclays Bank would have no responsibility of any kind for policy matters. There seemed little point in its existence, except for form's sake. After a few meetings we told our friends at Barclays that perhaps it would be better if it were wound up; and it was.

The Martins Bank Trust Company was promptly renamed the Barclays Bank Trust Company but it took the management of Barclays many months to decide whether or not to put its bank's name behind Unicorn. I discussed the subject with John Thomson, the Chairman of the bank, several times. He was courtesy itself and I recall our meetings with pleasure. All the same, it was a wretched period. The failure of Barclays to back Unicorn immediately was widely noticed in the investment world and it did our public image a certain amount of harm. I did not find it easy to maintain morale at Unicorn during this period nor did we find it conducive to our marketing effort that Barclays was apparently not supporting us in the wholehearted way that Martins had. It was difficult even to retain the loyalty of our existing investors in such circumstances.

A number of our senior people at Unicorn wanted to leave, but they were persuaded to stay. I undertook to see matters through until Barclays made its decision, and that is what I did. I reasoned that if Barclays eventually decided to incorporate Unicorn into its family then I would be needed to see the transition period through; if it decided against the business – a distinct possibility – we would have a real problem finding a new parent and the situation would need careful and sympathetic attention.

Time, however, was going by. In total, what with the months occupied with the business of the Martins takeover followed by Barclays' procrastination, I wasted a whole year. Eventually Barclays decided to back Unicorn and put out a statement saying so. It purchased the 25 per cent of Unicorn's share capital still in the ownership of the London and Edinburgh Insurance Company for £156,250 in November 1968. So for a total of less than half a million pounds it acquired a business which by then managed assets worth some £87 million. It was not a bad bargain. The next year, 1969, Hambros Bank paid £6.5 million for the Allied Unit Trust Group, then managing assets of some £70 million, and Save & Prosper paid £3.85 million to acquire the management of £50 million. I wished I still had my 24 per cent interest in Unicorn to benefit from this bonanza.

We at once renamed the business Barclays Unicorn. The Chairman of Barclays was kind enough to tell me that I could remain as Chairman of Barclays Unicorn until I retired if I wished. That was a vote of confidence: he was talking about a date more than a quarter of a century ahead.

Again I tramped the country, meeting all the Barclays Bank managers, telling them about Unicorn. I enjoyed the process. It was fun to talk about a business that I had created and was proud of, and they were all personally very friendly, as the Martins managers had been; but their style was more detached and they were markedly less enthusiastic for Unicorn.

Not all the senior management at Barclays understood the Unit Trust business as well as they might have done. Barclays was a much larger bank than Martins – it had over 2,500 branches compared with Martins' 700 plus – and its procedures were inevitably more institutionalised. In the early days of Unicorn's association with Barclays the bank was practising management by objectives (MBO) as a method of administration. I was horrified one day to discover that, without consultation with anyone at Unicorn, every Barclays Bank branch manager had been set a financial target for sales of Unicorn's Unit Trusts through his branch. The idea that Barclays Bank managers all over the country should encourage their customers to invest in Unicorn's unit trusts, quite irrespective of their particular needs or wishes, merely in order to meet some arbitrary target figures struck me as being foolish and irresponsible. Of course I protested and the proposal was cancelled. I had long prided myself that we built up Unicorn's business without any sort of high-pressure salesmanship. In consequence our figures for surrenders were consistently well below the industry's averages and this made our business financially more secure than many of our competitors. It was a matter of anxiety to find this principle suddenly and carelessly put at risk.

Then, from time to time, I found the direction of Unicorn's business under criticism from Barclays' senior management, invariably as a result of ignorance. I would receive messages that senior people in the bank, reading the tables comparing the performances of different unit trusts in the Sunday newspapers, were 'disappointed' not to see Barclays Unicorn invariably at their head. It was an unreal expectation and what they apparently did not notice was that our performance was consistently above average, month after month, year after year, rarely at the very top but never at the bottom of the lengthening list of Unicorn's competitors – never even below average. We did a good and responsible job for our investors; they knew it and that is why they stayed with us.

Looking back now from a distance of almost forty years what I recollect chiefly are the excitement and the sense of achievement I and my colleagues enjoyed when we were first bringing Unicorn into existence. I have no doubt at all that the movement we inaugurated has done much to increase the prosperity and security of millions of ordinary men and women.

I feel a deep sense of satisfaction when I see myself described as 'the father of the modern British unit trust industry'. I wish, all the same, that I could have patented the idea. My father used to say, 'Never take your payment in politeness.' He was right.

CHAPTER 4

YES
MINISTER

'Will you be asked to join the Government?' said my fiancée. It was early in 1962, I was engaged to be married and the wedding was fixed for July.

'No,' I said, 'I don't think I will. If I am it will only be in some junior office and I've decided to refuse. I should have to give up my job at Unicorn and we couldn't both live on a Junior Minister's salary. Anyway, why should I be asked? The Government's half way through its term, it seems pretty settled and if there are any changes they'll be quite small. There won't be much room for newcomers.'

Sometimes you can be wonderfully wrong. I had reckoned without the night of the long knives.

In the 1959 general election my majority in Taunton had risen from 657 to 6,499, the biggest Conservative majority there for twenty-five years, and the Party had done well throughout the country with a gain of 21 seats and an overall majority of 100. It was the third general election in succession that the Conservatives had won with an increased majority, an achievement unprecedented for more than a century and a tribute to Harold Macmillan's brilliance as a politician. When he had taken over the premiership in 1957 it was in the aftermath of the Suez debacle, and even before that the Party's fortunes had been on the slide. Then in 1958 the Chancellor of the Exchequer, Peter Thorneycroft, resigned his great office in protest at the size of the estimates of Government expenditure for the coming year. He was accompanied by two other Ministers, Nigel Birch and Enoch Powell, Economic and Financial Secretaries to the Treasury. 'Little local difficulties,' said the unflappable Mr Macmillan as he set off on a Commonwealth tour, and, though disunity is usually fatal to a Party's electoral prospects, it seemed as if his optimism was justified. He fought the 1959 election campaign on the 'great double' – stability of prices and full employment – and by then the economy was on one of its upward swings. He chose his moment well. Picking a good time to declare an election is, of course, one of the strongest weapons in the armoury of a ruling Party but, as many have found, it is usually easier said than done.

For a while after 1959 the Party was riding high under the leadership of 'Supermac', as the cartoonist Vicky dubbed him, but at the end of 1961 things again began to go wrong. Selwyn Lloyd, the Chancellor of the Exchequer, introduced a pay pause and increased purchase tax and bank rate (and thus the general level of interest rates). All this contradicted the general expectation fostered by the Prime Minister of continuously rising living standards, and the public was not slow to show its disapproval. In a by-election in Blackpool the Conservative majority slumped from some 16,000 votes to under 1,000. Worse, in another by-election in March 1962 a Tory majority of 14,000 in Orpington became a Liberal majority of almost 8,000. Something had to be done. Macmillan decided on drastic surgery. Overnight, in the summer of 1962, seven senior ministers – one third of the Cabinet, including the Chancellor of the Exchequer and the Lord Chancellor – were forced to resign. An equally ruthless disposal of junior ministers followed. It was summed up by Jeremy Thorpe, my Devonshire neighbour in Parliament, who observed 'Greater love hath no man than that he should lay down his friends' lives for his own survival.' It was a cruel, prescient remark. Macmillan was fighting for his political life, and the following year he was to lose it. The unhappy Vassal and Profumo scandals added to the Government's problems.

The day after the announcement of these resignations I received a summons to see the Government Chief Whip at Admiralty House. I assumed he would offer me a minor Government position on the Prime Minister's behalf, and, as I had told my fiancée, I was resolved to refuse. I did not want to sound ungrateful, so I carefully rehearsed what I would say and how I would say it. What followed was extraordinary. At that time, the Prime Minister was living at Admiralty House and not at 10 Downing Street, which was being repaired. Outside the front door when I arrived at about noon there was a mass of press photographers: aspirant Ministers had been coming and going all morning but the photographers took no notice of me. I wasn't sure whether to be pleased or disappointed. Who did they mistake me for? A messenger, perhaps.

I went in. There is a convenient arrangement for entry to the Prime Minister's house. You don't knock at the door yourself, a policeman standing there does it for you. A porter must be permanently on duty on the inside because the door is opened instantly. I was shown into a waiting room. It belied its name. I hardly had time to look about me before I was off again.

Half a minute later I was shown into the Cabinet Room. The Prime Minister was the only person there. It was plain that Mr Macmillan was not too sure who I was, so I tried to help him by identifying myself. Where on earth, I wondered, was the Chief Whip whom I had been summoned to meet?

'I want you to join the Government,' said Mr Macmillan.

'Thank you very much, Sir,' I replied.

He consulted some papers in front of him on the table.

'As Economic Secretary to the Treasury,' he said.

'Oh,' I said.

This was a surprise. To be a Treasury Minister, even the most junior, would be exciting. It was a splendid chance for me, not at all like the offer of a lowly office that I was expecting. The Financial and Economic Secretaries at the Treasury rank as Ministers of State and are paid accordingly, somewhat higher than the lowest scale.

'That's settled then,' he said.

'Well, Prime Minister,' I said, 'there are some problems.'

'Problems' – he pronounced it as if it were two words, 'prob-lems'. 'Oh.' There was a pause. Then – 'Would you care for a glass of sherry?'

I said I certainly would. He pressed a button and glasses and a decanter of dry sherry were brought into the room: like the front door opening, it was instantaneous service.

The Prime Minister was waiting for me to speak.

'I'm going to be married in a fortnight,' I said.

'Your first marriage?' asked the Prime Minister. He put heavy stress on the word 'first'.

'Yes,' I said.

'The girl' – he pronounced the word as if it were spelled 'gel' – 'will be very pleased.'

'I'm not so sure,' I said.

Obviously he didn't think much of that 'prob-lem'.

'You said prob-lems,' he said. He emphasised the plural.

'Yes, there's a second one.' I said. 'I'm Managing Director of an investment business.'

'Your partners will look after your interests. Your promotion to the Treasury will be an honour for your firm.'

It would take too long to explain the circumstances to the Prime Minister. I needed time – to think, to talk to my fiancée and to my colleagues at Unicorn.

'Prime Minister, may I please have some time to make up my mind?'

'How long do you need?'

'Forty-eight hours,' I said. I knew that George Stewart, the Chairman of Unicorn, was somewhere in the United States; Heaven knew how long it would take me to get in touch with him. And my fiancée; I should go up to Liverpool and have a talk with her.

The Prime Minister pressed another button. In came his Principal Private Secretary. He caught my eye and winked at me. I nearly had a fit. Wherever had I seen him before?

'Yes, Prime Minister?' he said.

'How long do we have before the announcement?'

'It will be made at four o'clock,' said the Private Secretary.

And then I knew who he was, Tim Bligh. The last time I had seen him, seventeen years before at the end of the War in Europe, he had just returned from the Mediterranean where he had been a most successful and much decorated flotilla Commander – something of a hero to younger officers like myself.

'You have until four o'clock,' the Prime Minister was saying. He stood up. 'I hope you will decide to join us. Mr Bligh will show you out.'

I talked a little to Tim on my way to the front door. He found my discomfiture very amusing.

The photographers were still outside. This time I was a little put out that they again took no notice of me. After all, I was more important than when I went in: I was a Minister-elect, no less.

It was lunch-time. I had just over three hours to complete my consultations. I raced back to my office in the City to get on the telephone.

My fiancée was splendid. 'Who cares about the cash,' she said. 'It's marvellous news and of course you must accept.' I reflected that it was lucky the honeymoon was already paid for.

Unicorn's Chairman, my friend George Stewart, when eventually I got through to him on the transatlantic telephone, was equally supportive. 'This is excellent news,' he said. 'You've no choice but to join the Government. Comparatively speaking you're a young man: you can make another City career in due course, and we'll always be pleased to welcome you back on Unicorn's Board.'

So it was settled. I telephoned Tim Bligh and told him I would be happy to accept Macmillan's offer.

I found years later that a wretched colleague in the House of Commons had been kept hanging about in Admiralty House for more than two hours, without the reason being disclosed to him, so that he could be asked to take the job of Economic Secretary if I refused. I shouldn't really feel guilty. It was hardly unreasonable for me to ask for time to consider the situation. The offer was wholly unexpected, and it is an odd system which requires a man, at a moment's notice only, to alter his career fundamentally, to abandon friends and responsibilities, to take on new ones, to accept a heavy financial sacrifice for himself and his family, and to exchange the comparative security and comforts of his existing position (including perhaps such fundamentals as a pension and health and life assurance cover) for a ministerial career of uncertain duration and prospects and no assurance that his old employers or partners will have him back. Few of us, however, when we are asked to join a Government, refuse the invitation.

I hoped the Chancellor of the Exchequer would not mind if I took time off, only a fortnight after my appointment, to go on my honeymoon. Macmillan had made it entirely clear by inference during our discussion that he expected his Ministers to be married only once: a honeymoon therefore was a once-in-a-lifetime opportunity, not to be missed or curtailed.

Working at the Treasury was to prove one of the happiest periods of my life. Reginald Maudling, who was the new Chancellor, was a splendid man to work for. I found myself involved in everything he was himself doing. John Boyd-Carpenter, a most able and conscientious man, was Chief Secretary and also a Member of the Cabinet. Anthony Barber had been promoted to become Financial Secretary to the Treasury after having been Economic Secretary for three years. He and I worked closely together. Each of us had responsibility under our senior colleagues for supervising one of the two revenue-raising departments, Barber for the Inland Revenue and I for the Customs and Excise.

Within a month of my return from honeymoon I found myself due to set off for Washington with the Chancellor of the Exchequer and the Governor of the Bank of England, Lord Cromer, for the annual meetings of the International Monetary Fund and the World Bank. I asked the Chancellor if I might take my wife with me. 'Of course,' he said, 'I hope you will. It will be nice to have her there and she will be a support to you.'

My private secretary told me that the Government would not pay for her flight. That seemed a bit mean to me, but if it was the rule that Ministers of my rank could not take their wives abroad with them even if they were newly married and needed their support, then so be it. I said that my wife and I would travel economy class; the Treasury could allow me the difference between the first class fare they would have paid and the cost of an economy ticket and I'd put that towards the expense of my wife's travel.

'Not allowed,' they said.

So I paid the full cost of my wife's ticket. For the second time in my life I found my Parliamentary career involving me in increased expenses to be afforded out of a lower remuneration. I swore to myself that if ever I had responsibility or influence I would see to it that public service, even if it involved some degree of personal sacrifice, should not demand it on too savage a scale; and I did my best to keep that vow when I later became Chairman of the backbench Tory MPs.

As my wife and I sat in the economy class in the aeroplane (perfectly comfortably I may say) the Finance Minister of a newly independent Commonwealth country in Africa, plus his wife and a number of other relatives and friends were all making merry in the first class. I could not help reflecting that if Britain was still a great power, influential and wealthy, we hardly gave that appearance as far as the treatment of our Ministers was concerned. Perhaps our friends did not notice. At any rate, if the African Finance Minister saw me travelling steerage he was too polite to say so when he came to see me a few days later to demand – he did not ask – that the British taxpayer send a further large subvention to bolster his country's badly administered fortunes.

This trip was my first experience of the international financial scene. Mr Maudling spoke early in the IMF meetings and put forward a proposal for the introduction of an international currency unit, an idea which he had allowed me to help him develop. This initiative led to the introduction of the Special Depositary Receipts, SDRs as they are commonly called, which are slowly gaining acceptance as a world currency and so assisting the functioning of the international currency mechanisms. I busied myself with more routine matters, receiving delegations on the Chancellor's behalf and the like, though I also had the chance to meet a number of interesting and important people including John and Robert Kennedy. I cannot say that I took to either of the two brothers: Jack Kennedy with his incessant womanising and Robert with his self-centred ambition were men with whom I did not find it easy to be at home. I thought, too, that their relationship with the UK owed vastly more to convenience than to affection.

Important as the formal meetings of the IMF and World Bank might be, it was the ancillary and informal meetings that made the occasion really worthwhile. More than a hundred of the world's finance ministers came together each year at the IMF, and many hundreds more of the world's most important central and commercial bankers. All day long, and far into the night too, they discussed their countries' problems and prospects, and much business was done in the corridors, over lunch and dinner tables and in the offices.

I am not sure this is as true today as it was then. The jamboree has become excessively large. There may be as many as 150 finance Ministers present, with three thousand bankers and a greater number in their entourages. The British Chancellor of the Exchequer did not attend the 1985 International Monetary Fund meeting in Seoul in South Korea; he preferred the Conservative Party's Conference in Blackpool. Nor did the Permanent Secretary to the Treasury attend: he was minding the shop in Whitehall. Decisions are no longer taken during the main sessions of the annual meeting: gatherings of Ministers and senior advisers from the five or ten most industrialised nations are more productive by far. Twenty years ago it was different. With international meetings there is a sure rule: the larger the gathering the more certain it is to achieve little.

I used to meet the British City press representatives sometimes in the evenings for a drink at a bar opposite the Sheraton Park Hotel, a barrack of a place where the IMF and World Bank meetings took place. Patrick Sergeant of the *Daily Mail*, an old friend from my Navy days, was often there; so were Ansell Egerton of *The Times* and the City Editors of the *Daily Express* and the *Daily Telegraph*, Fred Ellis and Francis Whitmore. Mr and Mrs Maudling joined us on more than one occasion. I learned a great deal from these senior representatives of the British financial press: they were invariably well informed and a splendid source of intelligence of a sort one could not get elsewhere – for example, what the American Secretary of State had said at his press conference, or the line being taken by the Common Market Commission.

One day a foreign Finance Minister stopped by. He sat at a table on the pavement, as we all did, and summoned the proprietor.

'How much?' he asked, in the hearing of everyone in the cafe.

'For your drink?' asked the proprietor.

'No, you fool,' said the Finance Minister, 'for the waitress.'

We returned via New York, where we had two days of engagements. Mr Maudling made a series of public speeches and TV appearances in both cities. He was always a good ambassador for Britain.

'Tell us, in a single sentence,' a tough interviewer asked him in a Washington TV programme, 'what your Tory Party's principles are.'

It was a loaded question. 'Tories' was the name given to the loyalists in the American War of Independence so the question was in fact an attack and would be recognised as such by the audience. (It is foolish to think that Americans are automatically friendly just because they speak a version of English. They are deadly rivals, commercially and politically.) I felt for Reggie: to answer that question I would have needed half an hour. He rose to it. 'The Conservative Party,' he said, 'is conservative to keep, to conserve, all that is best in our way of life in Britain; radical to change and improve everything that is in need of development in the light of experience.' It was a model reply. I have many times since taken it as my text for speeches about Party policy, and gone on to speak for at least half an hour.

When we returned to London I went to see Maudling to ask for his permission to initiate a programme of minor legislation. I stood by his desk and told him what I had in mind.

'Why are you standing there?' he asked.

'Well,' I said, 'I'm telling you what I'd like to do.'

'No,' he said. 'Go and get on with it. Report to me occasionally about progress; if you have trouble, come and see me at once.'

Treasury officials were delighted. We were able to produce Bills for a new, simpler Stock Market transfer system and to give the Trustee Savings Banks permission to issue cheques, the first of various modernising measures which have followed in recent years. Both were useful minor reforms which had lain in the pending tray for some years.

Government in the UK is organised pyramid fashion. Most decisions are made at the top, invariably by Ministers and usually by the most senior among them. In consequence they are overworked and not every problem can be given the time and attention it merits. I noticed that many of the files that came up to the Chancellor originated at a fairly low level in the Treasury. The file would pass from level to level, ever upwards, with each more senior civil servant adding his ha'porth of comment until it reached the decision maker. Why not, I thought, interrupt this stately and lengthy process by arranging for a number of decisions to be made lower down the ladder? Had I been fortunate enough to become a Minister in charge of a Department of State that is what I would have done. I have no doubt that a Secretary of State who was a determined and consistent delegator would do wonders for morale and efficiency in his Ministry, and give himself an easier time.

The 1963 budget contained a number of reforms on which we all worked hard. It abolished the Schedule A tax on property owners, which had always seemed to me to be a monstrous penalty on them; it introduced a depletion allowance on mineral workings; it halved the *ad valorem* stamp duty on share transfers; and it relieved some three quarters of a million people from liability to pay direct tax.

Maudling's presentation of this budget followed a wholly new and admirable format. His budget speech contained at its start a list of all those smaller measures that he had in mind to introduce in the forthcoming Finance Bill, including his proposed changes in tax rates. This list announced, he then went on to the serious macro-economic matters he wanted to discuss with Members of Parliament. It is not an experiment that has been repeated, and more's the pity. The sight of MPs, year after year, sitting though successive Chancellors' hour-long economic dissertations with barely concealed impatience while they wait to hear whether income tax or VAT is to be raised or lowered a point or two or benefits marginally altered, is not the most attractive spectacle in my Parliamentary experience. It panders to the most selfish and blinkered question a voter can ask – What's in it for me? It is true that in the end that is how most people judge a Party's economic programme, but however much one may take that into account (and it is certainly dangerous to forget it) a Government must also be capable of taking a broader view, and that should be reflected in the way that national finances are presented in Parliament.

I have frequently said, over many years, that budget day in the House of Commons is an over-rated occasion. The crowded House, the newspaper headlines showing a heavy preoccupation with trivial adjustments in taxation are manifestations of the idiotic way in which we conduct the nation's financial affairs. Budget day is in effect the equivalent of the presentation of a company's report and accounts; it is the moment above all in the financial year when the balance should be struck between revenue and expenditure. However, in my time in the House revenue and expenditure were hardly ever considered together; and debates in the House on the Public Expenditure White Paper, which set out the Government's plans and strategies for some years ahead, were rarely well attended – by comparison with budget day very poorly attended indeed. Throughout my political career I continued to press for a radical revision of our methods of financial appraisal and decision (after one speech I was taken to task by David Wood, then senior parliamentary correspondent on *The Times*, though he was kind enough to tell me later that on balance he thought I was probably right). But it was not until 1993 that the change was made and forecasts of revenue and expenditure were brought together into a single statement by the Chancellor. What a time it takes to achieve Parliamentary reform in Britain!

Maudling was a big man in every way. He was impatient with trivia and had the wit always to concentrate on the most important things. Shortly before the debates on the 1963 Finance Bill, Barber and I, as his two junior Ministers, asked him if we could have responsibility for taking the Bill through the House of Commons without help from our senior Ministerial colleagues. He seemed a little surprised but readily agreed. 'Send for me,' he said, 'if you have any problems.'

I remember seeing him lurking behind the Speaker's chair when we began our work, watching how we got on. We never needed to send for him: we accomplished our task in under three weeks and without undue difficulty. Nowadays it takes considerably longer to take a Finance Bill through Parliament and three Ministers, not two, are usually needed to steer it through. That was a good Parliamentary experience for me. I had already taken other legislation through Parliament, but the Finance Bill is a stern test. I enjoyed it.

In October 1963 I again accompanied the Chancellor to Washington for the International Monetary Fund and World Bank meetings, and again returned via New York. This time my wife did not come with me. She remained at home to look after our first child, Sarah, born in September. The visit to the US was made memorable for me for a wholly political reason: it was already clear before Reggie Maudling and I left London for Washington that there would soon be a competition for the leadership of the Conservative Party. Macmillan was ill and it was doubtful whether he would be attending the Conservative Party conference in Blackpool which would begin a few days after we returned. In the event he was unable to. His time as Prime Minister was coming to an end.

He would be hard to replace. For a start, he so well understood the business of political management and leadership. He was happy to trust his chief lieutenants, a trust that was not always repaid with the same generosity, and he went out of his way to encourage his junior Ministers. He asked their opinions because he was genuinely interested in them; he treated them as equals. I was twice asked to join him alone for lunch during my year as Economic Secretary and was flattered and delighted. In consequence he was more loyally served by a wider spectrum of his colleagues than are some Prime Ministers. Heath was his Chief Whip. He could, and should, have learned from Macmillan's example. The two of them would frequently dine together in the House of Commons. One can only guess at their conversations but Macmillan always did most of the talking. He seemed to be at his most urbane, expansive and relaxed. No doubt matters of Party management were the chief topic of conversation. No doubt, too, Macmillan would tell his attentive listener that the best scenario for winning an election was economic prosperity. If Heath learned that lesson he was to bungle it when his opportunity came.

In New York, Patrick Sergeant and I spent considerable time putting together a draft speech for Maudling to deliver at the Conservative Party Conference. I was one of a number who were anxious to see him established as Macmillan's successor. I had come to respect and to like him greatly. I knew how consistently good his economic judgements were. I had many times observed his ability to summarise a situation rapidly and to make a decision, and I had learned by standing at his side for more than a year how agreeable a man he was to work with. He was a good friend and a splendid colleague, but he had one great handicap in the forthcoming contest: he was only a moderate speechmaker. He was good in discussion, but the formal occasion, when oratory was called for, was not his forte. He was intellectually contemptuous of those who played to the gallery. He preferred to appeal to the head, not the heart.

So Patrick and I wrote what we believed was a first-class speech, and we offered it to him as a present. He was a little embarrassed but seemed nonetheless pleased. He promised to read it with care, but he never promised to deliver it. In the event he used not one word of it. Back in London, Tony Barber and I offered him further material for his speech: this also was unused.

The Conservative Party Conference at Blackpool in October 1963 was overshadowed by the leadership contest. Harold Macmillan's preferred choices as his successor were Quintin Hailsham or Iain Macleod. Hailsham announced that he was resigning his peerage, as recent legislation entitled him to, and so would be free to become a candidate.

I had been a Member of the Select Committee which reported to the House of Commons that renunciation of hereditary peerages should be permitted. That report had been accepted and it also led to the creation of life peerages. I had long believed that the role of the House of Lords should be not simply as a revising chamber, but that it should have a more important status as the Senate of the nation, its membership dominated by men of experience in every practical field of life. That has as yet happened only to a limited extent and no one can agree on what further reforms should be made. While I was Chairman of the 1922

Committee I established a Constitutional Committee of backbench Conservative MPs whose brief was to propose a solution. It failed to do so and despite endless debate there is still no consensus.

The accepted wisdom is that important constitutional changes should not be attempted unless a broad agreement exists between the major political parties. This makes reform of the House of Lords virtually impossible since there is a strong left-wing element in the Labour Party which is committed to its abolition. If there is to be a reformed second chamber the Conservatives must take the initiative and pass the necessary legislation. So far we have wasted the opportunity given to us by successive election victories and to my mind that is unforgivable. There is still a danger that an extremist-dominated Government might one day be elected in the House of Commons and we should then urgently need a reformed second chamber with enhanced powers. One day we may rue our over-lengthy inaction.

Hailsham's supporters set out to turn the Conservative Party Conference of 1963 into a barnstorming session. Macmillan had done his best in advance to dish Butler's chances. Neither Hailsham nor Macleod was fully trusted by the Conservative Party. Hailsham, almost the only major figure with a taste for philosophy in today's Conservative Party, demonstrated enthusiasms which attracted some and repelled others, and showed a weakness for playing to the gallery. Macleod caused unease among the more conservative in the Party. 'Too clever by half,' Salisbury had said in the Lords in 1961. There was thus no agreed successor to Macmillan. The opportunity for Reggie Maudling was there if he was willing to take it.

When Reggie's time came he made a dull speech at the Conference which bitterly disappointed his supporters and the Party as a whole. Later he said privately that he had gone to much trouble in preparing it. No doubt he had, but it was the wrong sort of speech for such an occasion. Patrick and I had warned him that he must take care that the microphones were properly positioned; he was a tall man and they were set low. He negected our warning, with the result that many in the hall did not hear what he said. In short, he threw away his chances.

I had remained at the Treasury in London under instructions to mind the shop while my elders and betters were cavorting by the seaside. I wish I had been at Blackpool. I would have done my utmost to persuade Reggie to make the speech that Patrick and I had long laboured over or the points that Barber and I had prepared for him. I don't say either would have won him the leadership but they certainly would have given him a better chance. Others who were there have told me that they gave him the same advice. He was not short of friends, but he ignored us all.

In the event, Alec Douglas Home won the succession fairly comfortably. There was an awkward pause while he resigned his peerage and stood for election to the Lower House of which he had previously been a Member. That process was soon happily accomplished. However, there were some who were not happy. Iain Macleod and Enoch Powell refused to serve in his administration. Reggie Maudling remained a loyal team member but his political career was to end sadly when he was dismissed by Mrs Thatcher from her Shadow Cabinet in 1975.

When Alec Home became Prime Minister he telephoned me. My wife and I were at her parents' home not far from Liverpool. A telephone call from 10 Downing Street is guaranteed to cause a sensation even in the most sober household.

'I'd like you to accept a new position in the Government,' he said.

'Thank you very much, Sir,' I replied.

'You will forgive my not seeing you myself,' he said, 'but it is impossible to meet everybody.'

'I absolutely understand,' I said.

'We can meet and talk on some other occasion and I will look forward,' he said.

'What is it you would like me to do?' I asked.

'Oh,' he said – it was almost as if he had forgotten why he rang – 'Mr Heath is going to take over the Board of Trade. He will be Secretary of State and I would like you to go there as Minister of State and be his deputy.'

'That's very good of you, Sir,' I said.

'Not at all,' he said, 'you will make a great success of it. Good luck.'

I was sorry indeed to leave the Treasury but delighted to receive this apparent promotion. Somewhat to my surprise, I found myself with a Ministerial car at my disposal. True, it could only be used for official purposes but it was a help all the same. I moved to a new office opposite the Cenotaph in Whitehall; now the Ministry of Defence, at that time it was occupied in part by the Board of Trade. Subsequently the Board of Trade would move into splendid new offices originally built for Shell, Number 1 Victoria Street, where I had a marvellous room on the eighth floor overlooking Westminster Abbey and the Houses of Parliament.

Ted Heath had the splendid title of Secretary of State for Industry, Trade and Regional Development, as well as that of President of the Board of Trade. This new post was originally to have been that of

Secretary of State for Trade, Industry and Regional Development but somebody pointed out that its initials lay close to 'TIRED', so the order was reversed. Apparently Heath had insisted on the title of Secretary of State. I was sorry to see the ancient title of President of the Board of Trade relegated to second-line status.

He was to be very different in style from his predecessor at the department. Freddie Errol, a most pleasant and able man with considerable experience of commercial matters, had seen his role primarily as promoter of British trade and commerce, and during his time as President he had been an energetic leader of Britain's export effort. Heath saw the department more as a personal power base. Not all of its officials at the time approved or welcomed this change. As always, he started with great enthusiasm: he is a doer. He estimated to his fellow Ministers that we had one year before the next general election. He wanted to put his legislative mark on his term of office. The question was, what sort of legislation should he introduce? Various alternatives were discussed and discarded, but he took his decision alone. He settled for the abolition of resale price maintenance. Philosophically, this suited him well. He would be seen as the thrusting champion of competition, leading to lower prices. On the face of it, it seemed like a splendid proposal, but in the short-term it was a serious political misjudgement. It may (or may not) have pleased the economic purists but certainly it upset the Conservative Party and many of its supporters. Retail opinion was up in arms, not least the proprietors of many smaller businesses, generally Tory supporters to a man, who felt that their economic future and their whole way of life were threatened. MPs' postbags bulged with complaints. The Conservative Party twitched uneasily. Heath was summoned before Tory MPs at the 1922 Committee on at least two occasions to explain his policies. He made the point that this measure must be regarded as part of a package dealing also with monopolies, mergers and restrictive practices. That argument went down like a lead balloon.

He and I had a rough time in the House. Together we had responsibility for taking the Bill through all its stages in the Chamber of the House of Commons and I shall not easily forget the discomfort that we endured from the contributions and criticisms made by our own side. The committee stage of the Bill (that is to say, its detailed examination, clause by clause, and the discussion of amendments to it) was taken on the floor of the House itself rather than less publicly in a committee room upstairs. The complaints and criticisms made by Conservative supporters were therefore obvious to the whole of our Party in the House and to our opponents, adding to our discomfiture and unease; the wide and persistent publicity inevitably given to these criticisms further upset our supporters in the country.

It was a hard ride. I remember receiving violent complaints from John Morrison, then Chairman of the 1922 Committee, with a strong request to pass them on to Ted Heath. 'I have always been his supporter,' said Morrison, 'but he strains loyalty to the limit.' Heath seemed curiously careless at the time about Party opinion. No doubt he was under heavy strain, but he was so dilatory about correspondence that I had to make sure that most of the many hundreds of letters of complaint from MPs came onto my desk in the first instance so they could be promptly answered. It was the wrong time to be alienating our supporters, not long before a general election. A number of Conservative MPs voted against the Bill at various stages and it scraped through by some narrow margins.

The measure was economically sensible but the timing of its introduction was tactless and politically stupid. Heath's predecessor had put forward a similar proposal some time earlier. His timing was better, but even so the matter was not proceeded with. There had been objections to the proposal when Ted Heath had first put it forward in the Cabinet but in his determined, stubborn way he had managed to overrule them. Perhaps the Prime Minister should have vetoed the proposal, but he did not. I do not doubt that the unpopularity of this measure among Tory supporters was a contributory cause to our loss of the general election later that year. It is a good general rule to do the unpopular things as early as possible in a Government's term of office, not immediately before an election. Heath revealed himself as a man whose ambition for economic purism had outweighed his political judgement.

Here lies the perennial dilemma of the politician. The electors insist that they be served by men of courage, men of opinion, men of conviction. Yet they do not always back them with their votes.

Much of my own work at the Board of Trade was concerned not with Parliamentary battles but with the promotion of trade. Between 1963 and 1964 I travelled to South America, to the United States and also to Africa. My wife and I visited Kenya and Tanzania shortly after their armies had mutinied. On that same African tour we were in Zanzibar a short time after Mr Karume had deposed the Sultan and murdered many of the Arabs there and in the island of Pemba. My wife and I and the British High Commissioner in Tanzania flew to Zanzibar in a small aeroplane, feeling not at all certain how kindly we would be received. A number of those who had taken over the Government were very much under the influence of the Communists. I remember leaving a Wedgwood ashtray with the arms of the Palace of Westminster next door to a bust of Lenin in what had been the Sultan's main reception room in his palace, now occupied by the Revolutionary Council. Zanzibar was a beautiful island, the odour of cloves was pervasive, but the smell of death was everywhere. There were Chinese-made heavy weapons at the airport. We were right to be concerned.

Travel for Ministers is essential. It is stimulating too. I have never visited a country or even a factory without learning something new. It was a risk to go to Zanzibar, of course; but it was important that one of the new, brutal regime's first visitors should be a British Minister of the Crown.

I had my first meeting with President Nyerere on that visit. When the army mutinied he flew to the bush and left it to one of his Ministers, who acted with conspicuous courage, to restore order. He will be remembered in history chiefly for the thoroughness with which his socialist dogmatism led him to impoverish his people. I have never understood why so unsuccessful a leader of any nation was able to survive so long in office, let alone to exercise so much influence outside his own country. Years later, as a luncheon guest at 10 Downing Street when another African leader made a visit to the UK, I was astonished to hear even Margaret Thatcher on her feet in front of her guests eulogising this man. If she did not know better she should have done.

My wife and I also visited Ethiopia. We stayed two nights in the Embassy compound in Addis Ababa with John Russell, the British Ambassador. His wife, a Greek lady, was a former Miss World. At one end of the mantelpiece was a signed photograph of Alec Home from Alec's days as Foreign Secretary; at the other a photograph of his cousin Bertrand Russell. Russell was pictured squatting on the pavement in Trafalgar Square participating in an early anti-nuclear protest. This scene was framed by a Metropolitan policeman's arm, with his duty armlet prominent. The two pictures made a left and right, as a shooter might say.

We drove in the British Ambassador's elderly Austin Princess motor car out to the Emperor's summer palace along dusty roads, the Union flag fluttering bravely on a mudguard. Along the road natives prostrated themselves in the dust as the car passed by. I was impressed, though not altogether surprised. It was Britain who gave the Emperor asylum when his country was invaded and conquered by the Italians; and it was British forces under Wavell who had liberated it after a remarkable campaign.

'I am glad to observe,' I said to the Ambassador, 'that the prestige of the British Raj is high. You do well to uphold it.'

'It's not quite like that, Minister,' said John Russell. 'The fact is, they mistake this heap for the Emperor's Rolls Royce.'

In my year at the Board of Trade I also travelled to the Communist countries, I signed trade agreements with them and others, and I negotiated with the Russian Trade Minister. I also attended meetings of the Organisation for Economic Co-operation and Development (OECD), the General Agreement on Tariffs and Trade (GATT) and the European Free Trade Area (the alternative grouping to the EEC) and many others. I toured factories, I travelled widely in the UK on commercial business, and there were Parliamentary duties also, answering questions in the House, a vast correspondence. It was a busy life.

Meetings with men like Nyerere and Kenyatta in Africa were as exciting and as interesting as meetings with Jack and Robert Kennedy in the United States had been when I was at the Treasury. Of all the many heads of state that I met in those days the one I most enjoyed talking to was President Ben Bella in Algeria. We got on extremely well and I was sorry when later he was deposed and his place taken by President Boumedienne. When I went to Algeria in 1963 the Algerians had recently taken over their country from the French, and British companies were trying hard to establish themselves there, always a difficult thing to do in a French-speaking country. They were competing to obtain important contracts in connection with the development of the infant Algerian oil and gas industry and I visited the country in support of their endeavour. It was an interesting but rough experience. The French had recently left the country after some bloody and bitter fighting, and the scars were everywhere. We slept in bullet-marked buildings. On one occasion our planes had been sabotaged and we had to travel by road from Algiers to Oran in blazing heat. We arrived en route at one prefecture, hot, dusty and extremely thirsty. The Algerian prefect complained that his cellars were bursting with wine but he offered us not a thimbleful, being himself a Moslem and teetotal. Services of the most elementary kind were frequently lacking. Arriving eventually at the prefecture in Oran where we were to stay the night we found no water supply in the town. We were reduced to washing our hands and faces with water from the lavatory cistern. It was all in the cause of our patriotic duty, I told my wife, and I am glad to say that the British companies won their contracts.

After a time, we half expected to see bullet holes in every building where we stayed the night. We arrived in Caracas, Venezuela, on New Year's Eve, 1963, ready to start an export promotion tour the next day. To our astonishment, the British Ambassador, at whose residence we were staying, recommended we went to bed at ten-thirty p.m. We had hoped at the very least to see the New Year in. He suggested we get undressed in the dark in our bedroom; the building, he explained, had been machine gunned two days before, and there was no need to tempt fate, and the machine gunners, unnecessarily. 'Close your windows,' he added, 'don't tempt the grenade throwers by leaving them open.' It was hot, and there was no air conditioning.

My meeting with President Ben Bella had an interesting sequel. In the midst of the 1964 general election campaign he asked me to go and spend two days in Algeria. This I did. In effect, I left the electoral battlefield with forty-eight hours leave, port to port. An international audience had been summoned to attend the ceremonial welding of an oil pipeline in the Sahara desert. It took place at a little oasis, in fierce and sweltering heat, ten miles from the nearest village, and the celebration took the form of an address by President Ben Bella to an Algerian multitude and a smaller non-Algerian group of assorted dignitaries, politicians, officials and commercial people. As we assembled, some dozens of desert dwellers, riding horses and camels, galloped to and fro firing their muskets indiscriminately in the air. Their ammunition was live. I hoped it was their way of saying welcome. I reflected that perhaps the hustings in the UK would have been safer.

I had a seat in a rickety covered stand. Peter Gregson and Jack Gill, two brilliant officials from the Board of Trade who were accompanying me, had to sit in the sun. The Russian Trade Minister, Mr Podgorny, my old antagonist as a negotiator, sat with me in the stand, dressed in a heavy overcoat. There was a large Chinese delegation dressed in siren suits and caps. The tribesmen took their places in front of the stand in their hundreds accompanied by their ladies who were dressed from head to foot in black, none of them allowed to expose more than a single cyclopean eye.

Ben Bella spoke for one and a half hours in Arabic. After each of the more exciting passages of his speech the shooting started again and the women ululated in empathy. I looked forward to release from the hard, cramped wooden benches when the speech ended. It was not to be. The speech was repeated, word for word, in French. Sitting there was vastly harder labour than electioneering in Taunton: I was melting, and I was in the shade. Poor Gregson and Gill, sitting in the sun, must have nearly liquified.

There was one particularly happy passage in Ben Bella's speech which made the journey worthwhile. I had not understood the Arabic version and there was no English interpreter present, but I was sure I had been mentioned at one point. I understood the French version much better. A part of his speech went something like this:

'We are a new nation, a proud people, independent and free.'

Much shouting, shooting and ululation.

'Many nations have offered us the hand of friendship – some in genuine sympathy with our aspirations, some perhaps in part at any rate for their own selfish political advantage. Of all our distinguished guests present today on this historic occasion there is one who stands out as a true and sincere friend – the representative de la Grande Bretagne, Monsieur le Ministre, Monsieur du Cann.'

He paused, looked over at me and grinned.

I am glad to say that a suitably modest amount of shooting and ululation followed. I looked across to the Russians and the Chinese. They were po-faced. They probably spoke less French than I. I hoped that my civil service colleagues had not altogether melted in the Saharan sun and had heard that friendly tribute. It was their devoted work in support of British industry that had brought the contract to fruition.

Back home in London, it had been a horrid shock, some three months before the general election of 1964, to observe on the desk of the Permanent Secretary at the Board of Trade a copy of the Labour Party's election manifesto. The Permanent Secretary caught my eye. 'It is my duty, Minister, as a conscientious civil servant, to be prepared for any eventuality, however distasteful or unlikely.'

We both laughed. He was an engaging, and tactful, liar. But under the joke we both understood the point. The political neutrality of the civil service in Britain is one of its greatest strengths and one of our nation's best assets. Today, this neutrality is increasingly in jeopardy.

The election campaign of October 1964 was fought by Alec Douglas Home with enthusiasm and skill. He paid a fleeting visit to Taunton and was well received, and no doubt his visit helped in producing a creditable enough result. In a three-cornered fight the Socialist and Liberal votes both increased and my majority fell from almost 6,500 to 4,748, but that was still more than seven times the majority I started with, so I felt comfortable.

Nationally it was another story. The Conservatives lost forty-seven seats and the Labour Party finished with an overall majority of four. We were out of office. My Ministerial career had lasted just over two years. I could not have known it, but I was not be a Minister again.

CHAPTER 5

CHAIRMAN
of the PARTY

Alec Douglas Home never lost his ability to charm and to astonish me. He surprised me on two counts one day in January 1965 when he asked me round to his flat in Whitehall Court. The first surprise was to find him in bed and in his pyjamas. He had a bad cold.

We had a cup of tea together and he sprang his second surprise. 'I want to ask you to be Chairman of the Conservative Party,' he said. 'The organisation needs considerable attention and you will do the work very well.'

I was astounded.

Looking back, I can see that he thought to humour the mood of the nation with this new appointment. I would be the youngest Chairman since 1926 and as a grammar school boy I would be far removed from the 'grouse moor image' of which the Tory Party's critics complained. (By coincidence, my school had been in the Parliamentary constituency of my Etonian predecessor, Lord Blakenham.) Alec made it clear that if I took on the job I would also be invited to join the Shadow Cabinet.

I asked for a few days' grace to give time to talk to my wife and my colleagues in Unicorn. I had only just rejoined the business after leaving Ministerial office: now, if I took on these new duties, I would have less time to spare for the direction of the business than perhaps my colleagues had expected. Would they regard that as fair? Also, after two years on a low Government salary I needed to earn a reasonable income again. There would soon be four mouths to feed in our family as my wife was expecting our second child in April. The Chairmanship of the Party would be a wonderful opportunity, a great promotion. It would give me immense scope for imaginative and constructive work and I would be glad to undertake it, but it was an unpaid post and therefore sure to cost me money and that would be a worry. However, my colleagues at Unicorn concurred at once. So did my family. I accepted.

It was only three months since the dramatic events of 1964 when, after thirteen years in office, the Conservative Government fell and Harold Wilson became Prime Minister. Wilson had been made Leader of the Labour Party after the death of Hugh Gaitskell in 1963, the same year as Alec Home became Leader of the Conservatives. His most formidable rival for the leadership, Aneurin Bevan, the charismatic Deputy Leader and darling of the left, had died three years earlier, so when the contest came it was effectively between Wilson and George Brown.

Stories about George Brown abound, many not entirely to his credit. I talked to him often in the House: his observations were always shrewd. He was a patriot and a good companion. Alas, he had a reputation for careless drinking, and a weak head for alcohol. One day, it is said, when Foreign Secretary, he was dining in London next to an Ambassador's wife, a lady of beauty and obvious charms. As they sat down to dinner he made some slightly improper remark to do with the depth of her cleavage. She took offence.

'Oh come on, be reasonable,' said George. 'Surely I can't be the first man to have made a risqué remark to you.'

'No,' replied the lady, 'but you are the first to do so before the soup.'

From Labour's point of view the choice of Wilson as leader was to pay an excellent dividend. It was his achievement, like Tony Blair's today, to make the Labour Party seem fresh, exciting and relevant. In his speech to the Labour Party Conference in October 1963 he had said:

> We are redefining and we are re-stating our socialism in terms of the
> scientific revolution . . . the Britain that is going to be forged in the
> white heat of this revolution will be no place for restrictive practices or
> out-dated methods on either side of industry.

In reality restrictive practices took an even firmer stranglehold on British industry under Wilson and his successors until finally an effective assault was made on them by Margaret Thatcher; but in the 1964 general election campaign Wilson's ebullient promises caught the mood of the nation. 'Let's go with Labour' was the slogan and the Tory Party was characterised as fuddy duddy and out of date.

Alec Home was lampooned as an elderly aristocrat peering over the top of his half glasses. It must be admitted that, although he had been an MP before he succeeded to his peerage, he was never fully at home in the rough and tumble of the 1960s House of Commons, a less gentlemanly place than the Commons of his earlier day. His supporters were nervous for him before every appearance he made at the dispatch box. Wilson taunted him: 'After half a century of democratic advance, the whole process has ground to a halt with the fourteenth earl.' Alec retorted, 'As far as the fourteenth earl is concerned, I suppose Mr Wilson, when you come to think of it, is the fourteenth Mr Wilson,' but the riposte was hardly convincing.

In the 1964 general election 317 Labour MPs were elected, 304 Conservatives and 9 Liberals. Labour's overall majority was only 4 on paper, but Labour MPs were confident: their Ministers were enthusiastic new brooms and Wilson promised a hundred days of dynamic government. After a long spell of Conservative administration, the country was ready to allow its replacement a fair opportunity to prove itself, and within the Labour Party its leadership was unchallenged.

The same could not be said of the Tories. When a Party loses a general election the inquest lasts for months, and the scars of the recent leadership contest which had put Alec in place had by no means healed. That would need more time. Meanwhile Alec's critics outnumbered those publicly expressing gratitude to him for his courageous efforts to restore our Party's fortunes after the disasters of the French veto on Britain's bid to join the EEC, the Profumo scandal, the undignified scramble to succeed the ailing Macmillan and the electorate's boredom with the Conservatives at the end of their long period of office. Those critics saw only that we had lost the election: they did not understand that, in the circumstances, losing it by so narrow a margin was a measure not of Alec's failure but of his success.

The question on everyone's lips was how long would the Labour Government survive? The precedents were mulled over, like entrails by the priests of ancient Rome. Labour's majority over all other parties was even smaller than the majority of six held by the last Labour Government elected in February 1950. It would only need two by-elections swinging against the Government to wipe out its overall majority.

Immediately after the election Alec Home had asked me to be Opposition front bench spokesman on Trade and Shipping and I had agreed at once. I felt very much at home in this position, partly because I had had a year as Minister for Trade in the Department of Trade and Industry and felt I knew the Ministry and its responsibilities, and partly because my continuing commercial experience kept me in touch with British business. Alec had apologised for not including me in his Shadow

Cabinet. It already had too many members, he said, twenty one in all, and he could not increase the number further. He thoughtfully compensated me for that by including my name in his dissolution honours list as a Privy Councillor.

Reggie Maudling congratulated me in a division lobby in an absent-minded sort of way. 'Always thought you were one,' he said.

For the few people outside Government who are occasionally made Privy Councillors it is a valued honour; some say it is the best to receive in a man's Parliamentary career. To MPs it confers one great advantage, priority in addressing the House of Commons. My duties proved far from onerous. I have only attended two Privy Council meetings, the first when I was sworn in as a Member. There is some ceremonial involved, and the Queen told me that one of my predecessors, overcome with emotion when he entered the room in which the ceremony was to take place, fell at once to his knees. It was a long room and to take his place in front of his sovereign he had to cross it. He was uncertain whether to get to his feet again. There was a hiatus, and then he covered the whole length of the room on his knees. It must have been an odd sight. My second attendance was at a splendid gathering of the whole membership of the Privy Council at a dinner to mark the Queen's Jubilee.

I had only been a Privy Councillor for a few weeks, and front-bench spokesman for Trade and Shipping for not much longer, when Alec surprised me by making me Chairman of the Party. The appointment seemed to surprise most other people, too, but it had a universally good press and was seen as marking a break with the past. Iain Macleod said I might have been designed for the appointment by computer.

There were some unpleasant aspects, however. In the biography of me that the Conservative Central Office issued it noted that I had qualified for my BA degree at Oxford at the age of eighteen, that is to say when I left the University to join the Navy. It was true, of course, but it excited a number of miserable people to write me offensive letters. You're a liar, they said, we've looked you up and you don't have a degree at all. What typical Tory arrogance. I was surprised and hurt. A thick skin is an essential shield for any political gladiator but I have never found it easy to grow one.

A clergyman wrote to say that he understood the position exactly. Of course I was qualified but understandably I had never registered my qualification after my War service, so I was not on the official list of graduates. If I cared to send him a particular sum of money (I forget how much, it was perhaps £5) he would do me that small service and I would be enrolled on the lists as a fully-fledged Bachelor of Arts. If I cared to send a little more money (I fancy it was a further £10) he could arrange to convert the Bachelor's degree into a Master's. (This was quite legitimate. To qualify for an Oxford MA at that time one needed only to take a BA, allow some time to pass and then pay a small fee.) In case I doubted his integrity I might consult various distinguished people for whom he had performed a similar service, and he mentioned some significant names, including Harold Macmillan. I sent him the cash. He did as he promised and I became a Master of Arts, no less, and more to the point, was on the books as such. That was the end of the criticism.

The Conservative Party's morale at that time was low. During the election campaign the rank and file of the Party had been increasingly impressed by Alec and Elizabeth Home's dedication, but our credibility in the country as a whole had been heavily damaged by the refusal of Iain Macleod and Enoch Powell to serve in Alec's Cabinet when he became Prime Minister the year before. I thought their actions selfish and disloyal: I remembered my uncertain feelings about them both when we had first met in the 1950s at the time of my candidature in Walthamstow. Macleod, Powell and Maudling had all warned Alec that his acceptance of the leadership would be unpopular in the Conservative Party and unsuccessful in the country. Maudling continued in Government as Chancellor: Macleod and Powell remained outsiders. Even the growing appreciation of Sir Alec's sterling character could not overcome the handicaps with which he began his premiership; and the Tory Party does not like a loser.

It was clear that another general election was bound to follow within months, as soon as a suitable opportunity presented itself for Labour to increase its working majority. Public opinion generally remained favourable to Labour, overlooking the Party's shortcomings in Government, the divisions within its ranks and the serious uncertainties prevailing in the fields of economic and defence policy. In the House of Commons, the Conservative Party was trying all it knew to engineer a defeat for Labour. I did not like to tell my colleagues that my heart was not in the task; I was afraid we might succeed too soon. It was too early to have a realistic chance of defeating Labour at the polls. In popular circles Labour was far from discredited, the Conservatives far from credible. In the event of an early general election I could foresee a re-run of 1964 with, probably, a worse result for us and a better result for Labour. Time was what we needed for success. I was afraid that time was what we would not have.

I was, therefore, immediately faced with a dilemma as the new Chairman of the Party. In the short-term it was necessary to prepare for a general election but my real task was to build up the strength of our Party's organisation for the longer-term, a four- or five-year programme. The precedent to follow was the one set by Lord Woolton after our election defeat in 1945, that of the behind-the-scenes organiser. I would not use the post for personal advertisement, nor seek to be a flamboyant advocate like, say, Quintin Hailsham. Advocacy could safely be left to other leading Party figures. My priority was to remould the Party apparatus. The long-term plan would inevitably involve some radical structural moves and include changes in senior personnel; but it would be foolish to embark in too dramatic a fashion on this long-term reorganisation if, when it had hardly begun, we found ourselves overtaken by events and forced to face a snap general election.

Events have a way of taking charge. There had been much private speculation about Alec's position, and some of Edward Heath's supporters, like Macleod and Walker, were clandestinely lobbying against him – unknown to Heath, I dare say, though one could not be sure. This sad fact was consistently reported to me by Lobby correspondents. I went out of my way to make public speeches in Alec's support but I was fighting a losing battle. Much of the press was against him and it was undeniable that his television appearances had not done him justice. His public manner was unimpressive and he made some *faux pas*, such as when he referred to state schools as grammar schools.

Some, even Members of Parliament, argued that Alec's shortcomings as a television performer were of minor consequence, but that was a foolish opinion. It is essential for a political leader to be competent on television: enthusing packed public meetings, such as Party conferences, is no longer enough on its own; they are now chiefy a spectacle for the TV. True, the leader must competently deliver innumerable speeches in a multitude of different circumstances but without doubt it is television that now counts most in influencing popular opinion. De Gaulle understood this well. He paid little attention to the newspapers but he controlled the news presentation on French television with a fist of iron.

With typical modesty, Alec decided that the Conservative Party would probably do better under new leadership. He attended a meeting of the 1922 Committee on 22 July 1965 and announced his intention to resign, after less than two years as Leader. During the early part of 1965 he had asked me and William Whitelaw, the Chief Whip, for our private opinions about the situation in the Conservative Party but, looking back, I think he had already made up his mind to retire. Perhaps his heart was no longer in his task but I have no doubt that he did what he believed was in the Party's best interest and that he was right. Still, I felt wretchedly sad. Neither the Party nor the nation repaid him with generosity for all he had done. Those who should have been his friends pushed him aside when, through no fault of his, he did not lead them to an impossible victory. As someone wrote at the time, although suicide was on Alec's death certificate, it was murder nonetheless.

There were complaints about the way he had been chosen as leader, by a 'magic circle' some said. Yet, in truth, the consultations within the Conservative Party that had led to his choice had been the widest yet held. It was a far cry from the time when it was virtually only the members of the Cabinet who chose the Party Leader. If there was a fault in the process of selection it was that of the Party, not of the one who was chosen, and it was Alec who brought in a new system for the election of the Party Leader to ensure that there would in future be none of the argument and criticism that followed when he was chosen. Yet despite the unfairness of the general complaints about him no one heard a word of complaint or recrimination from him at any time, then or since. Instead, he was the first to profess support for his elected successor. It was an example which, when his turn came, that successor did not follow.

There were three nominations for the succession of whom one, Enoch Powell, never had a serious chance. The two chief contenders, Heath and Maudling, could not have been more different in temperament and style. Heath had shown himself to be a fiercely combative figure in the House of Commons in those early days of the 1964 Labour Government. As Shadow Chancellor of the Exchequer he had a position which enabled him to shine and he took full advantage of it. Reginald Maudling on the other hand was not ambitious enough to thrust himself into the limelight. He had a brilliant intellect and a better mind than his chief rival, but his relaxed manner made his detractors accuse him of indolence. Detached he may have been, idle he was not.

Heath has a formidable capacity for work. It was his application rather than his outstanding intellectual qualities that took him to the forefront in politics. He too is an honourable man but his shyness, if shy is what he is, has put a shell around him and he could only on rare occasions achieve Maudling's easy camaraderie.

Heath immediately mounted a wholly professional election

campaign, masterminded by Peter Walker, a former National Chairman of the Young Conservatives who was to become Secretary of State for the Environment in 1970 – and who had helped me start the Unicorn Unit Trusts. He was supported by a dedicated and thrusting group of younger Conservative Members of Parliament who no doubt had a laudable desire to promote a candidate who would be a potential election winner – though, to be realistic, a candidate's backers usually have in mind the fact that if their man wins they are more likely to get promotion. In contrast to Heath's campaign Reggie Maudling's was amateurish. He put his confidence chiefly in his former PPS, Freddie Bennett, but while Bennett and others did their best it was far from good enough.

In the event Heath won the election over Maudling by 150 votes to 133. The narrowness of the margin shows that with a different style of campaign Maudling might easily have won. (Powell with 15 votes was a long way behind.) The Conservative Party preferred to choose an obvious fighter to counter that most skilful and astute of politicians, Harold Wilson. The adversarial format is the basis of our political system in Britain, as it is of our legal system; the design of the House of Commons abets it; media reporting emphasises it. The Conservative Parliamentary Party chose, above all, a man they saw as a bruiser: the deeper qualities of the alternatives were forgotten as Tory MPs allowed themselves to be over-influenced by the prevailing mood which demanded a radical change in style at the top. But the decisive point was probably the defection of Maudling's friend, Iain Macleod, to Heath's camp. It was in character: Macleod had let down Alec, now he let down Reggie. Naturally his allies followed his example and this torpedoed Reggie's chances of success. Macleod was to have his reward: Heath made him Shadow Chancellor between 1966 and 1970 and, when he became Prime Minister, Chancellor of the Exchequer, a post Macleod had eagerly sought. He died, unhappily, a mere four weeks after his appointment, so he never fully enjoyed the success that his inconstancy had brought him. Anthony Barber was his (more pliant) successor. It was a substitution which eventually was to have significant economic and political consequences: Macleod would probably have had the strength to restrain Heath's disastrous 'dash for growth' in 1973 when a sudden wild expansion of the money supply did not lead to sustainable growth but did inevitably produce one of the big surges of inflation that dogged the British economy for decades.

I did not find those early days as Chairman of the Conservative Party entirely comfortable. My term of office began with a public argument with my predecessor (featured in the *Daily Telegraph*) which I much regretted. It came about in this way. After a few weeks at the Conservative Central Office it became clear to me that the Party organisation was not in good shape. Furthermore, money had been poured out before the last general election and the Party was woefully short of both income and reserves. No doubt the motives for spending the money were excellent. One can argue that everything possible had to be done in the attempt to win the election, but now we had to face uncomfortable reality. The cupboard was bare, another expensive general election was in the offing, and the beginning of a new Parliament is a miserable time for a Party in opposition to raise funds.

This serious situation was suspected by my colleagues in the House of Commons. After all, if Alec Home had believed everything was as well as could be at Number 32 Smith Square he would not have appointed a new Chairman.

I was asked to meet the Parliamentary Party at a meeting of the 1922 Committee and to say something about our situation and my plans for the future. I rehearsed my speech with care and I thought I was being guarded in what I said. Certainly I made no criticism of anybody but there were full reports of my speech in the newspapers. These reports infuriated my predecessor as Chairman of the Party, Lord Blakenham, and a former Treasurer, Richard Stanley. They called to see me at my home in Lord North Street and demanded a public apology. This, of course, I was quite unwilling to give.

Lord Blakenham quickly got to the point: 'Your speech was a direct criticism of our stewardship of the Party's affairs.'

'Nonsense,' I replied. 'When I talked to the 1922 Committee I did no more than describe the situation as it is, and pretty mildly at that. There may be some people who take over a new office and set out to paint their inheritance as black as night so that they'll get the credit for any improvement, but that's certainly not what I was doing.' It had in fact been a deliberate tactic on my part to tell the truth. I badly needed the co-operation and help of the Parliamentary Party in putting things right and the only way to get it was to be as frank as possible from the outset.

It was an uncomfortable moment but somehow we got over the difficulty without a climb-down on my part and I began to put into operation some of the longer-term plans that I had in mind. I saw the 500 plus constituencies in England and Wales as, in effect, subsidiary and independently managed divisions of the Conservative Party. Each had its Chairman and the equivalent of a Board of Directors (its Management

Committee) and of a Managing Director (the professional agent). I believed it must be right to build up the status and the professionalism of those 'Managing Directors'. It was impossible for the Central Office to chivvy up every constituency or even to keep an eye on each of them, but in almost every one there was a dependable, professional ally – the qualified, trained agent. I wanted to see the best, most competent and most dynamic agents appointed and I wanted the profession to be more highly regarded.

Our Party has always been extremely well served by its professional workers. Although each constituency agent is the employee of his local constituency association, by whom he is paid, nonetheless he looks to the Central Office for his prospects of promotion. At election times the law rightly imposes strict formal responsibilities on a candidate and his agent. Misconduct by either, spending beyond a legal limit on election expenses, failure to comply exactly with timetables, and so on, can have serious consequences, including voiding an election. It is essential therefore that agents are properly instructed and qualified. Examinations for the qualification of agents are organised by the Central Office. In that way it sets standards for the profession and can, if it wishes, exercise a considerable discipline over the agents' profession without in any way interfering with the autonomy of constituencies.

I determined to work through the professional agents. The first need was to ensure that they were well paid so that we could recruit, and retain, agents of good calibre. The second was to help them become well versed in the complicated techniques of modern politicking. We had to move the Party away from the old semi-amateur basis into the new world of public opinion polls, the sampling of opinion, the techniques of mass canvassing through computer-based operations, direct mail, sophisticated fund raising and the like.

My immediate problem lay in the likely reaction of the constituency activists to the idea of paying realistic salaries to agents. Many of those who carry out voluntary work in the constituencies, retired people and the like, do not have large incomes. When they contribute generously to the Party's funds it is not unnatural that they should look on the comparatively well paid agent with a suspicion tinged with some envy. However, I felt I could encourage the more sophisticated people in the constituencies, especially those with experience in employment matters, to carry the plan through. I was not disappointed. We began systematically to raise agents' salaries, to raise standards and to increase their numbers. It is a measure of the extent to which organisation has slipped in the contemporary Conservative Party that the number of trained agents in the field is now only about a third of the number of Parliamentary constituencies.

The second innovation I introduced was in the field of policy-making. It seemed to me that too many of my colleagues in the House of Commons (and local councillors also) thought that the only job of the rank and file in the constituency parties was to get them elected. I wanted to change that and to involve a growing number of Party workers in the task of formulating policies.

In the Conservative Party policy is ultimately the province of the Leader. The manifesto at general election times is published over his signature and he is the final arbiter of what it contains. I did not want to alter that but I did want to associate the Party at large more closely with discussions and decisions about policy matters. My aim was a simple one: to encourage policy discussions in the constituencies up and down the land and to make it clear to our members that the policies adopted by the Leadership could and would be influenced by any rank and file Member of our Party. I wanted also to ensure that the Party leadership was continuously exposed to opinions at the grass roots and could draw ideas from all sections of society, especially from people active in business.

One important way of doing this was to integrate the Conservative Political Centre into the Party constitution. The CPC had been formed in 1945 by Rab Butler to provide a forum for discussion and debate within the Party. It was time, I was sure, to develop further the two-way movement of ideas of which Rab had written and the CPC was the ideal vehicle for this purpose. I had strong support from the Chairman, Reginald Eyre, and by the time of the Party conference in Blackpool in October 1966 I was able to report good progress. CPC committees were already functioning in 322 of the 547 constituencies in England and Wales and the number of discussion groups had increased by half: their reports to the Party leadership had doubled.

In my time as Chairman of the Conservative Party the CPC had two more splendid leaders, David Howell (who later became a Member of the Cabinet, for which his intellectual gifts well fitted him) and subsequently Russell Lewis, always an influential political commentator. The Party owed them much for the intellectual stimulus they offered. Between the 1964 and 1966 general elections twenty-eight publications came from the CPC covering every aspect of policies and expressing the widest span of Conservative thought. Many of the ideas we put forward at that time eventually became established Party policy.

Two of the most important practical proposals were that sitting tenants in council houses and flats should be allowed to buy their homes and that nationalised industries should be privatised and those who worked in them should be given shares or allowed to buy them at favourable prices. Some of our colleagues thought at the time that these ideas were absurdly far fetched and the Conservative Government of 1970-74 led by Mr Heath did little to follow them up; but during Mrs Thatcher's Administration they became accepted policy and ownership by the British people of property on a far wider scale has become a reality. More than ten million people own shares in British industry and commerce and two thirds of British families now own their own homes. Privatisation has been a considerable economic success with substantial benefits for the consumer, and the British example has been imitated worldwide. The development of ideas such as these in the Conservative Political Centre, and the association of the whole Party with them, meant that the Party slowly but surely began to win the practical and intellectual arguments in politics.

It is sad that by 1995 that lead, so hard won, has been carelessly lost. The Tory Party has gone back to sleep again and has largely lost any pretensions to intellectual leadership. Even the existence of its bookshop is hidden behind security guards. The experience of 1964 repeats itself. Over the thirteen years of Conservative Government after 1951, Ministers came to rely increasingly on official advice and less on outside opinion. At a meeting of backbench Conservative MPs in the 1955 Parliament I once heard the Transport Minister, Harold Watkinson, say 'Now I am a Minister I have to be above Party considerations.' I was appalled and said so. He was unrepentant. Such carelessness has lost general elections for the Tories in the past, notably in 1906 and 1945.

Now, in 1995, the critics rightly complain that a Conservative Government has 'run out of ideas', that the pace of the Thatcher revolution is faltering and so on. That is untrue, but the Government gives an impression of uncertainty and there is a reason for this. Too many Ministers, seduced by the aura of office and usually overworked, allow their attention to be diverted from their political objectives. Their attitude becomes defensive. They seem stale. In opposition in those years after the election defeat of 1964 we harnessed opinion makers in the professions and the universities and stimulated them to join us in publishing ideas and proposals for use in our time in Government. We made them our allies. That was a blueprint for success. Now that we have been in Government for a number of years, we have allowed those same groups to become our critics. That is a recipe for disaster.

The third thing we needed in 1965 was the best intelligence we could get. I determined to make certain that the Party had at its command effective tools for the measurement of public opinion. In this I was lucky. Among those I recruited to help me was an outstanding man called Tommy Thompson, Assistant Editor of the *Daily Mail*, who among his other duties was responsible for overseeing the National Opinion Poll results published by that newspaper. He was joined at the Central Office by Humphrey Taylor and the three of us proposed the establishment of an opinion research company which, while it would share its overhead by working for other clients, would work under contract for the Conservative Party as a priority. We set up a company under the name of the Opinion Research Centre and it became highly successful. The Conservative Party had access to up-to-date, continuous and exclusive information about the movements of public opinion and that intelligence was to prove invaluable to us.

I had originally suggested that the Party should take a share-stake in ORC but the Party's Treasurers did not like this idea and it was not pursued. More is the pity, because in due course Taylor and Thompson sold out their interests in ORC to Harris of America which Taylor subsequently headed. They made a great deal of money for themselves, as they well deserved to do. We could have made some cash for the Conservative Party too, perhaps £250,000 or more, but the Party Treasurers of the day were better money-beggars than money-earners. That was their temperament and the tradition of their office; an example of that contempt for commercial endeavour which is the English disease.

I had done my homework by checking on the work being done in the United States by the Republican and Democratic Parties. The Kennedy camp used public opinion research methods to an extreme degree. For example, before President Kennedy made an important speech the public acceptability of different themes would be evaluated by samplers. His advisers would select the most suitable and a speech based on those themes was drafted in outline, and then tested in detail by a second round of research. I found the process cynical in the extreme. It is the duty of the statesman, surely, to lead opinion, not to follow it; to seek to persuade his fellow men to accept his ideals, his principles and the policies by which he plans to give them effect. Only a lunatic would ignore the need to present ideas in an attractive style, but a political leader ill serves the public if he panders to fashion or prejudice as Kennedy and his advisers seemed to do. I have never believed that the

106

most successful politician deserves to be the one who shouts populist slogans in the loudest voice.

The fourth of my tasks as Party Chairman, and to my mind the most important, was to find ways of demonstrating to the electors the practical relevance of Conservative principles and policies. It would inevitably be some years before we could have the opportunity to form a national Government, but elections in local government were occurring all the time. I reasoned that if we could demonstrate in the towns, counties and villages that the local Conservative Party contained competent and wise administrators, it would be the best possible support for our claim to be well equipped to provide competent Government nationally. I set out to build power bases for the Party in the shires and towns of England and Wales by doing everything possible to help our candidates win local government elections.

We made a pretty good start on this policy. In the borough elections held in May 1965, only some three months after my appointment as Chairman of the Party, the Conservatives won 562 seats and the Labour Party lost 449. I had not expected such early success. We were to have more: later local election results were a continuing triumph.

Next, we set out to reinforce every section of the Party's formal structures, and three in particular. First we needed to consolidate our successes in the organisation of Women's Groups (for the Conservative Party traditionally has a majority of the votes of women in Britain). Second, the Young Conservatives were of increasing importance. In the decade 1974-1984 the total of new young voters coming on to the electoral register rose from just over 500,000 to a maximum of 750,000 in 1982 – a total of some 2 3/4 million electors voting for the first time in the general election of 1983. The importance of making an effective appeal to young people cannot be over-estimated. Third, under this head, we set out to attract and to influence Trade Unionists through the Conservative Party's Trade Union organisation. It was from this group, mostly male, that I had the highest hopes of winning support in the medium to long-term. The Labour Party had had things its own way for too long in this area. As the C2 classes, the skilled workers, became increasingly affluent, taking for granted the material benefits available to them and keen to retain them undisturbed – television sets, new carpets, houses, refrigerators, telephones, cars, foreign holidays, investments and the like – and as they became increasingly critical of a politically oriented leadership in their trade unions, I was sure that here was a fertile ground for the propagation of Conservative philosophy. This reasoning proved to be sound and the policy worked well for us. The Party's trade union membership continued to expand steadily. Liaison with national trade union leaders had to be left to the Conservative Party's official spokesmen: they could not be seen to be consorting with the Chairman of the Conservative Party. Nonetheless I had a close liaison with trade union leaders in my Taunton constituency; we met regularly and I learned much from them.

Like the Duke of Wellington before a battle I wanted to ensure that our political battleground was properly surveyed. My experience of marketing unit trust investments had taught me a number of important lessons in demography. To put the matter shortly, I became convinced that, more often than not, the bald voting figures at election times conceal substantial shifts in voting behaviour.

I arranged for every constituency to receive its demographic profile. Many long held beliefs were shattered as a result, even in my own constituency of Taunton. At the time of my first candidature in 1956 Taunton was represented to me by the officers of the Conservative Association as an agricultural constituency. This was hardly surprising since it contains some of England's loveliest countryside. However, the reality in terms of numbers of electors was different. There were many more retirement pensioners than there were farmers and the proportion increased every year. Almost a quarter of the voters in every constituency now are retired people. One thinks of a place like Taunton as unchanging in its electoral mix. It is not. Each year about 1,300 young people there attain their eighteenth birthday and reach voting age; so at each general election, assuming a Parliamentary life span of four or five years, it is likely that between 5,000 and 6,500 will be first-time voters, perhaps 10 per cent of the electorate. That is only part of the picture: the adjustments in the electoral register – new voters coming of age, deaths and people moving house – affect some 20 per cent or more of registered voters over a five-year cycle. The composition of the electorate in any constituency at any general election will be markedly different from what it was at the previous one. Electioneering must take this into account.

We continuously emphasised the importance of recruiting young people into the Conservative Party. In the 1966 general election no less than one third of Conservative Parliamentary candidates were Young Conservatives or former Young Conservatives, and 63 were elected, nearly a quarter of our Parliamentary strength. I set the Party a membership target of a quarter of a million YCs and they responded well.

It was not only the Party's formal organisation that required strengthening. For a Party to succeed in gaining office it must identify itself with as many strands of opinion as possible. I spent much time also encouraging peripheral groups in the Conservative Party's support. Such organisations as the Bow Group, the Monday Club, the Anglo-Polish Conservative Association (to name only three, dissimilar bodies) helped mobilise wider support for the Party, and they also had much to offer us in terms of fresh ideas, even if not all of them would be acceptable. I came increasingly to the conclusion that it was essential for the Conservative Party to involve itself with special interest groups – teachers, doctors, local government workers and so on: the list was virtually endless. Steadily and surely we drew more people into our work, into policy discussion and into the Party's affairs and ambitions. Steadily and surely we involved more of the electors: and we made allies in consequence.

The professional workers in the Party were enthusiastic supporters of our strategy, none more so perhaps than Michael Fraser (now Lord Fraser) one of the most cultured and intelligent of its long time servants, a loyal, discreet and trusted friend of its leaders from Churchill and Butler to Heath. He was the chief author of the Party's published policy documents and secretary of the Shadow Cabinet. He was a mine of historical information about our Party and an invaluable companion and supporter, in good times and bad. The Central Office staff, too, were excellent people, loyal, competent and increasingly enthusiastic as time went by. The Party owed them much and so did I.

One drastic decision I made was to scrap the list of approved potential Parliamentary candidates and prepare a new one. Out went the time-servers and all those who rated their egos as more valuable than hard constituency graft, people who boasted at dinner tables that they were candidates but who did no work for the Party. There were many hundred names on the list: scrapping it was unpopular but essential.

Since then the process of approval of potential Parliamentary candidates by the Party has been greatly formalised, modelled on the procedures of the War Office Selection Board for officers. Those observing the Tory Parliamentary Party in 1995 who ask the question 'Where have all the good men gone?' may doubt whether this new method is really an improvement and may reflect that there is no better reference than the personal recommendation of an experienced observer. Remembering my own inclusion in the list of candidates solely on Earl Winterton's recommendation, perhaps I am prejudiced, but I don't think so.

We don't want to lose you, but we think you ought to go . . .

Finally, I set out to establish a warm working relationship with the voluntary workers in the Conservative Party. Everything depended on that. I travelled the country a great deal. I had regular meetings with leading Party workers in their own areas (astonishing as it may seem, this was a new practice) and I initiated regular discussions with Area Chairmen in London (another new practice). We became a team of trusted friends.

The National Union of Conservative and Unionist Associations is the co-ordinating body for constituency workers in the Conservative Party. In England and Wales the Party is organised by regions with eleven provincial areas (the Scottish Conservative Party is separately organised) and each elects area officers and the like with the responsibility of co-ordinating political work in its individual constituencies. Party members in the areas send their representatives to the National Executive Committee of the Party, as do the Young Conservatives, the women's organisations, and so on. I was fortunate that for most of my time as Chairman of the Party the Executive had as its Chairman an outstanding man called Clyde Hewlett. He was a Mancunian, a former Royal Marines officer, a worker for charity, an industrialist in the chemical business, a man of strong opinions, and an indefatigable worker for the Conservatives. He and I became close friends. It was only after his death that I learned of an interview he had sought with Heath during my Chairmanship. He believed that Heath gave me less public support than I deserved and he called on him in his set of rooms in Albany to complain. The Party in the country, he said, was fully supportive of the work I was doing at the Central Office. It was having a marked effect. Heath's obvious and declared support for that effort would make the task of the leaders of the voluntary workers considerably easier, and so on. Ted was as ungracious as ever but Hewlett was not to be put off.

Reflecting on this history and later events I believe that both Heath and Thatcher shared a common failing in their disloyalty to colleagues. Heath received total loyalty from me: he hardly reciprocated it. If he knew that members of his staff were sometimes privately critical of his colleagues he did not prohibit their comments. When Margaret Thatcher was Prime Minister, one would from time to time read comments in the newspapers critical of one or other of her Ministers; and it was plain that the opinions, if they did not have official approval, did not receive her disapproval. Many names were quoted by those close to Margaret as having lost her confidence before they lost office: Stevas, Hayhoe, Lawson and even so loyal a figure as Pym. Later, as Chairman of the 1922 Committee, I would register my strong disapproval of such practices. Those who most deserve loyalty are those who offer it themselves.

After strategy, tactics. I needed to establish a new machinery for representatives of every section of our Party to settle the day-by-day tactics through which our strategy would be carried out. I arranged weekly meetings with the heads of departments at Central Office which were joined by representatives of the voluntary workers, the Chief Whips from both Houses of Parliament and the Chairman of the 1922 Committee, or their deputies. The aim was to encourage the various parts of our Party to co-ordinate their activities, and the system worked well. It also had another valuable effect in helping us to avoid trouble. 'What,' I used to ask, 'will be next week's trip wires, what are the likely problems, what events will cause us difficulty or embarrassment?' Forewarned is forearmed. We did our best to avoid trouble and we usually succeeded, a knack which in recent years the Tory Party seems to have lost.

Alec Home and I engaged together also in an international project. In Germany we met leaders of a number of European and other Conservative Parties. We argued in favour of the co-ordination of our political efforts, partly as a rival to the Socialist International and to counter its progress, and also because we believed that political initiatives and successes for the right-of-centre parties in one country would teach valuable lessons to us all. This project, for which we both argued so fiercely to a largely indifferent audience, had to wait almost twenty years for realisation, but since 1983 there have been regular meetings and some degree of co-ordination between the Christian Democrats, Conservatives and Centre parties in seventeen countries.

111

The domestic strategies and objectives I have outlined were warmly endorsed by Alec Home, but less than six months after my appointment as Chairman of the Party in England and Wales he resigned. In his resignation speech to the 1922 Committee he said this:

> When I took over the leadership of the Party in 1963 there was nothing that I could do but ask the Party to fight on the ground on which we stood. Unity was too fragile and time too short for anything else.
>
> After our narrow defeat in 1964 I knew exactly what I had to do. First to strengthen the organisation of the Party and to eliminate its weaknesses. This I am satisfied is being done by Edward du Cann.
>
> Secondly, I was determined that the Party should rethink its policies to make certain that they would be up to date and meet the needs of our countrymen who are not Socialists but who are progressive and radical. This work has been largely done . . . Thirdly, I tried to organise the Party in Parliament so that we would present an effective opposition. In this we have been successful.
>
> The object of all these moves has been to turn public opinion back to the Conservatives so that we would be in a position to win a general election. You have only got to look at the results of the local elections in May and since then to see that this is happening.
>
> . . . I come to two promises which I have always made to you. I have always considered them binding. The first is that I would never allow disunity in the Party, least of all over myself; the second, that I would tell you when I considered that the time was right to hand over the leadership to another.
>
> The decision had to be mine and mine alone.
>
> . . . I have asked our Chairman to set in motion the new procedures. I myself set up the machinery for this change and I myself have chosen the time to use it. It is up to you to see that it is completed swiftly and efficiently and with dignity and calm. I do not intend to stand for election.
>
> It only remains to me to thank all of you . . .

I was not surprised that evening in July 1965 to see more than one hard-bitten Conservative Member of Parliament in tears. I knew I would miss Alec's strong support, and I would never work for a better man or have a more considerate master. He was to be succeeded in turn by people of very different timbre, style and perception of the tasks of leadership: his going was the end of an era. Make no mistake about the circumstances of

112

his departure. A number of Conservative MPs were determined to bring him down and to elect Heath in his stead, and they succeeded. Perhaps a change was inevitable; perhaps it was, all things considered, for the best; but there should be no doubt about the agitation that forced it on him. Heath could not have been unaware of this; among the agitators were his prominent and principal supporters, but none of us in the House heard him raise a whisper to contradict or stop it.

One of Heath's first needs as Leader was a competent Parliamentary Private Secretary. Jim Prior, MP for Lowestoft, had recently been recommended by me to take over as Vice Chairman of the Party in charge of the selection and approval of Parliamentary candidates: I now proposed him as Heath's Parliamentary aide, reasoning that this reputation as a practical countryman would be a useful, indeed essential complement to Heath's outer-London suburban image.

For a time it seemed that the change in the Conservative Party's leadership had brought us a new tide of fortune. We even went ahead of the Labour Party in the public opinion polls immediately after the leadership change. It was not to last. Although Heath was the first Conservative leader to be directly elected by Conservative Members of Parliament, his attempt to attain credibility among the national electorate by discomforting the Labour leadership was unsuccessful. As *The Times* put it, Heath was still lumbered with the record of thirteen years of Tory Government. Also, he was not a natural orator: speaking from a brief was more natural to him than impromptu remarks, and his early speeches as Leader of the Opposition in the House of Commons were far from impressive. Wilson easily succeeded in diverting attention away from the shortcomings of his own administration, and his public relations were undoubtedly handled with brilliance.

Heath had seemed an obvious counter to Wilson and he had been elected with high hopes, but the disappointment in his actual performance made it hard to keep the Party solid in his support. His dismissal of such leading figures as Sandys, Marples and Boyd-Carpenter from the Shadow Cabinet made enemies and the Party's divisions over Rhodesia did not help him either. Unnecessary suspicions were aroused among Conservative MPs by his decision to establish numerous non-Parliamentary groups to formulate policy recommendations. It was lucky that there was no one to challenge him for the leadership, for his relationship with his supporters started uneasily and seemed set to continue frosty.

I had early, disconcerting evidence of this. One night in early spring during a wintry spell, he and I attended a dinner of leading industrialists in a private room in a London hotel. Ted was guest of honour, the newly elected leader of the Party. He arrived dressed in a white dinner jacket, the only one in the room. Our host, a peer and chairman of one of the UK's most successful companies, turned to me and asked 'Who's that bloody waiter you've brought with you?' Perhaps it was meant as a joke but I disliked the remark, thought it in poor taste and said so. As he left, our host said to me 'I know you'll do your best to make bricks with the straw you have, and we'll all do our best to help you, but you can't expect us to like the man.' Remembering remarks of that kind, and some of the snobbish criticisms of Heath's voice or pretensions that one so frequently heard, I have often thought that his prickliness becomes more understandable. Many years later I heard German industrialists make slighting remarks of the same style about Chancellor Kohl. Heath will be remembered for his signature of the Treaty of Rome and Kohl for his accomplishment of German reunification long after the names of such critics are forgotten.

Although Wilson's small Parliamentary majority was apparently a handicap, it had one great advantage in terms of his management of the Labour Party inside and outside the House of Commons: it gave him the opportunity to ignore his left-wing Members of Parliament, who were obliged to maintain him in office and mitigate their criticisms. Despite that, it was hard going for the new Labour Government: defence spending was cut back, new aircraft projects were cancelled and public expenditure was reduced on many socially desirable schemes in order to meet the economic crisis. A general election was bound to come sooner rather than later and meantime survival for the Government in Parliament was a knife-edged affair. In the general election of 1964 Patrick Gordon Walker, Wilson's nominee for the post of Foreign Secretary, had been defeated at Smethwick. He stood again for Parliament at a by-election in Leyton and lost again, by 205 votes. The Labour Government's overall majority in the Commons was reduced to two, but for all the euphoria in the Tory ranks, I thought the result was an aberration.

More alarms and excursions for the Labour Government followed. In May 1965 the Government's White Paper containing its proposals to nationalise the steel industry was only narrowly approved in the House. In the Summer Recess the Speaker died and had to be replaced in that politically neutral office by an MP from Labour's attenuated ranks. Their small majority was thus reduced by one more. In July 1965 a new clause to the Finance Bill was carried against the Government. In September

George Brown, who was then Secretary of State for Economic Affairs, published his National Plan: it seemed that Government would face a crisis over its wages policy early in the new Parliamentary session beginning in October. All the omens predicted a most uncomfortable period ahead for Labour in the medium to long term. The prospect was that sooner or later the Government would be defeated on an issue of confidence in Parliament with a general election to follow at a time not of Labour's choosing. Wilson, I reasoned, would be on the lookout for his best opportunity to go to the country.

Then, at the end of the year, Mr Solomons, the Labour Member for Kingston upon Hull North, died. A by-election became inevitable. On the face of it, it seemed as if the contest was an open one. In an electorate of some 64,000 the figures in the 1964 general election had been: Labour 20,664, Conservative 19,483, Liberal 7,570.

A Labour majority of just over 1,000 votes, with over 7,000 Liberal votes to be gathered, seemed a reasonable prospect from the Conservative point of view – if the timing of the by-election was not too soon in the life of the Government for an opposition to expect success. Any new Government has a honeymoon with the electors: it can last for a shorter or longer time but six months is the usual maximum – as I had learned the hard way in Taunton in 1959. My instinct told me that it might be protracted in the case of a new Labour Government, taking over as it had after a long period of Conservative rule. The prospects for a Tory win at Hull were likely to be less good than they seemed on paper.

The by-election date was fixed by the Labour Government for 28 January 1966. In accordance with what was to become my habit of visiting every by-election and speaking to the electors, I travelled up to Hull. The moment I stepped out of the train my heart sank. Long experience of politics gives one a facility for judging a constituency. Just as a sailor can sniff wind and weather, a politician can sniff trouble. I knew in my bones this was a seat the Conservatives could not win. Everything I saw confirmed my first impression. I toured the constituency, stopping to talk with people in the housing estates. There was a sea of red posters, and hardly a blue Tory poster to be seen. Conservative Party workers I spoke to and with whom I discussed organisational matters were listless. It was the same with the evening public meetings. The attitude of the electorate seemed to be clearly that the Conservative Party had had its chance, now it was Labour's turn. The Labour Party's slogan 'Thirteen wasted years' had gone home.

In vain did I point out that under the Labour Government Britain's defences would be weakened (as they were), that the value of the pound was slipping (and it continued to do so until devaluation resulted the following year); in vain did I argue that there was substantial criticism of Britain's economic management under Labour in all serious quarters, that the abandonment of aircraft projects was foolish penny-pinching and a denial of Wilson's promised support for technological progress; in vain too was a warning that the Labour Party's fragile unity would not survive an argument between the various wings of the Party over escalating wages, that with wage rises running at 9 per cent and productivity gains at 1 per cent inflation was inevitable, and so on. The electors simply did not want to know. They wanted to trust Labour. They were bored with the Conservatives.

The Anatomists

Even the sudden and unexpected announcement during the by-election campaign made by Mrs Barbara Castle, Labour's Transport Minister, that funds were to be allocated by the Government for a road crossing over the Humber that would cut fifty miles off the journey from Grimsby to Hull seemed not to excite more than a sniff of cynicism, though it was a blatant attempt to capture votes.

The bridge promised by Mrs Castle eventually opened in June 1981. It was scheduled to take a maximum of five years to build: in the end it took nine. The estimated cost was £29 million, the original Government loan was £98 million and by 1994 the total debt amounted to £434 million. Despite high tolls it continues to rise at the rate of many millions of pounds a year. The bridge, which is grossly under-used, has never represented value for taxpayers' money, and if there had not been a by-election in Hull the decision to build it would probably not have been made. The saddest thing is that it was a bribe that need never have been offered. This was a by-election that Labour just could not lose.

In the result the Labour candidate increased his majority to over 5,000. This favourable result was bound to influence Wilson strongly in his choice of a date for the general election. Immediately I returned to London, two weeks before the result was announced, I told the new Leader of the Conservative Party that I was quite certain we would do badly at Hull, that a general election would be called soon, and finally that I was not at all sanguine about our prospects of doing well whenever it came. My predictions were proved right.

Heath had irked me by insisting at about this time that I make faster progress in changing the senior professional personnel at the Central Office. The changes were part of my long-term plan for reorganisation: the paths to promotion had to be opened and the Party's professional organisation needed the new impetus that only new leaders would provide. But with a general election imminent, this would be a short-term mistake. It would be better for the Party to make changes after the election, not before. I would prefer to fight with old campaigners at my side, not with an untried and inexperienced senior team. Heath continued to insist. I thought his orders stupid, and said so, but I could not prevail in argument nor could I myself resign, so I told two of the senior professionals what was planned and said that I required their resignations. Almost at once the general election was announced (as it was bound to be) and I was then obliged to ask them to continue in office. Loyal troopers that they were, they agreed at once, and in the weeks to come they worked as hard and well as ever for the Party. I was bitterly embarrassed to have to trade on their loyalty in that way.

The general election took place on 31 March 1966. Wilson had said that 1966 would be make or break year; now he was asking for a mandate from the electorate 'to get on with the job'. He received it in generous measure. Labour increased its majority in the House of Commons from three to almost one hundred.

Still, it was good to know that the Conservatives had not lost the election through incompetence or lack of enthusiasm. We were well prepared; the usual high standard of Central Office publications was achieved; our candidates were all in place and well briefed. We had no major alarms during the campaign, few bricks were dropped. We had planned to raise a series of issues as the campaign developed and to try to put Labour on the defensive: our strategy was that of Marshal Foch in 1914: 'My centre is giving way, my right is in retreat; situation excellent – I shall attack.'

The Labour and Conservative Parties each held a daily press conference, theirs at Transport House, the headquarters of the Transport and General Workers Union, ours at the Central Office. Both were in Smith Square, Westminster, within fifty yards of each other. By agreement, Labour went first and the Conservative Party second, both at fixed times. I procured a press pass for a Junior Member of the Research Department, Chris Patten (the same Chris Patten who is now Governor of Hong Kong). Dressed in a shabby mackintosh and sporting a Napoleon Solo haircut he gave a brilliant impersonation of the seedy young provincial journalist. He would attend Labour's press conference each day and just before its end would hurry across the square to my office to brief Heath, myself and our colleagues before we went downstairs to the meeting room for our own press conference, at which I always took the chair. His reports were delivered in a lugubrious style, short and accurate. I found them hilarious but they were indispensable intelligence. Through them we were in a position immediately to counter Labour's propaganda and to decide how best to launch our own broadside. In addition we had a well developed system for receiving intelligence from the constituencies plus the results of our own long-term polling of opinion. We fought as competent a campaign as was possible in the circumstances. 'Action not Words' was the title of our election manifesto: it epitomised the theme we sought to pursue, that Labour under Wilson was better at self-advertisement than at the practice of competent Government. But the timing of the election was against us: it had come too soon for our arguments to have a chance of being taken seriously by the electorate. Wilson's honeymoon continued.

I spoke all over the country and spared what time I could for my own constituency. I was re-elected happily enough in Taunton, where in yet another three cornered fight my vote increased by 1,000. But nationally the Conservatives lost 51 seats and Labour gained 46, though our share of the total national vote fell by only 1½ per cent.

So Labour was re-elected to Government, and this time for a potential five-year term and with a substantially increased majority. So far as the Conservative Party was concerned it was back to the task of reorganisation, but from a lower base than previously. Morale among

Party workers was undoubtedly at rock bottom but we stuck to the task and I never ceased to enjoy my work.

My relationship with Heath was not easy. It has sometimes been suggested that we quarrelled but that is untrue. We have never had a cross word. I respected him, and still do, but he and I differed fundamentally in our views on politics and in our approach to the Central Office and to the Conservative Party generally. Heath regarded the constituent parts of the Party as instruments for the Leader's support and little else. Of course they are that; but to me the Leader of the Party is simply the supreme servant of the Conservative Party, *primus inter pares.* There is none of us, Leader, Minister, Shadow Spokesman, Chairman of the Party or ward representative, who should be anything but a faithful servant of the general membership. I regarded the voluntary workers in the Conservative Party as our partners in the quest for victory at the polls. I could not see them as Heath's servants, nor as inferior in status to Members of Parliament. The difference between Heath and me in our attitudes to the Party was fundamental. It spoilt our working relationship. I find it disturbing that thirty years later there is evidence of a new drive towards central control of the Party organisation.

One difficulty Heath's supporters faced was that a bachelor is not popular with some sections of the electorate. The Labour Party was happy to exploit this: Wilson was often photographed next to his wife and the contrast with Heath was obvious. Letters appeared in a number of provincial newspapers on this theme: 'Mr Heath is undoubtedly a very clever man, but what does one who is not married know about the problems of family life, the cost of kiddies' shoes, etc., etc.,' usually signed by a pseudonym such as 'Mother of four'. Photographs taken of Heath at the weekend, showing him in anything but family surroundings, appeared in several newspapers on Monday mornings. It was hard to counter this unsympathetic image which our political opponents plainly did their best to foster. Heath himself did not always help. His personal relationships were often less than warm even with senior Party workers, and complaints were made. At the Party Conference in 1966 I was made aware of how difficult he found it to respond to his own supporters. Until he became Leader it had been practice for the Leader of the Party to make a final appearance only at the end of the Party Conference. Heath insisted on attending the whole conference, and I saw that the necessary arrangements were made to fall in with his wishes. He spoke at the outset of the conference and made a major speech at its conclusion, but his constant attendance, although welcomed, was wholly at variance with his private attitude to the representatives who applauded him so vigorously at the conclusion of his final conference address. We were standing together on the platform and the ovation lasted some minutes. I was moved by it and pleased for him, but he made some remarks to me suggesting I cut the proceedings short. The applause embarrassed him. Instead of taking inspiration from it he was impatient with those who offered him a demonstration of their loyalty. The people present on the floor sensed something of how he felt and it made them less happy.

On the eve of that Party conference, in October 1966, a story was given some prominence in one of the national newspapers, and immediately picked up by others, saying that I was under criticism as Chairman of the Party and even that my resignation was in prospect. Of course the story was nonsense but it had to be countered. How, I was not sure. The evening before the conference began in Blackpool I met the agents in formal session, a meeting arranged long beforehand. We talked together about our plans for the future. They gave me a most enthusiastic reception and a standing ovation. My friends in the Central Office saw to it that this fact was well advertised in the newspapers the next morning and the critical stories vanished like sea mist burned off by the rising sun. I started that conference in a most cheerful mood. I like winning.

'Don't shoot the pianist'

'These people who are trying to get rid of dear Mr. du Cann seem to imagine we have an inexhaustible supply of scapegoats.'

Immediately after Heath's election as Leader, I had offered my resignation as Chairman of the Party so that he could choose his own man. He refused to accept it. I appreciated that and I did my best in his support but after a further two years I felt that I had done all I could do to get our Party on the path of success and I told him that I must now insist on resigning. This time he did not try to persuade me to stay and I resigned in September 1967 after almost three years as Chairman. Those three years were some of the happiest of my life.

Were our strategies correct and were they successful? One of my principal aims when I took over as Party Chairman had been to capture local government seats, and an important measure of our success lies in the statistics of local government elections when the Conservative Party was in opposition. The table below shows the gains and losses in those years.

Gains (+) and Losses (-)

at Local Government Elections

Year of Election	Conservatives and Supporters	Independent without Conservative Support	Labour	Liberal	Other
1995	+ 901	- 43	- 590	- 267	- 1
1966	+ 400	- 59	- 287	- 54	0
1967	+ 1,373	- 41	- 1,410	+ 39	+ 39
1968	+ 1,630	- 24	- 1,602	- 20	+ 16
1969	+ 945	- 63	- 889	+ 3	+ 4
Total	+ 5,249	- 230	- 4,778	- 299	+ 58

There was one Local Government triumph of which I was especially proud. Well in advance of the elections for the Greater London Council in April 1967 we laid our careful plans to win control. Candidates were adopted in good time. The Leader of the Conservatives, Desmond Plummer, and some of his lieutenants attended regular liaison meetings to my office. Desmond Plummer was a hardworking and able man, utterly committed to his daunting task, and daunting it certainly was: Labour held 64 seats on the GLC, we Conservatives held only 36. Our preparation paid off well. We captured control of the GLC, winning 82 seats to Labour's 18, the first time we had succeeded in prevailing politically in London since 1935, over thirty years previously. It was a great triumph.

The morning after, Heath, Plummer and I were photographed outside the Conservative Central Office. 'Look cheerful,' the photographers asked. In response to a suggestion by one of them Heath raised Plummer's right arm aloft. The camera shutters clicked. The photographs taken, Heath threw Plummer's arm down again, almost as if in disgust.

Our opinion polling was invaluable to us in our campaign to win control of London and other councils. I was particularly impressed to learn that the electors who were council tenants longed to get out of the thrall of their municipal landlords and become owners. It was a lesson I never forgot.

By the time the next general election came, in 1970, the Socialists controlled only 3 of the 59 county councils in England and Wales and only 6 of the county boroughs with populations of over 10,000, some of those by only a slender margin.

The Leader of the GLC, the Leader and the Chairman of the Conservative Party outside Conservative Central Office, on the morning of a Conservative victory in the Greater London Council Elections, 14th April 1967.

The establishment of Conservative control in most of the large local authorities in England and Wales was followed by major drives by our Party's representatives to improve the efficiency of local government and to give ratepayers full value for their money. I have no doubt that this demonstration of Conservative competence in local government did much to influence opinion in our favour when the next general election came in 1970. In local councils all over the country our Party was stronger in numbers, in organisation and in leadership – a firm foundation on which to build a Parliamentary triumph.

It is sad that these inherited riches have been subsequently squandered, especially by the Conservative Government elected in 1983. The attitude towards local government in the contemporary Conservative Party has been suicidal folly, allowing its local bases to erode. My home county of Somerset has a non-Conservative administration for the first time in a hundred years. So too has the county town of Taunton. Inevitably Somerset has a non-Conservative Euro-MP. When the foundation crumbles, the castle falls.

Paradoxically, it was Labour that first took strong action to tie the purse strings of local government. ('The party's over,' said Crosland, the Labour Party's Secretary of State for the Environment, in 1974.) But the process accelerated under the Conservative administrations led by Margaret Thatcher. Irked by the profligacy and irresponsibility of some local councils under the control of 'loony' left-wing activists, the Government drastically cut the powers of all local authorities and capped their spending. The nadir of political clumsiness was reached with the introduction of the sensible but unpopular poll tax. It always was an excellent idea to bring home to individuals their own responsibility for financing the heavy burden of local services but the contribution levels were set too high for most people to meet without severe discomfort and the attempt to introduce the tax was a fearsome source of friction with local authorities. The public disaffection was predictable. In my old Taunton constituency voters who under the old system of rates had paid little or nothing were faced with immediate bills of several hundred pounds per head. Naturally they revolted: no one had the cash.

The financing of local expenditure is complex and, to the ordinary voter, largely incomprehensible. At one time the calculation by Government of the physical and social needs of each local authority involved no fewer than sixty-three separate assessments. Happily the system is now somewhat simplified. Put shortly, the position is this. In 1994 well under 20 per cent of local authority spending was raised locally through the council tax. The business rate accounts for a further quarter, but this is set nationally and its level owes nothing to local decisions. The remainder of local authority spending, 60 per cent of the total, is provided by central Government from the national exchequer.

Thus the independence of local authorities has been largely destroyed. They raise little of their revenue locally and they have hardly any discretion over how they spend it. It is unsurprising, therefore, that small public interest is shown in local elections. On average, not much more than a third of voters bother to vote in them. In most other industrial countries, the United States, France and Germany for example, local politicians are well known and local elections excite a greater interest. In Britain most local voters are wholly unaware of the names of their locally elected representatives, and the campaigns are fought on national issues. It should be a priority for a for a Tory Government to put the local back into local government.

In the local government elections of May 1994 the Labour and Liberal Democrat parties were naturally anxious to organise their campaigns as a referendum on an unpopular central Government. Unwisely, the Conservatives allowed this to occur. The results were a disaster. The local election results in 1995 were also dictated by national issues, and the Conservatives suffered their worst ever defeat. In the contest for 346 Councils in England and Wales, Conservatives lost 1,700 seats, Labour gained 1,500 and the Liberal Democrats 400. Over the last five years the Liberal Democrats have increased the number of their local councillors to more than 5,000. In England and Wales Labour now has over 12,000 Council seats – more than the Tories and Liberal Democrats put together. Of these 346 Councils Labour controls 155, the Liberal Democrats control 45, the Conservatives only 8. Nationwide, Conservatives control around 20 Councils: when the Party was successful in the general election of 1979 the figure was around 250. Tory representation in local government has virtually ceased to exist. Our strength in the country, so hard won in opposition in the years before the general election victory of 1970, has been destroyed.

Much ill feeling was caused by the so-called reform of local government boundaries by Peter Walker when Secretary of State for the Environment in 1972. The excellent campaign guide published by the Conservative Party's own research department some years later summed up the situation:

> Lingering resentment at some of the effects of the 1972 legislation has ensured that structural issues have seldom been off the political agenda. Many of the councils it created have failed to inspire a sense of local loyalty identity.

Now the Major Government has had to put right some of the blunders made over twenty years ago by a new reorganisation of local government, reached after a long and often bitter debate.

Back in 1970 the Conservative Party did not make mistakes of that kind. Our success in local government was an effective demonstration of our administrative competence. In matters of national policy we were also well prepared for office. We had begun to make our views heard and felt, not least in the Universities. Steadily we were winning the intellectual argument as we had planned and determined to do.

I well remember the shock I experienced as a Minister when the Cabinet decided on the abolition of RPM in 1963. I asked officials at the Board of Trade to provide a reading list of material for me. This they did. All were written from a left wing point of view. This intellectual vacuum I was determined we should fill, and we did.

One pamphlet published under Conservative auspices in those days deserves special mention because it well illustrates the long-term success of this policy. It was written by Alderman Griffin, a prominent worker in local government in Birmingham, and it recommended the sale of council houses to sitting tenants. He and I talked together about this many times when I was first appointed Chairman of the Party, and that pamphlet, published all those years ago when the Conservative Party was in opposition, has been the blueprint for sales of council houses since, making a reality of Anthony Eden's dream of a property-owning democracy. I was proud that the policy was a significant factor in the Conservative Party's victory in the last general election I fought as a Parliamentary candidate, in 1983. Calling at houses on predominantly council estates in Taunton and Wellington during that election I was immensely heartened to hear so many occupiers say that they would vote for me and the Conservative Party because they were now house-owners; and other electors say that they would not vote for the Labour Party because it had threatened to ban council house sales in future. I just wished Alderman Griffin had been still alive to accept the credit he deserved.

After I resigned as Chairman of the Party Heath was generous enough to ask me to continue as a Member of his Shadow Cabinet. I declined and so no doubt ruined my chances of subsequent office. He did tell me then that he would like it if I would join his Cabinet when he became Prime Minister, but I asked him not to commit himself. 'Who knows what this uncertain future may hold?' I said. I had the clear impression that he undertook even so to offer me a post when the time came but in the event he did not. I was not asked to join the Cabinet he formed in 1970.

'Never refuse an appointment,' the political wiseacres advise; but I have no regrets. I did not like Heath's style of management. He was too dogmatic as Chairman of the Shadow Cabinet for my taste and too inflexible in his ways. My ideal chairman is one who seeks the views of everyone who has an opinion to give and arrives at a consensus by skilful chairmanship. Heath prefers to impose his own opinions.

It would be rare for him to attempt to solve a problem by just defining his objective: rather, he would assemble a team of experts to devise a practical answer for him. He was a pragmatist, never an idealist. I do not think I ever heard him in any discussion, private or formal, draw an historical analogy or quote from an historian or an author of a political view. At one Conservative Party national conference on local government in Western-Super-Mare I watched him read out the text of a speech written for him by his staff apparently without rehearsing it or even reading it through: the occasion was apparently of little significance to him, and he made nothing of the opportunity to exchange ideas and thoughts with some of the Tory Party's most experienced campaigners and organisers. I was profoundly shocked that he should be so insensitive. He lacked the capacity to inspire and to enthuse his supporters, or any audience: he had stamina, determination and will, but he would not unbend and there was no friendliness. Perhaps emotion to him was a sign of weakness. I once asked him when we were alone together in his flat in Albany to play the piano for me. He played like an automaton. Sometimes, too often, it was the same with his speeches. Respected by the Party he certainly was, but he was never loved.

He seemed to take no trouble to make friends or to placate his opponents, of whom perhaps the most formidable was Enoch Powell. In the early days of Heath's leadership he and Powell sat directly opposite each other across the table at meetings of the Shadow Cabinet. The two men treated each other with a studied politeness but their natural antagonism was electric. I never saw two men dislike each other more, or so obviously. They were old enemies (Heath was Chief Whip when Powell and Thorneycroft resigned from the Treasury in 1958) and it was inevitable that they would fall out publicly sooner rather than later. So they did, over the emotive issue of immigration. Powell was never a team man, never dependable. Possessed of a brilliant intellect, he lacked the judgement and the patience that might have given him the chance as a Minister after 1970 to put his ideas into practice, though his advocacy of a populist view that the number of immigrants into the UK should be more limited has been adopted as Tory policy.

Heath's style of politics for me has too much of the fact in it (or the supposed fact) and too little of the philosophical and emotional. But it was his personality that separated him from me and from so many others in the Party. I do not remember him ever taking the trouble to be gracious to anyone during the three years I worked closely with him at the Board of Trade and as Chairman of the Party. Often in the latter capacity I found myself in effect apologising to those he had offended (even once in my own home after dinner with people prominent in my constituency). If politics is about the business of influencing opinion and getting people on one's side Heath started (and continued) with a heavy self-imposed handicap.

In 1970 when the Conservative Party's victory came, on the anniversary of the Battle of Waterloo, it was a narrow one with an overall majority of 30 seats. Heath deserves much of the credit for this success. Throughout the campaign and until its very end Labour led in the opinion polls. Wilson's easy style and quick wit were vastly more attractive than

127

Heath's woodenness and lack of humour, but by the end of the election period Heath's doggedness and sincerity had begun to make an impression. Potential disaster, widely feared even by the Tory hierarchy and, so far as one can judge from contemporary evidence, even by Ted Heath himself, was transformed into success.

I like to think that the work that was undertaken at the Conservative Central Office while I was Party Chairman played a significant part in that success. At any rate, the voluntary workers in the Conservative Party showed that their members thought so when they invited me to become their President for the year 1981-82.

The Conservative Party conference Blackpool 1981: Chairman of the Party, the Leader, President of the National Union.

When Heath came to form his Government in 1970 he included Maurice Macmillan, Harold's son, as Chief Secretary to the Treasury. It came as a surprise to Maurice (so he told me and others more than once) and to most other people as well.

'Why was it?' I asked him.

'I can only guess,' he replied, 'that he was grateful for a telegram I sent him during the election campaign assuring him that I was confident he would win it. I believe I was his only Parliamentary colleague to do so.'

Perhaps I should have done the same.

CHAPTER 6

RIDING *the* FINANCIAL WAVES

After I resigned as Chairman of the Party each of my careers entered a comparatively calm period. There was still plenty for me to do as an MP but I was able to find adequate time for my work as Chairman of Unicorn. Then in 1968 the bankers Keyser Ullmann invited me to join them to take charge of their industrial investments. I was happy to accept.

Keysers was very much a family affair. It was a public company whose shares had been quoted on the Stock Exchange since 1962, but half those shares were family-owned; Charles Keyser was Chairman and two able brothers-in-law, Ian Stoutzker and Roland Franklin, were Managing Directors. I was elected to the boards of the group holding company and its subsidiaries but my specific job was as Chairman of the subsidiary through which Keysers held investments in some twenty industrial companies. Our portfolio was a diverse one; it included a chain of retail shops in Scotland, electrical and mechanical manufacturing companies, steel manufacturing in the North East and the Midlands, clothing retailing and lens manufacturing. I was delighted to have the chance to play a part in the management of industry and to learn about practical banking. Hitherto, all my investment experience had been in portfolio management, that is to say in indirect rather than direct investment in commerce and industry. Now, I hoped, my colleagues and I would have the chance to bring a small part of the City's resources directly to bear on the reinforcement of British industry. In 1970 I was elected Chairman of the holding company which controlled the Keyser Ullmann group, in succession to Charles Keyser who retired after serving for thirty-six years.

Although Keyser Ullmann was a fully fledged merchant bank with a full banking licence and the ability to issue its own cheques and operate in the money markets it was still a small enterprise by comparison with a clearing bank. Profit before tax and transfer to inner reserves in the year ended 31 March 1970 was some three quarters of a million pounds. Capital employed in the business was less than £10 million and the balance sheet totals were some £70 million.

Starting from that base we made steady progress over the next several years. We formed a medium-term loan bank in partnership with five major US provincial banks, we launched a subsidiary bank in Geneva, and we formed our first unit trusts.

We attracted influential and powerful support. In 1972 the Prudential Assurance Company, the largest insurance company in Britain, invested in new shares which we issued to provide funds for increasing the scope of our operations. This was a remarkable vote of confidence in our management. The Pru nominated a director to our Board and became Keysers' largest shareholder, owning some 12 per cent of our equity. Four of Britain's largest insurance companies also invested heavily in exchange for shares in the investment trust companies that we managed. We celebrated our centenary with a dinner at which the Governor of the Bank of England was the principal guest.

There was every reason to be happy about Keysers' progress, but we were not the only ones to feel pleased with ourselves. The whole climate of business in the years between 1971 and 1974 was optimistic. With hindsight it was far too optimistic and many were lured into being greedy or careless, but the crash that followed was not attributable to any individual or institution in the private banking sector. Authorities had positively encouraged optimism and certainly did nothing to discourage or redirect it. This short-term attitude had destructive results.

The process that was to lead to so much trouble started almost imperceptibly with what seemed to be a purely technical change in Government policy. I well remember Ted Heath addressing Conservative Members of Parliament in the 1922 Committee at the end of the summer Parliamentary session of 1971 and describing his Government's new idea of 'Competition and Credit Control'. This was a finance and monetary policy which had been launched a few weeks earlier as one of the main planks of his Government's economic programme. I looked around the room and wondered how many of the MPs present fully comprehended what he was talking about. I doubt whether more than half a dozen had the least idea. Even the most sophisticated audience tends to assume that glazed look when matters of monetary policy are raised, and this meeting of Tory MPs was no exception.

In principle the idea was simple. In May 1971 a consultative document had been issued by the Bank of England as a basis for discussion with banks and finance houses, following a statement in his budget speech by the Chancellor of the Exchequer, Anthony Barber: 'I believe it should be possible to achieve more flexible but still effective arrangements basically by operating on the banks' resources rather than by directly guiding their lending.' What this meant was that the amount the banks would be allowed to borrow would be regulated but what they did after that would be left to them. Vitally, this included decisions on how much credit might be extended to customers. The consultative document marked a watershed in the attitude of the authorities towards the banking industry and the scope of its activities. In short, the brakes were well and truly off.

It was not only Conservative MPs who did not grasp this. It was generally supposed that all that was occurring was the replacement of one system of control by another: it was certainly not appreciated, perhaps not even by the banking sector generally, that the competition part of the package in fact meant virtually unbridled liberalism, leading to new and unforeseen risks. In the days to come cynics and enthusiasts alike came to call those times the wheelbarrow days – just take your wheelbarrow to the banks and cart away the cash. The banking crisis which was to follow three years later was unquestionably triggered by these liberal policies and the way in which they were implemented.

Ted Heath made no secret of his intention to create boom conditions, at least in his conversations with a few journalists; and boom conditions did certainly follow. Between the launching of Competition and Credit Control and the end of 1973, when the introduction of an emergency budget by the Chancellor of the Exchequer in effect marked the abandonment of the policy and official recognition of the crisis it precipitated, lending by the clearing banks increased by more than 100 per cent. The secondary banks increased their lending perhaps three times, though proportionately it was only about one third of the amount lent by the clearers. The money supply increased by some three quarters. The heaviest borrowers were in the property sector. This produced an extraordinary imbalance. By the end of 1973 that sector had borrowed as much money as the whole of British manufacturing industry. Few people – certainly not the Government – foresaw the crisis to come.

Before the crisis broke Keysers took two more steps in the development of its business which were dazzlingly successful.

For some years Keysers had advised a property company, whose shares were quoted on the Stock Exchange, called Central and District

131

Properties. Central and District had assets of around £100 million and made an annual profit before tax of some £1.5 million. The Chairman of Central and District, a former clearing bank manager, retired and I was asked to take his place. I had been a salaried director of another large property company which had no connection with Keysers: out of loyalty to Keysers I resigned and joined Central and District. I took no salary but I had an option on a few shares. One of the two Managing Directors of Central and District, Mr Rubens, a cautious and able man, began speaking of his wish to retire and to sell his share interest. Although it was a very substantial move to make in financial terms, our Board at Keysers decided to acquire Central and District in exchange for cash and shares in Keysers. Mr Rubens accepted the cash offer and retired. His fellow Managing Director of Central and District, Mr Shine, did not retire but accepted shares in Keysers and joined Keysers' Board.

Our second major step was to acquire a smaller bank, Dalton Barton, managed by Jack Dellal who was also its principal shareholder. We had had a number of business connections with them, joint loans and the like, as we had with many other banks and institutions in the City of London.

The Bank of England kept a close eye on the operations of all the merchant banks in the City of London. Monthly returns of Keysers' business were lodged with the Bank of England and the figures would be analysed and commented upon. Thus Keysers' commercial and banking activities were regularly and closely monitored in common with all other banks doing business in the UK. This was not the only form of supervision: there were continuous informal liaisons with the Bank of England.

At each year's end I, as Chairman of Keysers, would call formally with a colleague, usually Ian Stoutzker, the joint Managing Director, on Mr Keogh, the head of the discount office at the Bank of England. For some hours we would respond to a close cross-examination about the bank's affairs. It was a process which, though always most politely conducted, was rather like attending the headmaster's study for a discussion about one's end of term report. A careful analysis of effort and achievement was made; it was sympathetic but meticulous and perceptive. Not much, if anything, was missed.

Keysers' proposal to acquire the Central and District property company was informally referred to the Bank of England before negotiations even began. It was warmly approved. The proposal also had the enthusiastic endorsement of our largest shareholder, the Prudential.

That done, the Bank of England then urged us strongly to take over the Dalton Barton business, asserting that Dalton Barton's successful experience of lending against property and of the property business generally would be invaluable to us. The merest hint of doubt given to us either by the authorities or by our largest shareholder, Prudential Assurance, would have meant that neither takeover would have proceeded: negotiations would not even have begun. Doubts there were none. Quite the reverse. There was enthusiasm for both takeovers and so both takeovers went through. Mr Dellal and a colleague joined Keysers' Board.

Central and District had been intended to be a permanent investment within the Keysers group. However, our subsequent purchase of Dalton Barton meant that Keysers now had a substantial additional interest in property. To reduce our property interests and so restore the balance between banking and property, and to help the expansion of our banking activities by raising additional capital, we decided to sell Central and District. We then proposed to increase Keysers' capital base to some £80 million. The intention was to make ourselves more competitive on an international basis: in this intention, judging by what has happened in the City subsequently, we were a decade or more ahead of our time.

In a brilliant coup Mr Dellal sold Central and District to another publicly quoted property company, Town and City, for the huge sum of £97 million, all in cash. The finance was provided by Rothschilds and Barclays Bank – not presumably in wheelbarrows. This sale, made at a peak in market values, gave Keysers a profit on our purchase of Central and District of some £28 million in less than eighteen months. This was a truly remarkable achievement. Keysers thus achieved one of the strongest bases in financial terms of any of the merchant banks in the City. We had made dramatic progress in a short period.

It was then that our problems began. Some were due to the collapse of markets, especially the property market, but the main part was of our own making. I have often reflected on the folly of our actions immediately after these very remarkable successes in raising so much capital.

Day-to-day decisions on the banking side of the business were made or endorsed by a banking committee consisting of the Managing Directors and other directors of the bank, who had been recruited from clearing banks at assistant general manager level. These were the watchdogs, senior and experienced bankers: the surprising thing, with the advantage of hindsight, is that they absolutely failed to bark. The systems were fine:

133

but the judgements faulty. A number of the loans of the bank's funds made at that time proved in the light of later experience to have been irresponsible: too much money was lent to a few borrowers whose security proved to be inadequate.

The Bank of England raised no questions at the time. Neither did our auditors. Nor did our principal shareholder, the Prudential, through its representative on our Board. Nor was any criticism made to me as Chairman either formally at board meetings or informally by any of my colleagues. Not an alarm was heard, not a warning note.

It was when the property market began to crash in 1974 that real trouble followed. Keysers, for all its basic financial strength, faced liquidity pressures. We were not alone: there were rumours of severe liquidity strains for several merchant banks and even for one of the major clearing bankers; and the rumours were accurate.

At first we were not unduly concerned. Our own clearing bankers had promised us financial support if we needed it, as we did. I had verified this myself. However, the general atmosphere was beginning to deteriorate, and sharply. Several banks had to be rescued by means of support packages put together by other banks, in one of which Keysers participated. In the course of this I spoke privately to the Chancellor of the Exchequer, telling him what was being done and alerting him to the position.

It might be assumed that, following these dramatic events, Government, the authorities and the Treasury would have been sensitive to the fact that caution was needed in dealing with the financial and property sectors of the economy. Not a bit of it. Eight days before Christmas 1973 the Chancellor of the Exchequer announced a harsh emergency budget. Bank lending was restricted by penalties, Government spending was to be cut heavily, personal taxation was increased in the upper reaches and, worst of all from the point of view of the property market, a development gains tax on disposals and first lettings was introduced.

Thus the proud policies of Competition and Credit Control about which the Prime Minister had boasted to his Conservative followers in the House of Commons a little over two years previously, advertising them to be one of the main aspects of Government policy and achievement, were now to be restricted. The Government had set in motion the events which had led to the availability of credit on a huge scale; now it was reversing its policies at the very moment when the market which it had so casually fuelled (I will not say deliberately) had clearly over-reached itself. The emergency budget hit the banking and property worlds hard just at the very moment when signs of serious crisis in both were becoming apparent. That budget was an act of unimaginable folly. It made certain that the problems of the banking and property sections of the market would accelerate.

In these circumstances, serious depositors began, as a reasonable precaution, to withdraw funds from all banking institutions other than the clearing banks and those merchant banks which were members of the Accepting Houses Committee; they no longer put deposits with the smaller and so-called 'fringe' banks. The moment this tendency became apparent I sought an interview with the Governor of the Bank of England. I explained that it was a matter of historical accident that Keysers was not yet a member of the Accepting Houses Committee. Membership was taken to be a badge of reliability, but in fact it was far from systematic. Such well known and respected names as Warburg and Philip Hill had only achieved membership by buying up businesses that were already members, Warburg by acquiring the business of Seligman and Philip Hill by acquiring Erlanger. It was an anachronism that Keysers, a larger bank than most, was not a member; membership would release the pressures on us, and so on. The Governor was sympathetic and promised to do what he could. I have no doubt he kept his word, but we were not elected. He said that the Accepting Houses formed in effect a club, the members made the rules and he did not. That was his excuse.

'They do not like some of your colleagues,' he said.

'What arrogance,' I replied, 'damned arrogance.' I remembered well the time when both Philip Hill, a mere West End issuing house, and Warburgs, newly formed by a foreigner, were hardly acceptable and both were referred to in the bars and luncheon tables in the City in unflattering terms. Now the formerly unacceptable were apparently the judges.

So the pressures upon Keysers, which membership of the Accepting Houses Committee would have substantially mitigated, mounted. Worse still, we were then told by the Bank of England that we could not draw on the precautionary financial support arranged with our clearing bank. With some of the smaller finance houses now in serious trouble, a committee was to be established by the Bank of England to channel loans from the clearing banks to those other banks that had experienced a loss of deposits, and all financial support would go through these so-called lifeboat arrangements.

I protested vigorously to the Governor at another meeting. I said that I thought it a profound mistake to mix together financial institutions of varying financial strengths and status under the aegis of this newly invented support mechanism. The stronger would be certain to be classified with the weaker in the popular mind and their prestige would suffer unnecessarily.

I was told that this would not be so, because the existence of the committee would be secret. I told the Governor quite plainly that I was sure that this was nonsense. I did not believe such a matter could be kept secret. He was somewhat offended. I said it was not his discretion that I doubted, nor my own, but the lifeboat arrangements would be known to a large number of people inside and outside the City. It would prove impossible to keep them secret and to hide the names of the institutions which needed the committee's support. General knowledge of the fact that a banking institution was in effect being bailed out would undoubtedly be damaging to it in the short and medium term.

And so it proved. Keysers would certainly have weathered the storm more easily had we been permitted to make our own private arrangements for financial support. The existence of the official support group and even the amounts of money provided by it to various banks and other financial institutions became widely known, as was bound to happen, and naturally this led to a loss of confidence in the banks that found themselves in the 'lifeboat'.

Nonetheless, in general, the Bank of England deserves credit for the leadership it gave in this situation of mounting crisis. It was speedy and effective. Keysers was more severely hurt than it deserved to be, but the whole banking industry was facing a deteriorating situation in which there would certainly be casualties, and the Bank of England did its competent best to localise the damage in what was by far the largest and most complex rescue operation in British banking history.

Bank failures, of course, are no new phenomenon, anywhere in the world. Historically there has been a huge number. Even in recent years no country has succeeded in preventing some banks from failing. Some of the failures have been spectacular. Deposits totalling many billions of dollars have been lost in the collapses of such giants as the Canadian Commercial Bank and BCCI. Credit Lyonnais has only been kept alive by massive subventions by the French Government. In 1995 the old and respected house of Baring lost its independence overnight, apparently by the dubious activities of a single ill-supervised employee in Singapore. Even Warburg has now lost its independence and in the process lost its reputation for competent management. And these are just some of the best known cases. There have been many, many others. In 1985 alone more than 100 US banks failed. So long as we have a private enterprise system there are bound to be failures: no regulatory system is, or ever will be, perfect. All business involves risk.

In 1973, as far as the banking system was concerned one has to say that on the whole it responded well to the crisis. What caused the near disaster was the behaviour of the Government. The sudden relaxation of controls under its policy of Competition and Credit Control had fuelled a sudden boom, in property above all. Ted Heath spoke of a 'dash for growth', but he wholly misread the situation. Nothing real grew; there was no sudden increase in our productive capacity, only a violent rise in property prices that was not founded on a rise in real values. Then, just when the market was being made aware that it had over-reached itself and badly needed a steadying hand, the Government gave it a hard push downwards. The result of this was not unforeseeable: I and many others foresaw it and warned the Government of what would happen. We were ignored, and the stubbornness of our rulers succeeded in turning a readjustment into a near panic.

At Keysers we struggled through and we survived, but it was a hard time. At peak we had received loans totalling £65 million from the support group and were paying interest at expensive rates. Where we were particularly unfortunate was in the matter of publicity. Two of our directors, for reasons of their own, engaged, in my opinion, in campaigns of vindictiveness which after all these years I still find hard to understand. We had been pleased to recruit a senior man from the Midland Bank to the banking side of Keysers' business. In the event he turned out to be a thoroughly disloyal colleague. As a member of the company's Banking Committee and a director of the bank and the holding company he was fully aware of every loan made by the bank and he acquiesced in them. It transpired that he had complained privately about the conduct of Keysers' business to the Bank of England and to the Prudential, Keysers' major institutional shareholder, perhaps in an effort at self-preservation. A former director of the Central and District property company, who unlike his co-director had accepted Keysers' shares in exchange for his Central and District stockholding, arranged other protests, public and private, presumably in revenge for the fall in value of his holding.

As I said earlier, Keysers did make some unwise loans – everyone makes mistakes – but all board members assumed their full share of responsibility for the conduct of our business. At the time, as the contemporary records show, neither of the critics suggested the adoption of different policies or management methods. To put the matter no more strongly, it hardly helped those of us who were battling in the general interest with an extraordinarily difficult situation that two of our colleagues were doing their level best to sabotage our efforts. They had too much success: the newspapers and others were hungry for gossip and background stories and they were ready listeners.

All in all, 1974 proved to be a wretchedly difficult year for Keysers. We agreed that the two directors who had joined us from Dalton Barton, Mr Dellal and his colleague, should resign. I was sorry to see them go, but they had had the major responsibility for initiating the large loans made against property, the chief cause of Keysers' problems – and ironically the area where the Bank of England had insisted that their experience would be of such value to us.

Reducing our involvement in property was one part of our strategy for recovery, and that strategy succeeded. In our next annual accounts we announced a £1 million rise in profits, an increase in our net assets of £18 million, cash and liquid assets of £150 million and advances to customers at the unusually low level for a banking group of only two and one half times the group's net capital. We also published a table showing our record of progress over the past five years. In that short time, Keysers' capital and reserves had multiplied 25 times. Net assets per ordinary share had risen from 33p to almost 300p and net earnings per share from almost 5p to over 19p. Last, but by no means least, we provided reserves against contingencies of £17 million.

This record of past progress, impressive though it unquestionably was, together with the demonstration of substantial current financial strength and the obvious conservatism of our approach in the present situation, did not appear to improve our image. The swing of opinion was inexorable: we were trying to play Canute and the cynical tide was too strong for us, as the economic tide was to prove for so many others. For if 1974 was a wretched year for Keysers it was a year of disaster for the Stock Market. At the beginning of the year the *Financial Times* thirty-share Index stood at 339.3. This was more than 200 points lower than the previous peak of 543.6 reached in May 1972. By January 1975 the index reached a new low of 146, a fall of almost 400 points from the peak.

Throughout the year, the industrial and political news was unhappy. Oil prices had quadrupled following the Yom Kippur War, and they were to rise still further. 1974 began with Britain working a three-day week. A state of emergency was declared. The miners saw their chance and demanded a hefty wage increase, backing their demand by going on strike. Ted Heath hesitated, then called a general election in February which he lost to Labour.

Political uncertainty continued. Harold Wilson had won the general election of October 1974 with an increased majority of 42 seats over the Conservatives, but an overall majority of only three seats. Inflation in Britain was accelerating to 20 per cent.

A combination of Parliamentary stalemate, the energy crisis and financial disturbances all contributed to the 1974 stock market crash. The situation forced the Labour Government to budget in November for relieving action so far as industry was concerned, after price controls and inflation had between them pointed to a fearsome liquidity crisis. It was a hard year to live through. And on 31 December, it was announced that the Bank of England was busy rescuing even the giant Burmah Oil company from its liquidity crisis.

Keysers' share price was badly affected by our own problems, the pessimistic way they were regarded by the market, and the depressing general economic context. The price had reached a peak of 385p per share in 1972: the low point in 1974 was 34 1/2p, less than a tenth of the peak. Every investor whose shareholding had been worth £100 now found it worth less than £9.

This put me in a personal dilemma. I had bought a number of Keyser shares from one of my colleagues. I thought it appropriate that I should publicly demonstrate my faith in Keysers, and of course I hoped the investment would be profitable. I could have sold at the peak and made a great deal of money for myself: the sale would have brought in more than £250,000. I considered selling and quite deliberately decided against it because I thought that a sale even of part of my holding would be a poor example for the Chairman to set – either to his colleagues or to the general public at a time when it was crucial to maintain confidence.

A complication was that I had borrowed the money from Keysers to buy these shares. It would have been easy to borrow from another bank but it was a house rule that personal financial transactions by directors should go through our own accounts. When the crisis came and Keysers needed all the money it could get it was impossible for me to pay back the loan: selling my shares at the price to which they had fallen would not have begun to cover the debt. There was nothing I could do, nor had I done anything illegal or improper in incurring this debt. It was all above board and normal practice. Nevertheless I came in for some rough treatment on account of it. Some disloyal colleagues were critical of me behind my back for having borrowed money – though not critical of themselves, it seems, for having done the same.

I was also quite literally attacked one evening in my London home by a *Daily Telegraph* reporter. He rang the doorbell. I answered the door. He told me his name and newspaper.

'I want to talk to you about your debts,' he said.

I told him that if I had any, my private affairs were my own business and not his and asked him to go away.

'I want to put your side of the story,' he countered, 'and if you don't help me, I'll print what I'm going to write anyway.'

There was more of this sort of conversation. He was aggressive, and became increasingly insulting and unpleasant. By now he had his foot in the door. He kept it there and tried to push the door open with considerable force. At one stage he pushed me back into the hall. I only got rid of him by threatening to call the police.

As part of the strategy for Keysers' recovery Prudential and the Bank of England voiced a demand for the appointment of a professional banker to replace me as Chairman. To this I agreed on condition that the Managing Directors remained: Keysers was after all a family business. This was accepted and I resigned from Keysers' Board. However, I was persuaded to remain as Chairman of the quoted Investment Trusts under Keysers' management and of the Cannon Assurance Company. I found the attitude of the Prudential insufferable. As the largest investor in Keysers they had nominated a director, and he had had as much responsibility for all that had occurred as anybody. I told them that at one evening meeting of directors of the holding company which I had called to discuss strategy for Keysers over dinner at my house he had arrived having had more to drink than was sensible and the meeting in consequence had been largely abortive. They appeared unperturbed at this intelligence. I was experiencing the sad fact that practical people do not always receive the support they deserve and need from their institutional shareholders. The Prudential's ventures into practical banking were not universally commercial successes. Its shareholding in the Dawnay Day Company, on whose Board it was even more prominently represented, was nothing but a disaster.

My successor as Chairman of Keysers was Derek Wilde, a senior member of the Board of Directors of Barclays Bank. He had spent most of his career on the trustee side of the bank's work and had no special reputation as a lender, but he had masterminded the launching of the Barclaycard in the UK in association with the Bank of America, a most successful enterprise and a leader in its field at the time. Shortly afterwards he invited both our Managing Directors to resign: so much for my understanding with the Prudential and the Bank of England. This I thought was wretchedly sad. Both had been with the business for twenty years and both have subsequently done very well in their different ways; they were most able men. Mr Wilde kept on the rest of the Board: in my view, he sacked the wrong people.

How clear things are in hindsight. I now wish I had insisted that the whole Board and staff of the bank went on leave and the banking operation closed down the day after the cash came in from the sale of the Central and District company. The money could have been put on deposit for a year, and after a twelve months' sabbatical we could have resumed business, re-entering markets at an appreciably lower level. Of course no one thought of that.

However, alternatives had been canvassed. A merger was proposed with Rothschilds: it did not happen. A plan was devised to divide Keysers into two parts, in effect separating the banking and investment business from the remainder and taking out the property loans from the bank, to be separately managed by Mr Franklin and Mr Stoutzker. We negotiated with Middle Eastern interests to buy control of the bank which, freed from its property book, would have been a thriving entity; but they were unimaginative and would not come to an agreement because the bank, they said, had been Jewish. (It is true that when I joined Keysers all the other directors were Jewish. I must say they made their new Christian colleague very welcome.) Philip Shelbourne, at one time the respected Chairman of Britoil, introduced Keysers to a Mr Sindona who held several important positions in the banking world and who wanted to buy control. None of us had previously met Mr Sindona and none of us liked or trusted him. We were not surprised later when he went to jail. It is not unusual in the City for apparently respectable people to keep doubtful company. Nothing came of any of these approaches.

Never complain, never explain, was Disraeli's supposed advice. Explanations are in order, in my view; complaints are not. I would add a more relevant instruction – never resign. I deeply regret my resignation as Chairman of Keysers. I thought at the time it was the best thing for Keysers and for my friends. I was wrong.

In the first accounts of the holding company published after he became Chairman Mr Wilde painted a black picture. He was probably right to do so both in his own personal interest and in the bank's. The accounting policies followed under his chairmanship were described by the press as 'hyper-cautious' and 'more conservative than most'. Massive amounts were written off the loan book with the result that losses were announced for the previous years totalling some £60 million. No doubt it was thought prudent to present publicly the worst possible picture: thereafter the bank was virtually certain to show an improvement, with consequent credit to those in command. And so it proved.

Not that the news was all gloomy by any means. The following year the new Chairman was able to announce that support from the 'lifeboat' had already halved from the peak of £65 million to £33 million, and the *Sunday Times* commented that the bank 'still rivals the big names in assets, Hambros, Schroders and Kleinwort Benson'. Nonetheless the auditors qualified the accounts with what were described as the 'now conventional warnings about property values'. They had said not a word in any previous year. How people love to be seen shutting the stable door after the horse has long bolted.

Keysers was thus strong financially in spite of its problems, and in spite of the sullying of its good name, especially by those to whom I have referred, which Wilde told me he regretted as much as I had. All its borrowings from the support group were repaid in full by 1976, interest having been paid meantime at above market rates. From the financial year 1977/78 Keysers were profitable again. Wilde had worked hard as Chairman but in the end he regarded himself as no more than a caretaker. The business could well have survived as an independent entity and, after the storm had passed, it would have prospered; but he did not have the stomach to see matters through and in 1980 Keysers was taken over by another bank, Charterhouse Japhet, for £43 million. Charterhouse got a bargain.

For myself, my time at Keysers was financially a disaster. Even so, looking back, I am pleased at many of the things we achieved while I was there. Most of our activities were profitable and useful and we built up the company on a sound basis of capital growth that should have put it in a very strong position. It is sad that a failure on one side of the business, the property side, led to the loss of its independence

I learned some lessons from that. There are two that stand out. One: never trust a Government to act responsibly; always manage your business so that it does not depend on such an unrealistic expectation. Two: although any well run company depends on a high degree of mutual trust between those in command it is never safe to assume that apparently well qualified people will always be doing their job as they should. If you are Chairman, look for yourself.

Those are good lessons to have learnt: I just regret that I had to learn them the hard way.

TWO BATTLES
among GIANTS

I never met Bernie Cornfeld, the founder of Investors Overseas Services (IOS), nor did I even wish to, but for some time I was closely embroiled in a struggle with his company, which in the end cost me dear.

Cornfeld began his career in the investment world as a salesman for mutual funds in the US, where his family had emigrated from Istanbul before World War Two. He then set up as a salesman on his own account in Europe. By 1956, the year I was elected to Parliament, he had established a team of salesmen. They became highly successful in selling the Dreyfus Fund, a most respectable and well managed US growth fund. By 1960 his sales force was some 150 strong and sales were running at an annual volume of $20 million, mostly to US servicemen based in Europe; in this way he avoided US legal restrictions. He financed his company's expansion by selling stock in it to his salesmen and he virtually guaranteed the continuance of sales of mutual fund investment programmes at a high level by establishing stock option plans for the salesmen in what became the IOS company. Like Jack's beanstalk IOS grew and grew and grew. Then came the moment to cash in.

The stock market in the US reached a peak at the end of 1968. In 1969 a fifth of IOS common stock was offered for sale to the public: whatever may have been said at the time about the reasons for the sale its chief purpose was unquestionably the enrichment of IOS senior personnel.

On the surface IOS had been phenomenally successful. It had developed world wide. It employed and motivated over 15,000 salesmen. It provided the public, in many countries, with a myriad financial services. It employed many distinguished and able people at every level of its operations, among them the eldest son of the late President Roosevelt, a former Vice Chancellor of the West German Federal Republic and former Director General of the General Agreement of Tariffs and Trade (GATT). You can always buy talent.

I neither liked what I had heard about Cornfeld and his associates, nor did I trust the management of the business. I was in a small minority at that time, but the evidence was there for those who wished to see it. Sales were too heavily based on commissions; as a financial operation it was unsound. As well as this, IOS's operations were, to put it no more unkindly, careless of the law in the territories where they operated. They fell foul of the Brazilian authorities in 1966; with the Securities and Exchange Commission in the United States in 1965; with the Swiss Authorities in 1967; and each adventure was well publicised in the world's press. One didn't have to be prescient to infer that disaster was only a matter of time.

Nonetheless IOS had influential backers and supporters. Stockbrokers and bankers practically fell over each other in their readiness to do business with IOS or to accept IOS's hospitality at their Geneva headquarters. IOS's public issue of 5,600,000 common shares on 16 October 1969 was supported by a list of 122 Institutions led by Banque Rothschild, Hill Samuel & Co, Drexel Harriman & Ripley, Guinness Mahon, Pierson Heldring, and Smith Barney & Co. The full catalogue of the institutions backing IOS read like an international Who's Who of merchant banking. Keysers too were on the list, I am sorry to say. I was against our accepting an underwriting participation but I was outvoted. We were in good company, however: even Rothschild had sufficient confidence to have agreed to market an investment fund in France jointly with IOS.

Early in 1970 IOS was in control of twenty mutual funds and investment trusts. Money under management totalled the staggering amount of well over $2 billion. Sales of investment programmes to individual investors were running at more than double that amount in face value (around $4.5 billion) each year: this was at least as great as the whole domestic US mutual fund industry, and that was by far the biggest in the world. Investors numbered more than one million. In addition, IOS's banking network held over $100 billion in customer deposits; its insurance companies had well over $1 billion of insurance in force; and its real estate operations totalled some $80 billion. IOS was a giant.

In the UK, IOS had formed a subsidiary company called International Life Insurance. Well organised and well managed, this company was different in character and style from Cornfeld's other operations anywhere else in the world. IOS did not own all the stock in ILI, only a controlling interest. The company was started by an American called Richard Hammerman, an insurance broker by profession, a capable man of proved integrity, who subsequently was to take part in an honourable attempt to rescue IOS when it got into serious difficulties.

ILI copied Unicorn's model and sold life assurance based on investment funds, primarily under the name of the Dover Plan. ('Dover' evoked the solidity of the White Cliffs, though in reality the name was chosen simply because ILI's original offices were in Dover Street in the West End of London.) The secret of ILI's success in selling investment programmes lay in the substantial commissions paid to salesmen. With that incentive they sold Dover plans very successfully, but of course the customer had to pay: he got less value for his pound than from a British competitor. That might not matter if stock markets kept rising and the costs charged to him were more than offset by the consequent rise in value of his insurance policy. In IOS's world, optimism was the keynote. Salesmen always talked of rising markets, never about the reverse. Life, alas, is not like that.

As Unicorn developed, I became increasingly aware of ILI as a successful competitor in the UK savings field. Its UK management was competent and honourable, if expensive to policyholders; but from 1970 onwards IOS's well publicised troubles began to affect its subsidiary's reputation. I knew one of ILI's directors, Anthony Montague Browne, who had been Sir Winston Churchill's private secretary for some years, and in 1970 he told me of his anxiety to ensure that the ownership of ILI passed into safe and responsible British hands. He invited me to help. I saw an opportunity for Keysers and agreed to look into the matter.

Coopers and Lybrand, ILI's auditors, had prepared a full report which made clear that the company was sound, had a good business and was profitable, but through a lack of investor confidence it was bleeding to death. Policy redemptions by investors far exceeded the volume of new sales. The figures were horrendous: during 1972, funds under management were declining by some £250,000 a week.

I met representatives of the owners of the controlling interest in ILI, whom I disliked. We had a protracted negotiation. Their point of view was easy to understand: they were anxious to find a UK partner of undoubted integrity so as to restore public confidence in ILI. They knew they owned a valuable asset, but it was an asset that was declining in value every day and the only way to maintain it was to secure a partner. The problem was that they were greedy: they would only sell a small part of the equity in ILI, hoping to see their own larger part grow substantially in value after the company's fortunes had been restored by their new partner. They wanted to have their cake and eat it too.

I also had in mind the effect that the developing crisis in ILI might have on the life assurance industry generally, and especially on that part concerned with equity-linked policies. Many of the older life assurance companies had never been enthusiastic about the growth of their upstart equity-linked brethren. If ILI failed, some of them would not hesitate to denigrate the whole equity-linked industry, waging a campaign by innuendo that would be powerful enough to affect Unicorn's marketing to a serious extent.

ILI at that time had on its books 125,000 policyholders, a huge number of individuals whose financial future was involved. Although the company was financially sound, no business could endure the loss of a quarter of a million pounds of its assets each week. To restore public confidence in ILI would require no great new capital investment, merely a divorce from IOS and a new control. The sooner it was done the better, before the bleeding became terminal.

I also talked to the minority shareholders in the company, original backers of Hammerman personally when ILI was founded, owning just under 20%. They were excellent people, both American in origin, George Delacorte and John Templeton. George Delacorte was the founder of the Dell Publishing Company of New York, an elderly but tough, urbane man, a generous benefactor to charities, wealthy, of undoubted integrity. John Templeton was an investment manager by profession, and very successful at it. He had been a Rhodes Scholar at Oxford, and he was a devoutly religious man. Between them these two held 21 1/2 per cent of the issue share capital of ILI. I asked them both if they would support Keysers and me if we took over responsibility for ILI. They were enthusiastic. So was the senior partner of Coopers and Lybrand, whose firm provided us all the help it could give. In addition I felt I needed the goodwill of the authorities if I was to become involved, so I approached the Bank of England and the Board of Trade (the regulatory authority for the insurance industry). Both made it clear that it would be a considerable relief to them to see the company's affairs in safe hands.

The Chairman of ILI was a colleague in the House of Commons, Sir Harmar Nicholls, and he too warmly welcomed the idea that Keysers should become involved. He was enthusiastically in favour of my succeeding him as Chairman and promised me all the support he could give.

My colleagues at Keysers were also enthusiastic and we had the support of the Prudential, Keysers' largest shareholder. For my own part, keen as I was, I recognised that the project would certainly involve a great deal of hard work for me. It would also involve risk. Perhaps I would suffer in reputation as a result of this association at one remove with IOS. And what if we failed? The pressures on IOS were increasing and quite possibly their influence on its UK subsidiary would be too damaging to survive. Furthermore I would have to give up the chairmanship of Unicorn and my connection with Barclays Bank (a job for life, as the Chairman of the Bank had promised me). On the other hand my innovative work on Unicorn was complete, and I did not feel altogether comfortable with Barclays' over-institutionalised approach to the management of Unicorn. I decided to accept the challenge.

The negotiations were to prove extremely difficult. Early in May 1970 Cornfeld had been ousted as Chairman and Chief Executive of IOS after a seven-day Board meeting in Geneva. He was succeeded by an Englishman, Sir Eric Wyndham White, the former Secretary General of GATT. Sir Eric did his devoted best to bring some stability to the scene but IOS just could not keep itself out of the newspaper headlines. The following month, after the announcement of the first quarter's trading figures which showed a loss of $4 1/2 million, the council of the London Stock Exchange suspended dealing in the shares of IOS Ltd. This followed suspension on the Toronto and Montreal Exchanges a few days earlier. A few days after that the shares of IOS were being traded unofficially at just over £1 each: a few months earlier they had been quoted at over £7.50 each.

The bad news about IOS continued in the newspapers: one day it was the resignations of key personnel; on another it was the redemption figures; then there were disclosures of substantial loans to directors, officers of the company and friends amounting, it was said, to some $30 million. Cornfeld's garrulity did not help: he talked – and never stopped talking – about making a comeback, about his love affairs, about his plans to start a rival group, and so on, and so on.

Then there were the rescue attempts; by a consortium of banks led by Banque Rothschild; by an oil-man from Denver, Colorado, who looked like the charging bull-elephant whose picture he displayed behind his office desk; and not least by Harold Lever (now Lord Lever), an ex-Labour-Cabinet-Minister who had the wise idea of placing the whole business in the safe hands of trustees. All came to nothing.

Finally there came on the scene a Mr Robert Vesco. Following IOS's seven-day Board meeting he had manoeuvred himself into a position where he exercised effective control of IOS, so it was with him that negotiations would have to be conducted if control of ILI was to be divorced from IOS. I asked the US Treasury representative at the American Embassy in London to give us an opinion about Mr Vesco's character. He reported, after consulting the Securities and Exchange Commission in Washington, that Mr Vesco was a gentleman of the highest character, and that furthermore his action in abandoning his other business interests to rescue IOS was something that had their gratitude.

A meeting was arranged and Vesco came to my home in Somerset on a flying visit. He struck me as a slippery fellow, not at all what I had expected from his reference; however, I put to him a proposal that Keysers should take over ILI, to which he agreed in principle. He would not sell a majority share interest in ILI but he would be willing to enter into firm contracts to place the management of the business in Keysers' hands. As ILI was not his chief interest he would leave any detailed negotiation to his subordinates.

It is interesting now to reflect on the opinion of Mr Vesco given at that time by official sources. The US Government and its agent, the SEC, were extremely concerned about IOS. IOS was huge. Millions of individuals had an interest in it, and it had assumed a high profile in many countries. Cornfeld had advertised it worldwide as a proof of American success in business, an advertisement for capitalism, a living symbol of the triumph of the US way of life. Its failure would reflect badly upon the American ethic. Naturally the SEC was anxious to ensure that IOS was brought under effective management.

Then, as now (though they have improved somewhat), the international policing arrangements in the securities industry were patchy: there were few, if any, formal arrangements for liaison between national authorities. Unquestionably the US Treasury's representative in London would hold a different opinion of Mr Vesco today. He has turned out to be a looter on a grand scale. He subsequently decamped to Costa Rica with a fortune appropriated from IOS.

My colleagues at Keysers had a clear view on the situation. It would be of undoubted financial benefit to us to obtain a contract to manage ILI's investment portfolio which we were organisationally well equipped to do since we had at the bank a strong investment management team. Also, it would bring us prestige if we could re-establish ILI's reputation. I had a duty to my colleagues to carry this project through: it was agreed that I might negotiate terms to suit myself by way of reward. We should attempt to obtain a majority of the shares in ILI, if possible. If not, it was considered that a minority holding in the company coupled with unbreakable management agreements and my own appointment as Chairman of ILI should be adequate to restore public confidence.

The negotiators appointed by Vesco were adamant that a majority holding in ILI was not for sale. They repeated that they were keen to re-establish the company's value by entering into a partnership arrangement with a respected British financial institution but refused to part with any of ILI's equity to Keysers or any other similar institution. They made it plain that they wanted me and were indifferent to Keysers. If I joined ILI as Chairman they would sell me some 18 per cent of the equity for a nominal sum; and they would willingly permit ILI to enter into contracts with Keysers binding themselves to delegate to Keysers all aspects of ILI's management, including investment management, if I insisted upon that as a condition. That was the best that could be achieved, and even that was not brought about without considerable argument. Keysers agreed, and on that basis I committed myself. I resigned as Chairman of Barclays Unicorn and as a director of the Barclays Bank Trust Company.

I felt that the shareholding in ILI would be compensation for the fact that I had made so little money on the sale of my stock in Unicorn when I joined the Government as Economic Secretary to the Treasury in 1962, a sort of poetic justice that allowed me a second opportunity to capitalise potentially on my expertise in the investment and life assurance world.

I then handled matters badly from my personal point of view. One of Keysers' directors demanded that Keysers have a half-share in my proposed stockholding in ILI. After much argument within Keysers this view carried the day and I was obliged to agree with as good a grace as I could muster. My boats were burned: I had given up my position at Unicorn. So – it was back to the drawing board and negotiations with IOS's representatives began all over again. In the end (and I was heartily sick of it all by this time) I was able to persuade the IOS people that Keysers should become shareholders too but at a price. Both Keysers and I were made to pay for our shares. I ended up with a holding of 131,250 shares out of a total of 862,500 in issue, some 15 per cent of the equity, and a large debt which I had not expected to assume. That debt was to prove a millstone round my neck for years to come.

On 30 June 1972 the deal, apart from the stockholdings – the final arrangements for which had not yet been completed – was announced: Keysers was entering into a series of agreements under which Keysers would assume management control of ILI; I would have the right to nominate a majority of the Board of Directors of ILI, and I would become Chairman of the Board.

Press reaction was friendly but most comment was only of the 'so far so good' variety. 'Everything about the deal is an improvement which should be welcomed,' wrote one newspaper. I was paid pleasant compliments for the 'moral commitment' I had assumed, but 'nobody should run away with the idea that ILI has been transformed into a clean uncomplicated situation overnight.'

One unfortunate coincidence occurred which, while it was accepted to be no more than that, made everybody, myself included, uneasy. The publicity which Keysers received at this time came to the notice of IOS fund managers. They took an immediate view that Keysers was a merchant bank which was making steady progress and consequently merited an investment. Unknown to any of us at Keysers, they bought, through the stock market, some £3 million worth of Keysers' shares. It was a compliment, a vote of confidence, we could well have done without. We needed no connection with IOS and sought none.

I came to the conclusion that if I was to re-establish ILI's reputation I had only one course of action open to me: to persuade, force, or cajole IOS to dispose of the rest of its holding in ILI. It took time and it was difficult, but in the end we succeeded. A year later Keysers bought out IOS completely and our investment in ILI was eventually to prove the second most successful and profitable investment in Keysers' history. Confidence was progressively restored and ILI began to make steady progress. My original judgement was confirmed: ILI had a fine management team, loyal, competent and vigorous. In March 1973 we changed our name from ILI to Cannon Assurance to mark our change of ownership and of style.

I hoped I had brought stability to Cannon's affairs, but there was a deepening shadow over our existence – the developing problems of our parent company, Keysers, in the slump that followed the UK's property boom, and the publicity it received. I had hoped that Cannon's managers and sales force would be able to point to the new controlling shareholders of Cannon as a merchant bank of high standing and reputation. This boast was denied them, but although Keysers may have been an unwise lender to some extent at one stage, unlike Cannon's previous owner it was not dishonest.

There were a number of visible signs of our success. Cannon became a member of the Life Officers Association by election: our

Managing Director was promptly invited to join its linked life assurance committee: we established a leading position in computer systems technology. Cannon's Investment managers put up an outstanding performance by comparison with our competitors. We diversified our product range. Our business grew. We did more work with a smaller staff and Cannon as a company remained very profitable, earning some £2 million a year before tax. Cannon even played a part on two occasions as a member of a consortium organised by the industry in the support and rescue of other insurance companies with liquidity problems. We worked hard, and we were a happy ship. The work I was doing was recognised when a significant section of the insurance industry elected me Patron of the Association of Insurance Brokers.

I drew no salary for my work at Cannon until after I resigned from the Board of Keysers in 1974. The salary was paid to Keysers, and as it was larger than the salary I was drawing from Keysers as their Chairman by some £9,000 a year Keysers in effect employed me at less than no cost. Keysers drew substantial fees in accordance with the provisions of the original investment management agreement which I had negotiated, averaging nearly a quarter of a million pounds a year. Including dividends on their investment, the total income received by Keysers during the years of the bank's involvement with Cannon was well in excess of £1 1/2 million. It was a highly profitable investment and brought in substantial annual revenue at a time when Keysers particularly needed it. It was eventually to become still more profitable.

Cannon's business was developing well but it became increasingly clear that the process would undoubtedly be assisted if the link with Keysers could be cut. It seemed sad to contemplate this but it was inevitable that we should. Although some of our competitors in the banking and life assurance industries had their problems at this difficult time they did not receive the unflattering newspaper comment that Keysers seemed to attract. Hambros Bank had substantial difficulties arising from its financial involvement with the shipping industry, but these were not held against its life assurance subsidiary. Numerous insurance companies lost millions in poor underwriting results in the United States – the Prudential, the Royal, the Commercial Union, for instance – but the public still placed its domestic insurances with them. We determined, if we could, not to allow someone else's crisis to become our drama; and, if possible, to persuade Keysers to agree to sell its interest in Cannon to another parent about whose status there could be no doubt.

That was easier said than done. Since it had become apparent that Vesco was no longer the knight in shining armour that had been described to us by the US Treasury representative. IOS had reached the point where the authorities decided that it was now essential to liquidate whatever sections of the IOS empire they could get control of.

It was as a result of this decision that the potential sale of the controlling interest that Keysers had acquired in Cannon hung fire: it proved impossible, through no fault of Keysers, to offer clear title to any intending purchaser. The original purchases of shares in ILI had been paid for, the stock had been transferred and registered in Keysers and my own names, but the subsequent sale of the majority holding could not be completed. The stock had been transferred and the title of the new purchasers was registered in the books of the company, but the purchase consideration had not been paid over. Owing to Keysers' growing doubts about Vesco and his associates, it had been prudently put in an escrow account gathering interest until the situation at IOS had been cleared up and it could be decided who had a legitimate claim to it. Vesco never demanded payment, and when the liquidators of IOS, a firm of Canadian accountants, took over responsibility they were in no hurry to take the money, and in no hurry to clear Keysers' title. My successor as Chairman of Keysers put modest pressure on them to do so. The situation was both absurd and unfair. Keysers wanted to sell these shares to raise the money that it so badly needed, and an attempt to be helpful to the authorities had certainly rebounded on us.

Then in November 1975 the liquidators, who had previously refused to take the money in escrow, issued writs against a number of defendants, principally Keysers and myself, demanding payment of the money – which by then had grown to £2.4 million – and certain other moneys. They did so as a formality to establish their title beyond doubt, but it was, as the Chairman of Keysers said, a 'deplorable' action. Their only achievement was to risk upsetting Cannon's policyholders, and of course, to incur legal expenses. Whoever wins or loses legal actions, the lawyers always profit. It took a further three years before we were clear to dispose of the majority shareholding in Cannon. I thus found myself with an unexpectedly large bill for interest on the money borrowed to pay for my holding, a bill I should never have incurred, more than £250,000 in all.

Meanwhile there was a further, most unpleasant hazard to overcome, in the form of a secret Board of Trade enquiry. What precipitated it I was never told; my guess is that one of Keysers' shareholders had lodged a complaint about the loan I had obtained to buy my shareholding in Cannon. I knew that the loan was perfectly legitimate, but the enquiry was conducted in such a way that I was not allowed to answer the charge of impropriety. It is a curious system that allows a charge which is not disclosed to the person investigated, made by an informant whose identity is kept secret, to be enquired into by anonymous civil servants who are likely to lack any commercial experience, and assisted by advisers whose opinions are kept private and unchallenged; but it happened. When I told my colleagues on the Board of Cannon they were as shocked as I had been to learn what the Department proposed (and proposed, moreover, without any prior reference to them, the managers of the company).

Cannon's directors were totally supportive of me. In a memorandum to the Department they pointed out that before I became Chairman the company was losing funds at the rate of £200,000 a week. Total failure was a possibility. In the four years of my Chairmanship Cannon's assets had increased from £88 million to £119 million, annual premium income from £15 million to £20 million, policyholders from 120,000 to 180,000 and sums assured from £293 million to £750 million. The financial base of the company had been greatly strengthened. It was some turnaround. My friend Richard Sykes, the well known solicitor, waged furious battle on my account. In the end, the matter was dropped: as he said, it should never have been started. The secret enquiry lasted a year. It was a hard period to live through. I dare say that officials thought they were doing their duty. Ministers, if they knew of the matter, had no business to let such silliness proceed.

It was not until March 1978, six years after I acquired my investment and the debt that went with it, that the liquidators freed Keysers to sell Cannon. I was immediately busy. One man showed great interest, a Canadian who had left his native Edinburgh as a young clerk, crossed over to Canada and arrived in Calgary with only $20 and a bicycle. It is said that he used the bicycle to ride all the way from Montreal to Calgary, a distance of nearly two thousand miles. Of course, he is a Scotsman, so the story may be true. He was shrewd, ambitious and a hard worker. On his arrival in Canada he started work in the construction business and before long was busy and successful in the property world. He then moved into the insurance business in Canada, acquiring small companies which were not too competently managed, and conceived the ambition to develop similarly in the UK. I was satisfied as to his integrity. He had excellent references from several sources. He gave me the assurances I needed about the future development and management of Cannon's business.

On 1st April 1974 the whole shareholding in Cannon was sold to Mr Graham's Cascade Group of Canada for a total sum of some £10 million. For its majority interest Keysers received over £6 million, a good profit on its original investment. It had been a most satisfactory investment for Keysers and for the other minority shareholders, Mr Templeton and Mr Delacorte. It was nothing like so satisfactory for me. I received payment for my share, but against it had to be set the sum I had borrowed when I bought it plus a heavy interest liability, compounded, which was not allowable for tax. I suggested to my successor as Chairman of Keysers that they should forego interest. He refused. A tiresome wrangle with the Inland Revenue followed which was not concluded until 1985: it too charged interest on the capital gains tax due with no mitigation. A tax saving scheme I had purchased was retrospectively ruled out of order. Thus in the end I found myself without the financial reward I had hoped to achieve, and perhaps deserved to. There is no fun in being a public person: some hateful person in the Revenue deliberately leaked a misleading account of my tax affairs to a newspaper reporter, a most serious offence. Despite complaints to the head of the Inland Revenue I could get no remedy.

Two years later Graham decided he wanted to appoint his own man as Chairman. Most of the other directors were asked to resign at the same time. He was, of course, perfectly within his rights and was under pressure at the time from the economic recession in Canada. All the same, it was a bitter disappointment for me, as I am sure it was for the others, not to have the opportunity to continue to develop Cannon after having seen the company through so problematical a period. It had been a rough time and we had come through well, as the facts show.

In the end Graham did not have the patience to develop Cannon's full potential. In August 1984 he sold it to an American Insurance Company, the Lincoln National Corporation. Cannon is now renamed Lincoln National. It has continued to make excellent progress and now has funds under management of more than £3 billion, approaching Unicorn's size. The 1984 sale price of Cannon was £42.5 million, a profit for him over his original acquisition price of more than £32 million in only six years. He had received in addition some £2 million in dividends each year, a total of £12 million. Quite a deal. His purchase had been no April fool's joke.

As a certain Mr Rothschild is said to have remarked, 'It is seldom wrong to take a profit.' I wish I could have followed that advice, but again I found myself in the position where I had worked hard and successfully to make a company profitable and in the end had failed to profit myself.

But, as they say, one door shuts, another opens; and a very big door had opened for me well before my time with Cannon came to an end. As a result I later found myself involved in another corporate battle which dwarfed my struggle with the Cornfeld empire.

It was back in 1972, while I was Chairman of Keysers, that I was approached by Duncan Sandys, Chairman elect of Lonrho, and invited to act as its merchant banker. Lonrho's position at that moment was uncomfortable. The company's British finance Director and others had been arrested in South Africa on charges of fraud and warrants for the arrest of other directors were issued. These affairs were much publicised both in Africa and in Britain, where the arrest of Lonrho's finance Director was, understandably, regarded seriously. The charges were later shown to be trumped up and he was exonerated on the command of the Transvaal Attorney General, but this clearance took three whole years to achieve. Bad news makes the headlines, long-delayed corrections rate only a line or two. The clear impression was left in people's minds that there was something wrong with Lonrho – the company was in bad trouble with the law.

At this moment, when their help and support were most needed, Lonrho's merchant bankers, S. G. Warburg, resigned.

Lonrho undoubtedly had problems. Although a substantial enterprise, with a turnover in 1971-72 of some £215 million and a pre-tax profit of approximately £18 million, it was thought in the City to be suffering from liquidity problems. A high proportion of its earnings came from its trade in Africa and remittances to the UK were not always prompt or certain; hence the theoretical squeeze on Lonrho's resources of sterling, the currency in which its accounts were written. Following the dramatic public display of lack of support shown by Warburg, Lonrho was experiencing a crisis of confidence.

For a start the company decided to appoint a new Chairman. Duncan Sandys was an MP and son-in-law of Winston Churchill. He had a remarkable record of service to the State, particularly during the War when he was appointed Minister in charge of armaments production and later Chairman of the War Cabinet Committee for defence against German flying bombs and rockets.

Lonrho's British auditors, Peat Marwick Mitchell, one of the largest and most respected accountancy firms in the world, had been commissioned to write a detailed report on the company. Jim Butler, the partner with specific responsibility for the Lonrho account, later to be the firm's senior partner, came to my home in Somerset to show me an advance copy and to reinforce Sandys's request. The report (over 1,500 pages long) was complimentary about Lonrho, though the company's heavy dependence on African profits was clearly stated and the consequent financial risks were equally evident: there were criticisms of its financial controls: they had not kept in pace with the company's expansion, but Lonrho's basic financial position was sounder than was generally supposed, its trading prospects were good and its management highly competent.

My colleagues at Keysers and I discussed the matter. We decided that we could, and should help. Keysers were immediately appointed merchant bankers to Lonrho and we were asked to nominate a director. Mr Franklin, as the Managing Director in Keysers with responsibility for the commercial department, would have been the natural choice, but because he was Jewish and in view of the Arab connections which Lonrho was developing at that time it was thought prudent that I should serve, with Mr Franklin as my alternate.

A third new director was also appointed to the Lonrho Board. The Bank of England keeps a register of potential non-executive directors for appointment to companies which require the services of such persons, and on the list in 1972 was Sir Basil Smallpiece, a former, hardly successful, Chairman of Cunard and of the British Overseas Airways Corporation. He had been pestering the Bank (we later learned) to find an appointment for him and his name was suggested to Lonrho. We all had reservations about him personally. *Faute de mieux*, and unwisely, as it turned out, we all agreed to his appointment. So in 1972 the Board of Lonrho received the reinforcement of three new directors: a Chairman who, in spite of his distinguished public life, had enjoyed only a secondary experience of commercial affairs; an accountant who was to prove pernickety and disloyal; and myself.

I drew neither fees nor other remuneration for my appointment. Keysers however received ad hoc fees for particular services and an option on two million shares (which was subsequently exercised at a substantial profit). Sir Basil Smallpiece received an annual remuneration – and I was struck by his insistence on punctual payment. He always chased Lonrho's accounts department for his cheques.

Duncan Sandys had asked for an annual remuneration plus a once-for-all signing-on fee to compensate him for giving up an advisory role at Ashanti Goldfields Limited (a subsidiary company of Lonrho), a position he had held for many years. This had been agreed at the figure of £130,000 and the payment was to be made abroad – a not unreasonable proposal, as much of his work was expected to be performed overseas. Part of Sir Basil Smallpiece's remuneration was also, at his request, to be paid abroad. The advantage of overseas payments, at that time, was that they did not bear UK tax, a situation which has since been changed. This arrangement in the case of Duncan Sandys, of which I was unaware when it was made, was soon to prove a source of embarrassment. Although it was not illegal it was seen by many people as an example of a rich man avoiding payment of UK taxes in a way not available to the less well off. A *Sunday Times* correspondent credited me with devising the arrangement and was obliged subsequently to issue an apology. What newspapers do not know, they often invent.

I was enthusiastic that Keysers should make a success of our appointment and we set to work with a will. Lonrho agreed our proposal for an issue of new shares by way of a rights issue to existing shareholders. This raised new capital for the company which at once eased the supposed liquidity crisis. More important, in the circumstances of the time, it was clearly seen to have done so. This prompt action, the new Board appointments and the establishment of a series of new financial controls headed by a Finance Committee of the Board – combined with Keysers' involvement – restored public and City confidence in Lonrho to a marked extent.

The confidence was deserved. Lonrho was a company with a romantic record of enterprise and achievement behind it and with a fine future ahead. It began in 1909 as the London and Rhodesian Mining and Land Company and for the next fifty years it slowly but steadily expanded its activities in mining, property, ranching and agriculture in what was then the British colony of Southern Rhodesia. Then in 1961 the company was transformed by the arrival of a single man. On the recommendation of Angus Ogilvy, the husband of Princess Alexandra, Tiny Rowland joined Lonrho as Managing Director.

Rowland proved to be one of the most extraordinary entrepreneurs of our time. He had an exceptional ability to nose out a commercial opportunity and he was a brilliant negotiator with an uncanny ability to size up an opponent. Above all, his talent was to make deals. Once he had set his heart on a deal he could be amazingly persistent. He had the patience to go through apparently interminable negotiations with African

Governments, and sometimes with European Governments too. It took something like fifty visits to Lisbon to arrange for the building of the oil pipeline designed to link Rhodesia to Beira in the then Portuguese colony of Mozambique.

He was born in India of a British mother and a German father but spent his childhood and early adolescence in Germany. In 1934, at the age of seventeen, he was sent to school in England and his parents came over to Britain two years later. After leaving school he worked for his uncle in London in an export/import business and at the outbreak of War joined the British Army. He saw active service in Norway. His father, a German national, was interned on the Isle of Man, where Tiny's mother loyally joined him. Tiny sought compassionate leave to visit her as she lay dying, was refused but went nonetheless. He was arrested, imprisoned and discharged from the Army.

After the War he set himself to trading and manufacturing. He had his reverses but by and large he prospered, and eventually went out to Rhodesia where he became interested in mining and farming. When he joined Lonrho his own mining interests were transferred to the company in exchange for shares and that was the foundation of his later fortune.

In 1961 Lonrho was turning over around £4 million a year and making a pre-tax profit of some £160,000. By 1989 the pre-tax profit had risen to £273 million and the turnover to over £3.6 billion. The company became a huge asset to Britain's economy, employing about 150,000 people in eighty countries and being listed by the *Financial Times* as the fourteenth largest employer in the private sector in Europe.

This success was due in large part to a single act of courage. When other companies were pulling out of Africa, as one former colony after another became independent, Lonrho stayed put. It continued to trade throughout Africa and Tiny Rowland built up close links with many African leaders. He used those links not only for Lonrho's commercial benefit but also to work for peace and stability in, for example, Angola, Mozambique and the Sudan. He was known and welcomed by presidents and rebel leaders alike, at home with President Machel of Mozambique and just as much so with Alfonso Dhlakama, the leader of the Renamo rebels against Machel's regime; welcomed by the Communist Government in Angola and by their opponent Jonas Savimbi of UNITA. Unlike so many Europeans who did little to hide their contempt for Africans and African Governments, he worked with them, cultivated their friendship and was respected and honoured for doing so.

Not in Britain, however. His reception in his own country was always grudging and suspicious and he has never been given the recognition, even honour, that is his due. Although I myself have met and worked with many notable figures, political leaders, commanders of great commercial empires, public servants and the like, I have never been associated with a man whom I liked and respect more than Tiny Rowland. He could be harsh on those of his associates or employees who did not measure up to a high standard of probity or competence. He could be unremitting, sometimes unreasonable, in the pursuit of a specified objective. He worked himself extremely hard and he expected the same dedication from his senior subordinates. To his friends, however, he demonstrated a generosity and a loyalty which were heart-warming. I never knew him to break a promise: I never knew him to let down a friend.

'It's all right, I think they're friends of Tiny's!'

159

He has a charming way with him and he is a man with infinite patience. He would always make time for discussion, although he did not have the tolerance to read the mass of paper that is inevitably involved in dealing with the affairs of a large trading company with a multitude of subsidiaries. He preferred to have his lieutenants and employees make their oral reports to him. After a three or four hour meeting of the Lonrho finance committee, one or other of us would encapsulate its deliberations and decisions for him in a sentence or two. But give him an essential piece of paper and he would read it with fierce concentration. The strength of the organisation of the team which we built up in Lonrho was that it left him free from the minutiae, free to plan Lonrho's strategy, to conduct interminable negotiations with African leaders, to seek out the deals and the opportunities.

He preferred African temperatures to those of the UK. The London office temperature was kept much higher than is usual in most City establishments, and sometimes I used to find this uncomfortable. Once he rang me from Africa especially to tell me that the temperature was over 130 degrees in the shade. I said I hoped he was not cooked. 'On the contrary,' he said, 'I have my overcoat on.' He suffered from asthma which meant that walking or mounting stairs was sometimes difficult. Occasionally he would have an attack of malaria. I never once heard him complain of physical discomfort.

He travelled frequently to Africa and prided himself that his office was wherever he happened to be, even in an aeroplane. He was constantly on the telephone and kept in frequent touch with everyone who worked in an important position in Lonrho. Wherever he was, Tiny was ever present to his colleagues, urging them on, soliciting opinion, telephoning to the ends of the earth, roaring with laughter, always cool in a crisis, strong, never out of temper though occasionally grumpy, always ready to do a deal and always looking for deals to do.

It was not long after I joined Lonrho's Board that a group of eight directors, led by Sir Basil Smallpiece, attempted to oust Tiny Rowland from his position as Chief Executive. The dissident directors were an ill-assorted group, some motivated by ambition, others by resentment. One saw himself as a potential managing director of the company and was so confident of success in the plan to dispose of Tiny Rowland that his wife timed a visit to our offices in the City to coincide with the ending of a monthly Board meeting. She arrived clutching champagne and flowers to celebrate Tiny's dismissal. Another, General Spears, a former Tory MP and Churchill's personal representative with the French Prime Minister of

160

France in 1940, had never forgiven Rowland for the fact that Lonrho had taken over his Ghanaian mining company, Ashanti Goldfields. As to Sir Basil Smallpiece, the ostensible leader of the group, his motive was a mixture of both ambition and resentment. Smallpiece disliked Sandys, I dare say he disliked me, and certainly the antipathy between him and Rowland was as mutual as it was strong. Smallpiece was a petty man with a nit-picking attitude, never happier than when examining the cost of candle ends. Naturally he was ill at ease with Tiny's grand concepts.

Yet another dissident was Nicholas Elliott, a director of MI6, the man who botched Commander Crabb's underwater investigation of the Soviet cruiser *Ordzhonikidze* at the time of Kruschev's visit to the UK in 1956. A former head of station in Beirut, he travelled there in 1963 to obtain the traitor Kim Philby's confession. He succeeded in this, but then allowed his old friend from MI6 to escape to Soviet Russia. On the face of it these were two of the most monumental blunders perpetrated by British Intelligence since the War. Presumably the reality must have been different from the way in which the public perceived these events or he would surely have been dismissed in disgrace. For a while, until the shareholders of Lonrho dismissed him for his disloyalty to Rowland by an overwhelming majority, we were both directors of Lonrho. I never heard him make a single contribution of substance at any of our Board meetings. I always sat as far away from him as possible: he suffered badly from halitosis.

The conspirators tried to convince the rest of the Board that Tiny's management of Lonrho was leading the company to disaster. I refused to join them. My colleagues and I at Keysers were quite clear that Tiny was the architect of Lonrho's success. With him, the company could be expected to make further, substantial progress; without him, it would be the poorer. We came out strongly in his support.

It was impossible to keep the dispute private. It began to be reported in the newspapers. Angus Ogilvy, doubtless under pressure from the Palace and his own advisers, found discretion to be the better part of valour and resigned from the Board. I spent long hours arguing with his advisers since I believed that he was so strongly associated with Lonrho in the public view that resignation would appear like desertion, whereas to stay and support his friend would be seen as honourable. Furthermore, it would be sensible to stay because Rowland was going to win. They would not listen: a decision had been made that Ogilvy should resign and resign he did. He was not entirely his own master.

The conspirators also put heavy pressure on Duncan Sandys. They attempted to blackmail him into joining them by proposing to publicise his overseas payments. The effect of this threat on Sandys was dire. Early each day while the battle lasted he would telephone me for reassurance, and I did my best to give it to him. His laboured breathing over the telephone haunts me still. Smallpiece and his supporters allowed themselves to be called the 'straight eight'. To my mind the pressure put on Sandys showed them to be anything but straight.

The Board appeared divided into two equal camps. To succeed, the dissidents needed Sandys's casting vote as Chairman. To his eternal credit, Sandys met the challenge head on: he refused to desert the Chief Executive and remained his staunch supporter. His overseas payment became public knowledge and caused a political furore.

Publicity continued to build up. Everyone likes to gossip about a power struggle, particularly if it can be personalised. There were court hearings, and Tiny Rowland obtained an injunction to prevent the dissident directors sacking him. One Lonrho Board meeting took place while the court hearing was in progress. Sandys passed me a note: 'Keep the discussion going until we have the result of the court proceedings.' I challenged Smallpiece to state his complaints to Mr Rowland's face and in front of all the directors, but he refused. Sandys, in a circular to shareholders, rightly made great play of the fact that none of the directors had disapproved of Rowland's actions or the way he discharged his duties.

It was arranged that the dispute should be decided by Lonrho's fifty thousand shareholders in a general meeting. The lobbying began. Each side issued circulars. Tiny's letters to shareholders were written in a fluent style, easy to read and understand, emphasising Lonrho's past successes and confidence in building on them. Smallpiece's circular to shareholders was, like the man, pedestrian and dull. Many newspapers commissioned articles about the arguments in the dispute, the personalities involved, and the role of the Companies Act in such situations. The Government even promised a new Act of Parliament. (It was the usual reaction in such situations – promises, some would say threats, of more controls, more regulation, more excuses to stifle enterprise.)

I found myself under attack – sometimes overt, more often covert – in my constituency, in the City and even in the House of Commons. Denis Healey MP, then Shadow Chancellor of the Exchequer, attacked Lonrho in a party political broadcast on behalf of the Labour Party: in it he described me as Lonrho's 'financial factotum'. Willie Hamilton, MP, without any previous warning to me (it is a convention, universally

162

practised, that a Member of Parliament intending to refer to another in debate will give him advance notice), referred in the Chamber of the House of Commons to the Board of Directors of Lonrho as 'a bunch of crooks who should be locked up in Brixton prison'. As it happened the Speaker was not in the chair at that moment or perhaps Hamilton would have been pulled up at once. When I complained in the House the next day in what Mr Speaker Thomas (later Viscount Tonypandy) in his autobiography called 'forceful but extremely courteous language' Hamilton apologised. If that is the sort of thing Healey and Hamilton were saying in public, Heaven only knows what they and others were saying in private.

Lonrho's managers came out to a man in loyal support of Tiny Rowland. From African Governments came threats of nationalisation of Lonrho's assets if he was replaced as Chief Executive. Meantime more politicians, especially the comedians, were having a minor field day. Sir Gerald Nabarro MP put himself forward to be Chairman. Marcus Lipton MP waded in. Even more senior and responsible figures involved themselves. At this time Ted Heath, then Prime Minister, was in the midst of discussions with the CBI and the trades unions about wage restraint, and in the House of Commons, in answer to a supplementary question by Jo Grimond, he referred to the 'unacceptable face of capitalism'. It was not clear whether he meant Lonrho the company or its payment to Lord Sandys. This phrase is generally thought to be the only memorable one he uttered as Prime Minister. He had used it a few days before at a dinner in Scotland, where it had been heard with astonishment. A few weeks later, at the Conservative Party's Women's Conference, he was again violently critical of what he called the excesses of capitalism, mentioning Lonrho by name. He represented the Conservative Party under his leadership as society's defender against such wickedness. Not once did he speak to Sandys or myself, his Parliamentary colleagues, before he vented his spleen in public. I sent a private message to Duncan to say that I would be pleased to see Prime Minister Heath and explain the situation: I had no reply.

Public opinion was sharply divided about Lonrho. *The Times* headlined a pompous main leading article 'Mr Rowland must go'. On the other hand the *Daily Telegraph* urged Lonrho's shareholders to support their Chief Executive. The *Economist* got very close to the mark. 'One face that British capitalism showed to the world this week,' it wrote, 'was the jealousy of less successful men as they joined the rush to pull Mr Tiny Rowland down.'

'I must admit Harold – some unpleasant and unacceptable faces are easier to deal with than others.'

Government was not to be left out of the action. It set up an enquiry into Lonrho, thereby following the golden rule – if there is an embarrassing controversy and you want to duck responsibility, get someone else from the massed ranks of the great and the good (naturally) to enquire into it. That shuts everyone up for a while. The announcement of the enquiry wiped £5 million off Lonrho's value on the stock market, but the Stock Exchange showed its confidence in the company by continuing to make a market in Lonrho's shares, an unusual step to take in the circumstances.

Mr Heath's attack on Lonrho and the announcement of the enquiry occurred almost exactly one week before the vote for or against Lonrho's Chief Executive was due to take place. Neither event was calculated to help his cause. The shareholders' meeting was held in the Central Hall, Westminster. Three thousand attended and the atmosphere was electric. Duncan Sandys presided. He lamented the occasion. Tiny Rowland spoke briefly and was given a rapturous reception. Smallpiece also spoke. He was lacklustre and heckled. I was called on to answer a question about Lonrho's unusual situation. I replied that, speaking as a director and the Chairman of the Company's merchant bankers, I could assure the meeting that there was no liquidity crisis and I foresaw none.

The meeting was an anti-climax. The bulk of Lonrho's fifty thousand shareholders had already cast their votes by proxy and the result of the vote was overwhelming. The shareholders gave Tiny Rowland a massive vote of confidence: 29.5 million votes for and 4.5 million votes against. In a second vote the dissident directors were dismissed by a majority of 18 million votes. It was a triumph for the Chief Executive.

'In victory, magnanimity,' said Churchill. Rowland shook Smallpiece by the hand as they left the platform. It was a generous gesture to make to the man who had tried to assassinate him.

That Government-appointed enquiry took no less than four years to complete. (It seems hardly fair to a substantial enterprise to keep its management and its workers in a state of suspense for so long: it is almost incredible that a speedier process has not been devised.) The report was 170 pages in length and cost more than £1,000 a page. The *Daily Mail* summed it up well:

> While newspapers may have a field day with criticisms of Lord Duncan Sandys, Angus Ogilvy, Tiny Rowland and other directors, the investigators have found no traces of fraud, nor of misfeasance, bribery or, indeed of any crime. The report contains nothing that we don't know already though it's there in enormous detail. There is much on Tiny's highly personalised way of running our fifteenth largest

company but the inspectors don't mention Lonrho's magnificent fifteen years record nor the near-doubling of earnings a share since they began their investigation.

I have never regretted my support for Tiny Rowland – quite the reverse – and I was cordially pleased to see the back of Sir Basil Smallpiece. The judgement that my colleagues at Keysers and I made at the time, that Lonrho under Rowland's leadership had much progress yet to achieve, came to be amply justified over the years.

So too, I fear, was another forecast I made. At an early stage in the dispute I had made a private call on Basil Smallpiece. I told him that I was sure that the continuing disagreement on the Board would attract much publicity and that it would be in no one's interest. It could well harm not just Lonrho but the City in general, and be a poor advertisement for capitalism. He would, I believed, lose the battle, so it might harm him too. He would not listen. I thought him then, and I see no reason to change my opinion now, an insufferable prig and utterly lacking in commercial judgement. He retired and, happily, was not heard of again.

There are occasions when there is no fun in being proved right. 'Nothing except a battle lost,' said the great Duke of Wellington, 'can be half so melancholy as a battle won.' It was a sad, unnecessary affair.

CHAPTER 8

BRINGING *the*
EXECUTIVE *to* ACCOUNT

'It is damaging to the public interest to have any decision-making process exposed.'

I quote Andrew Leithead, Assistant Treasury Solicitor to Lord Justice Scott's enquiry into the export of arms to Iraq in 1994. His staggering remark is itself evidence that the arrogance of the Executive is unlimited.

The attempt by our Parliamentary representatives to make the Executive more accountable has continued for centuries. In 1780 a famous motion was put before the Commons: 'that the influence of the Crown has increased, is increasing and ought to be diminished.' The majority in favour of the motion was only 18. Taunton's MP, I am glad to say, voted for it. One speaker said that the Crown's influence was 'productive of the happiest, most beneficial and glorious consequences'. Sycophants of the Establishment are to be found in every Parliament.

Two hundred years later, the influence of the Executive has increased markedly; it is hardly reducing even under Conservative administrations. The proper scope of the Government's influence is a matter of political argument between Conservatives and Socialists, but however we define that scope it is surely the over-riding duty of Parliamentarians to ensure that the Executive is more adequately supervised than it is by our present, too casual, practice.

In the last sixteen years Conservative administrations have been elected with a clear mandate – to hold back Government expenditure and to reduce taxation. They have done neither. Public expenditure has risen hugely in absolute and proportionate terms. Taxation too has risen. True, the top rates of direct tax have come down and there has been a shift from direct to indirect taxation, but overall the average taxpayer still hands over a hefty share of his money to the Exchequer. In 1993 the average tax rate (i.e. income tax – local and central Government – and social security) of a married man with two children earning £20,000 a year was over 25% of his gross income, more than in France, Germany and the US and about twice the rate ruling in Japan. If he earned £40,000 a year his average rate rose to 30%, again a higher proportion than his foreign equivalents. No wonder the British voter lacks the 'feel good' factor – even if *per capita* spending power has risen by more than 50% as a consequence of the rise in real earnings since 1979. Political theorists too often forget that people are more grateful to political Parties for possible future favours than for past benefits.

The situation has put Conservative supporters in an embarrassing position. The popular belief, fostered by the Labour Party and by a multitude of pressure groups, is that there have been massive cuts in public expenditure. This is the opposite of the truth, but Conservatives do not like to admit that they have failed in this fundamental area of their Party's declared policy, nor do they want to be made to appear guilty of making unpopular reductions in welfare expenditure. So they have riposted with the boast that, while of course the Tory Party stands for lower taxation, it has actually spent more money than any of its predecessors in virtually every respect where Government has responsibility, and especially on the social services. This attempt to have it both ways has not been convincing. To take a single example: calculated at 1992/93 prices spending on benefits has risen from £45 billion to about £75 billion, yet few people believe it has increased by 60 per cent under the Tories.

Early in my time in Parliament I came to the conclusion that there was a more important matter to consider than the usual Party political arguments, namely that whatever its absolute amount public expenditure is not controlled as closely as tax payers have every right to expect. Margaret Thatcher's successive administrations made an attempt at remedies, and achieved some economies through more competent housekeeping in Government departments, but much more needs to be done. The cynical observer may well ask: if Governments led by the Iron Lady have been unable to contain expenditure, what Government will succeed in doing so? In fact it is not difficult to bring about radical improvements: many such have been recommended over the years in the House of Commons by a small group of conscientious Members. But the will has been lacking.

Good government is too important to be left exclusively to Ministers, but attempts by backbenchers to rectify the situation have come up against formidable obstacles.

the house magazine

Number 41   Vol. 3   1977

NOV. 7–13

Edward du Cann –

Somerset, Taunton

Born in 1924, he attended St John's College
where he read Law. He did not follow his father to
the Bar but went into banking, where he founded
the Unicorn Group of Unit Trusts and later was
Chairman of Keyser Ullmann. He contested West
Walthamstow in 1951 and Barrow-in-Furness in
1955. In February 1956 he was elected to his
present constituency. He has held government jobs
as Economic Secretary to the Treasury from
1962-63, and Minister of State at the Board of
Trade from 1963-64. His strength politically has
been behind the scenes in his own party, of which
he was chairman from 1965-67. He is currently
Chairman of the 1922 Committee. In the
Commons he was the first Chairman of the Public
Expenditure Committee and now chairs the Public
Accounts Committee. He is a powerful figure.

A powerful figure

First, there has been a substantial growth in party disciplines and in the vested interest of placemen whose careers depend on the Party leadership. The number of Ministers in Government continues to grow. In 1900, there were 64. Ramsay Macdonald's first Labour Government had only 57, but during and after the 1939 War this downward trend was sharply reversed. Churchill's 1945 Government had 81 members; Wilson in 1970 had 98; Callaghan topped the century and Mrs Thatcher did not reduce the numbers.

It was *The Times* that first wrote of the 'ministerial vote' – a more polite expression than the 'payroll vote'. Including Whips, there are 86 Ministers in the Commons in the present Conservative Government (out of just over 100 in all), plus up to 50 unpaid Ministerial Parliamentary Private Secretaries, many of them aspirants for office – well over a third of all MPs on the Government side. Add to that a further 60 plus who are the Opposition shadows of the administration, and more than a quarter of the total membership of the House of Commons is dependent upon one or other of the two main parties for position and patronage. The Parties are more powerful than they have ever been. The scope for independence in the House of Commons is smaller than it has ever been. The main political Parties now dominate all forms of Parliamentary activity and one can achieve very little without the support of one or other of them.

Second, there has been a huge growth in the power of the Prime Minister's office. This process accelerated during Margaret Thatcher's period as Prime Minister. We move increasingly towards regarding our Prime Minister as a Presidential figure rather than the captain of a team.

Third, in recent years there has been an immense growth in the volume of legislation with which Parliament must deal. Fifty years ago Parliament passed into law annually 450 pages of legislation. Now it is seven times that amount, more than 3,000 pages a year. To that must be added more than 2,000 Statutory Instruments (another 10,000 pages) which can have important and far-reaching effects, plus a plethora of European material, most of which goes by unchallenged.

It would seem logical for Ministers and expert witnesses to be examined by MPs on the purposes and consequences of legislation, but although machinery exists for this purpose it has been used less than half a dozen times in the past two decades. Never is there a formal review of the consequences of legislation other than an occasional Select Committee enquiry. Surely the opportunity for review should be taken as a matter of routine?

Then there is the 'guillotine'. Whenever Government becomes impatient with the progress of legislation it curtails discussion by timetabling the progress of bills. When I was first elected to Parliament in 1956 the guillotine was used once or twice a year: in the four years after I left it was used to curtail discussion no fewer than 17 times. It is in effect a gagging mechanism, a device to strengthen the dominance of the Government of the day over elected MPs. Some MPs have even been trying to get the passage of *all* bills timetabled so that they can go home earlier at night. They are forgetting that delay is one of the few effective weapons backbenchers can wield.

Fourth, and by far the most worrying, is the fact that never in our

170

history, except in wartime, has Government possessed such power as it does today. Never has it provided incomes to so many people, directly and indirectly. Never has it exerted such patronage (apart from its Parliamentary patronage) in terms of personal appointments or aid to industry. Conservative Governments since 1979 have reduced the number of state-owned industries but even so the full extent of Government regulation in unowned commerce and industry is still vast. Never before in our peacetime history has Government operated in so many spheres: never has it been so ubiquitous or so dominant.

Advocates of the present Conservative Government speak with forked tongues when they refer to these matters; they more often boast of what Government does than of any reduction in the number of its activities.

I am not arguing here either for or against a greater involvement by the State in our daily lives, though I would wish to see individuals and corporations encouraged to be increasingly self-reliant rather than dependent on it. State influence is inevitable, but my point is that whether weighty or light, it requires competent policing, and the weightier it is, the greater the need for policing. How can that be done? An individual MP in the modern context has little authority. However, if he combines with others, then his influence increases markedly. There are two chief avenues open to him. The first is through his Party channels, for example, the 1922 Committee, its 20 plus satellite committees and their Labour equivalents – the other Parties are too small to have a comparable structure. The other is through an all-Party effort. That latter facility has been hugely developed since 1979; the tragedy, I believe, is that it is still inadequately used.

It is hard to realise how vast the influence of the State is in terms of our personal lives. Consider some statistics. More than half of all British adults receive an income from the State: 38 million people have a weekly income in some form, including earnings and State benefits – but the private sector delivers income to only 17 million of them. Central and local government, the health service, the armed services, the nationalised industries and the like together employ some 7¼ million people, that is to say some 30 per cent of the employed labour force. Those receiving social security benefits – pensions, unemployment and supplementary benefits and the like – now total over 15 million.

The bald figures conceal interesting trends in the component groups: in recent years, the numbers of those employed in central Government have fallen; local government staff numbers have also fallen; the police force has grown and so has the staff in the health service; the numbers of those working in the nationalised industries and the armed forces have fallen dramatically; but the overall increase over the years in the number of people who depend on the State for all or part of their income has been dramatic.

The statistics for Britain, it is only reasonable to point out, are only marginally higher than for other European countries. In the UK, Government provides incomes for 56 per cent of the earning population. In France the proportion is 55 per cent, in Germany 51 per cent. In the US the figure is lower at 42 per cent. Public sector employment represents 31 per cent in the UK. In the US it is 18 per cent.

A fundamental tenet of our constitution is that Parliament controls the Executive. In the final analysis, Parliament can dismiss a Government or deny it supply (i.e. finance) if it sees fit. This, however, is the extreme position. It rarely happens. If one asks: How thoroughly, day by day, does Parliament supervise the Executive's activities? no answer will amount to more than a cryptic mumble. Our priorities belong to a bygone age – like a stagecoach at Brands Hatch. It is simply not good enough. The British Parliament seems content to leave outside observers with the impression that it is an old-fashioned, fuddy-duddy assembly, keen to make debating points in the Chamber but unconcerned with its prime job of surveillance of the Executive.

In theory it is supposed to use its debates to interrogate Ministers and call them to account. In practice the result of each contemporary debate in the House of Commons is invariably decided on party lines and predictable before the debate begins. 'A ritual dance,' Lord Hailsham has called it. It is not an adequate system for the careful analysis of the detailed financial data on which policy choices must be based. It is not a sensible method for comparing out-turn with forecast; nor is it an appropriate method for budgeting, nor for supervising huge expenditures. Nowadays, when the House of Commons is asked to examine proposed spending and vote for or against its supply, it invariably seizes the opportunity to indulge in partisan debate on some topical, comparatively trivial issue. It is as if our Parliamentarians have decided to abandon even a token attempt to scrutinise expenditure.

Another Parliamentary procedure which in theory enables the backbencher to call Ministers to account is the hour-long daily question time. The public often hears the twice-weekly quarter of an hour of questions to the Prime Minister, and most people receive an unfortunate impression from the emphasis given by the broadcasters to the gladiatorial confrontation between the Prime Minister and the Leader of the Opposition. Listeners find the whole of question time a rowdy, ill-tempered affair. They suspect that it may not be untypical of much that happens in Parliament, and to an extent that suspicion is well founded. The question period is hardly an opportunity for careful analysis. It is not usually difficult for a Minister standing at the despatch box to duck the really hard question, and the single supplementary that follows; or so I found when I was a Minister. Certainly I have had a vastly harder time of it at Robin Day's or Brian Redhead's hands on television or radio than I ever experienced at the hands of my colleagues in the House of Commons, and I suspect that everyone who has been a Minister would say the same.

It is incontrovertible then that Parliament's two main methods of supervising the Executive, debate and question time, are no longer adequate in the modern context. This is not a Party matter. On the back benches in the House of Commons, irrespective of Party allegiances, there has been a growing awareness of the problem, a growing impatience with the failure of the leadership of any political Party to seek remedies, and a growing determination among a minority of MPs to find solutions.

The Executive resists any erosion of its powers – which is precisely why the rest of us should demand it. As Professor Griffiths has pointed out 'the modern executive is the heir to those great powers of the Tudors and the Stuarts'. The Commons has been reduced to a merely reactive body: the Executive has become, in effect, an elected dictatorship. So if British voters, perhaps unwittingly, decided to send to Westminster a majority of Parliamentarians with extreme political views, what safeguards would there be? The terrifying answer is – almost none. It is high time to set some visible, declared, limit to the Government's authority.

I became closely involved in this aspect of politics after the 1970 general election. Despite what I had seen as his clear undertaking, Heath did not offer me a place in his Government. Perhaps it would have been difficult for him to do so. As a senior member of the Party I could hardly be offered a junior post, and if I were given a senior post he would have had to displace someone who had held a Shadow Cabinet portfolio. More importantly, I had never been enthusiastic for the proposal that Britain should join the Common Market. I had said so in public, repeatedly, and I had written pamphlets proposing alternative economic and political strategies. (All these years later, I regret not one word of them.) Heath was already known as a fanatical supporter of the European ideal, and as Prime Minister he would undoubtedly strive with might and main to get

Britain's signature to the Treaty of Rome. Indeed, this determination was made a prominent point of policy in the Conservative Party's election manifesto in 1970, though I had not included it in my own election address and had made my personal view clear at every one of my seventy or so public meetings during the campaign in my Taunton constituency. Heath could never afford to include in his administration, let alone in his Cabinet, a senior figure who might be relied upon to argue against this aspect of policy and perhaps would resign from office rather than be a party to its achievement. Unlike some of my contemporaries, of whom the most prominent example was Peter Walker, this was not a subject on which I would change my mind. I would rather be outside the Cabinet for the right reasons than inside it for the wrong ones. Outside it I proved to be. I made no complaint then and I make none now.

Perhaps my absence from office was noted with a little sympathy by my friends; perhaps the ever-vigilant Conservative Whips thought it better I should be found a job of work to do than be left without particular occupation on the back benches where I might be tempted to create a little mischief. Most likely the Government needed a workhorse to do a job, but anyhow a few months later the Chief Whip, Francis Pym, asked to see me. He told me that the Government had decided to propose that the House of Commons establish a Select Committee on Expenditure, and invited me to be its first Chairman.

The proposal had come about in this way. The Plowden Committee on the Control of Public Expenditure had reported in 1961. Until that time Government expenditure was usually assessed annually and the Chancellor's annual budget related to one year's activities only. Many Parliamentarians and others felt that the attention of Ministers and Parliament should be focused increasingly on the longer-term implications inherent in Government expenditure programmes, for two main reasons.

In the first place, a decision made this year to increase expenditure in one field can have important results in, say, ten years' time. For instance, if retirement pensions are increased by £1 a week this year and there are 8 million pensioners, the additional cost to the Exchequer will be £416 million in the first year. In ten years' time, however, thanks to the habit we have developed of living longer, the number of pensioners may be, say, 9 million (and by the year 2000 there will be 250,000 more of us over the age of 80 than there are today – and I hope to be one of them). The cost then will rise to £468 million without allowing for inflation in-dexing. Thus inherited commitments to established spending programmes will limit the freedom of choice for Governments in years to come.

In the second place, intermittent variations in Government expenditure can be damaging to long-term programmes. Some years after a programme of capital expenditure is initiated there may be a sudden need for economy, so it is scaled down, interrupted or dropped. The curtailment of a programme that is already well under way usually involves a waste of money: the effort that has gone into planning comes to nothing and half-finished work may be abandoned.

Responding to the recommendations of the Plowden Committee, in April 1969 the Government announced its intention to publish annually a White Paper on projected Government expenditure for five years ahead, and also to develop 'forward looks' at public expenditure. So far so good, but Parliament had no procedure for scrutinising public expenditure in other than annual terms.

In July 1969 an All-Party House of Commons Select Committee on Procedure recommended the establishment of a Select Committee on Expenditure. This was to replace the old Select Committee on Estimates whose duties were to examine the form of the Estimates – the Government's detailed proposals for expenditure – and to report to the House how any of the policies covered by the Estimates could be carried out more economically. The function of the Estimates Committee was strictly limited to that objective and examinations of policy matters were not included in its remit. I had been a member of the general sub-committee of the Estimates Committee for some years, so I was not without experience of its methods.

The new Select Committee on Expenditure was to have a wider remit: its duties would be to discuss the Government's expenditure strategy, to examine the means being adopted to execute that strategy, and retrospectively to examine the results achieved and the value for money obtained.

That was how matters stood when the general election came in June 1970. In October that year the new Conservative Government published a Green Paper (a consultative document) stating its proposals. The Procedure Committee's recommendations were somewhat scaled down, but in November 1970 the Green Paper proposals were generally accepted by the House of Commons.

This little history illustrates a remarkable state of affairs. In practice it is not the House of Commons that decides how far and in what way the Government is to be scrutinised: it is the Government itself. The House of Commons has become the Executive's little doggie. It may bark only to the degree that the Executive permits.

175

Until my interview with Francis Pym I had taken a somewhat academic interest in these events. Thinking about his proposal I told him that I did not believe the Committee would be effective, or that the House would agree to its establishment, unless its terms of reference permitted the Committee to enquire into policy matters. The then Leader of the House, William Whitelaw, agreed at once. I therefore told Francis Pym I would willingly accept responsibility for getting the new Expenditure Committee under way.

In the House Mr Whitelaw said he saw the Expenditure Committee as having

> . . . a wider role than the old Estimates Committee, and would bring under examination the projects of public expenditure made available to the House. It would be free to consider the policies behind the figures and, therefore, might sometimes wish to examine Ministers on them.

He was as good as his word. In January 1971 the new Expenditure Committee was duly established together with a series of 'functional' sub-committees involving a total of 49 Members of Parliament of all political Parties. I was elected Chairman and served for two years, during which I did as I had undertaken: I got the Committee started.

In practice the Expenditure Committee did not prove to be as successful as all who had worked to establish it had hoped. A detailed analysis of its first four years' work concluded that it had 'helped meet the need of the House of Commons to be able to consider the many different aspects of public expenditure, including the policies inherent in the programmes set out annually in the White Paper on Public Expenditure.' That was true, but it was only a small step in the right direction. One indication of this was that out of 56 reports published in those first four years, only five were debated on the floor of the House. Furthermore, only a small minority of the reports concentrated on the financial aspect of Government programmes, and that was the Committee's chief failure. The reasons for this failure deserve analysis.

The number of MPs that made up the Expenditure Committee was smaller than its sponsor, the Procedure Committee, had recommended. Its enquiries, therefore, could not penetrate areas in which other House of Commons Select Committees specialised (for example, the Select Committee on Nationalised Industries). It therefore lacked comprehensive authority. That was not the fault of its members: it was the fault of

Government for not giving it a wider remit, and the fault of the House of Commons for not insisting that the Procedure Committee's report be fully implemented.

But its lack of success was, I believe, largely the fault of its members. The sub-committees that were established (Defence and External Affairs, Trade and Industry, Environment, Education, Arts and Home Office, Social Services and Employment, and a General sub-committee) mainly operated as the former Select Committee on Estimates used to do, that is to say they usually chose to examine particular subjects within their allotted areas of public expenditure rather than scrutinise and compare the figures of projected expenditures for five years ahead contained in the White Paper. In other words, my colleagues preferred the publicity and excitement that came from discussing a single subject of topical interest rather than the duller chore of careful, long-term financial analysis. There was no machinery for imposing a discipline on the sub-committees or for co-ordinating their work. Furthermore, the seven sub-committees were staffed only by seven clerks of the House of Commons (although some of the sub-committees appointed specialist advisers from time to time). Thus the Expenditure Committee lacked the back-up to do its job thoroughly and to realise its full potential. Once again, Government seemed determined to keep the blinds drawn down upon any shaft of daylight which might illuminate its activities. It genuflects before the altar of democracy but rarely takes a man-sized step towards it unless it is pushed. Experience showed that the Expenditure Committee – which had been designed by Government, not the Commons – lacked the teeth, the authority and the resources to do a proper job.

The October 1970 Green Paper had concluded with a familiar sentiment which exactly illustrates Government's invariably ambivalent attitude in these matters:

> Any system of Select Committees must make additional work for Ministers, the Departments, and, of course, for Select Committee members themselves. It increases the pressure on the Parliamentary timetable and risk of controversy over the proper limits to the confidentiality of the decision-making process. But this is the inevitable price to be paid for the significant strengthening of the Parliamentary system to which the proposals in this paper are addressed.

My interest had now been aroused and I decided to specialise in the subject. In April 1974, with the Conservatives in Opposition, I was appointed to the All-Party Select Committee on Public Accounts and its members elected me Chairman.

This Select Committee was established by Gladstone in 1861. The doctrine of Parliamentary accountability is based on the principle that Parliament grants 'supply' (i.e. money) to the Crown and then holds Her Majesty's Ministers accountable for the way it is spent. The purpose of the Public Accounts Committee is to do just that, to investigate the way in which money has been spent. The process begins with the presentation to Parliament of annually audited accounts, more than 570 of them. They range from the accounts of all Government departments to the accounts of a wide range of statutory Boards and Authorities. The audits are carried out by the Exchequer and Audit Departments (now called the National Audit Office), about 600 strong at the time that I became Chairman of the Public Accounts Committee, headed by the Comptroller and Auditor General (the C & AG for short).

The C & AG also examines the accounts of the Inland Revenue, and of Customs and Excise. His responsibilities do not include the local authorities or the nationalised industries and there are divers businesses and organisations in the private sector which receive public money but which are not within the scope of his remit and his audit; nonetheless, he has the right to inspect the books of around 4,000 such bodies.

When each audit is complete the C & AG writes a report and publishes it to Parliament. It is then that Parliament's All-Party Select Committee on Public Accounts (the PAC) comes into operation. The PAC has 15 members of all political parties. Its membership is a microcosm of the House of Commons. The Chairman is invariably a prominent member of the Opposition of the day, usually an ex-Treasury-Minister. By tradition, the Financial Secretary to the Treasury, a junior Minister in the Government, is a member of the Committee; but, by tradition also, he attends only the first meeting of the PAC in each Parliamentary session. The Committee's main function has always been to ensure that public money is spent as Parliament intended. It also looks for the exercise of due economy and the maintenance of high standards of public morality in all financial matters. It questions the Accounting Officers of Government departments about the reports written by the C & AG and seeks explanations for difficulties, anomalies, extravagances or wastage. At the end of each examination the Committee publishes its reports to Parliament.

The Committee has continuously emphasised the importance of high standards of conduct in financial matters, and for the honest handling of public money. The Comptroller and Auditor General, too, has commented on the need to combine private sector disciplines with public sector values. If there are strengths which amount to the effectiveness of the Public Accounts Committee they are, first, that it starts its enquiries from a firm base of facts agreed with the Accounting Officer of a Government department before he is questioned orally. The Committee does not have to spend time establishing the necessary factual foundation, but makes its enquiries with a clear idea of the areas in which there are potential weaknesses to be probed or matters on which the Committee ought to be more closely informed. Second, the members of the Committee work as a team, whatever their Party. Their common purpose is to improve the quality of administration, and there is almost no Party-political conflict within the Committee that might limit its effectiveness. Its recommendations, which are invariably unanimous, have so much the more impact. Third, the Committee's comments and recommendations are normally backed up by public opinion, and they make sense to the Treasury and Government departments. They cannot therefore be ignored.

The PAC has disclosed many hundreds of examples of folly or incompetence in the use of taxpayers' money by various Government departments, maladministration of programmes and the like. A few will suffice, from a single year's crop.

Item – The 1958 estimate for expenditure on the Driver & Vehicle Licensing Centre in Swansea was for an expenditure of £146 million. The actual cost was some £350 million, and it was thought that the number of staff employed would rise to 8,000, an increase of 50 per cent. The project was five years late, and the larger staff dealt with a smaller number of vehicles than expected. (The total cost, incidentally, would have built 1,600 new primary schools.)

Item – The cost of building a new hospital in Liverpool escalated from £14 million to over £40 million. I led the members of the Public Accounts Committee to Liverpool to conduct an on-the-spot enquiry, the first time the Public Accounts Committee had ever held an examination session outside the precincts of Parliament. (How many other new hospitals could have been built – or kidney machines afforded out of that extra £26 million?)

Item – In the days when the Inchinnan Bridge over the River Cart in Scotland was looked after by the Local Authority it took one man to open it and care for it generally. That responsibility was taken over by the Scottish Development Department: six men were now needed, working full time, to look after the bridge at a cost of £18,000 a year. During each year it was opened only once or twice. The total revenue gained in the years under enquiry was 80p including VAT.

Item – VAT was first introduced in the United Kingdom in 1973. The tax losses of the Customs and Excise Department in its first full year of control measures, 1974/75, were between £35 and £40 million.

I have taken these four examples from the speech I made in the House of Commons on 22 January 1976 introducing the reports of the Public Accounts Committee for the previous session. In the course of the debate I complained that Government expenditure was hardly under effective control and that the Commons had been less than competent in fulfilling its primary duty, control of the Executive through control of the purse. My concern, and the remedies I proposed, fell on deaf ears. The House was almost empty.

I do not recall learning that any civil servant was ever demoted or dismissed for incompetence as a result of the failings the PAC revealed, but I believe that the publication of its critical reports to Parliament, supported by the evidence of careful research, did sometimes lead to improvements in departmental procedures and the avoidance of similar mistakes in future. However, I was clear that we could and should do more, and I made my point, repeatedly, inside and outside the House of Commons, especially on television. I wrote a pamphlet *Parliament and the Purse Strings* which became a best seller. I was also lucky enough to be successful in a ballot for Private Members' Motions (the only time in all my years in Parliament) and I initiated a debate in the House on 15 May 1978.

Its terms were as follows:

That this House notes with concern that the degree of Parliamentary control over the Executive has diminished and is diminishing; believes the opportunities for regular supervision of the actions of the Executive by Parliament are inadequate in the modern context; is concerned with the implications for the Constitution and ultimately for the efficient operation of the democratic process in the United Kingdom; and is of the opinion that Parliament's powers of supervision and control now need to be strengthened and improved.

Shades of 1780. First to speak in the debate after me was Ian Mikardo, the left-wing Labour MP and former Chairman of the Parliamentary Labour Party. He spoke strongly in my support. His speech, like others made by Labour MPs in the debate, seemed to me exactly to illustrate my point that whatever the extent of the State's influence it is the business of every politician, irrespective of his party's usual prejudices, to ensure that it is brought under effective scrutiny.

It was clear to me that as a first step we must sharpen up and make more effective the machinery we already had. As Chairman of the PAC I was in a good position to influence this and I set out, with the Committee's steady approval, to achieve three objectives. The first was to ensure that the Committee continued to be 'influential' – the complimentary epithet usually applied to it by the press. The greater the publicity received by its reports, the more chance there would be to ensure that their lessons were learned in Government.

In the Parliamentary session of 1977/78 I persuaded the Committee to admit the public to those sessions where evidence was being taken on subjects not expected to raise issues of national security or commercial confidentiality. The Committee was by no means unanimous but my view prevailed. It seems extraordinary that until then the Public Accounts Committee had met in private for 116 years.

The Press and the television newscasters responded readily. The Public Accounts Committee's reports began to receive wider coverage and the Committee's influence increased accordingly. The threat of publicity was a powerful ally to us in our work. However, the Committee's attitude was consistently responsible. It was never pompously wise after the event. It did its honest best to examine matters in the light of circumstances as they existed at the time. It was invariably sympathetic to experiments. It never dwelt upon what had gone wrong in the past, but sought to draw instructive lessons from experience.

I thought that if the work of the Exchequer and Audit Department and the Public Accounts Committee were understood and appreciated by a wider audience it might be possible to raise their status, and thereby to improve accounting standards generally in the public service, my second objective. It may seem astonishing, but at that time one did not need a professional qualification to serve in the Exchequer and Audit Department. Exchequer and Audit staff were given a full professional internal training but since the mid-1970s the department has moved over to an all-graduate intake coupled with a training for a professional qualification. The statistics show this clearly. In 1965 only 4 out of the 345 staff in the professional audit grades were qualified accountants. By 1995 this had risen to 417 out of a total audit staff of 575. Since 1992 graduate entrants have undertaken the Institute of Chartered Accountants (ICAEW) training. I have been delighted at this success.

My third objective was to develop the scope of the Exchequer and Audit Department's work. Hitherto, audit had been a largely mathematical process, checking that a balance was struck between opposite sides of the ledger. Yet, I reasoned, the scope of audit should surely be wider. When Gladstone created the Department in 1866 it was appropriate that attention should be concentrated on a few questions only – basically, had money been properly spent on those purposes for which Parliament had voted the supply? Basic considerations were still important, but in the modern world there were additional questions to be asked.

The auditor of any substantial commercial organisation has a divided responsibility. His first job is to verify the corporation's own financial work, and in that he is the servant of the corporation. But in 1948 the new Companies Act gave the auditor an added responsibility, to judge the company's accounts for propriety and responsibility. Successive Companies Acts and the pressure of professional opinion have reinforced that duty.

Should not the public sector audit take a leaf out of the private sector's book? Why not introduce judgement into the State audit? If the status and influence of the Exchequer and Audit Department were rising (as they undoubtedly were) and if the quality of the personnel in that department was improving (as it was) why not arrange for it, on suitable occasions, to begin to judge the effectiveness of departmental programmes, to evaluate their worth? There would need to be rules, of course, and in particular the auditor should not question the political decisions which led to the adoption of particular policies. The Public Accounts Committee operated in a strictly non-political atmosphere and if it ceased to do so it would lose its impartiality and therefore much of its effectiveness. However, it would greatly help Parliament properly to consider the activities of Government if a dispassionate assessment of their effectiveness were routinely available, based on what the present C & AG has properly defined as 'sympathetic objectivity'.

'Value for money' would be a practical and constructive concept to introduce into Parliamentary discussion and debate. Here is one example of what this means in practical terms, quoted by the present C & AG in a brilliant lecture given at the University of Southampton. The NAO, in examining the management of assets in the NHS, surveyed the use of operating theatres. It found in 1987 that in spite of long waiting lists for operations, daytime utilisation in some cases was only 50 or 60 per cent. The NAO analysed the causes, and action was taken. In 1991 the NAO found that utilisation had risen to 90 per cent. In such instances a value-for-money audit has been hugely effective in thoroughly practical ways, although when we first introduced it the concept was novel and not universally popular.

In 1979, when the Conservatives had won the general election, it became the turn of the Opposition to provide the Chairman of the Public Accounts Committee. I was succeeded by the Labour MP Joel Barnett, a former Chief Secretary to the Treasury. His views and mine seemed to coincide exactly.

The Conservative manifesto (which I had a hand in writing) had contained the sentence: 'We will see that Parliament and no other body stands at the centre of the nation's life and decisions, and we will seek to make it effective in its job of controlling the Executive.' Looking back over that period it is difficult to avoid the conclusion that in reality the new Conservative Government was not interested in ensuring that Parliament could do any such thing. As Prime Minister Margaret Thatcher was personally involved in a number of initiatives, to make economies and to promote efficiency, but it appears to most observers that such initiatives were successful only to the extent that they kept her image bright. Economy is not a popular exercise. No attempt to impose it (including the scrutiny of functions inside the Civil Service initiated by Lord Rayner) has had more than a limited success. Nor did Conservative Ministers show any sign of wanting to tighten up Parliament's control of their actions.

One honourable exception to this rule was Norman St John Stevas. On being appointed Leader of the House, he acted promptly to fulfil the election manifesto's pledge. The proposal that he put to House on 25 June had first to be carried through the Cabinet, which cannot have been an easy task. He proposed – and note that these were Government proposals, not proposals made by the Commons – that twelve select committees, each covering a main Government departments, including the Treasury and Civil Service, be appointed 'to examine the expenditure administration and policy of the principal Government departments . . . and associated public bodies . . .'

During the debate St John Stevas amplified his proposal:

Each Committee will be able to examine the whole range of activity for
which its Minister or Ministers have direct responsibility [and] the

183

activities of some public bodies that exercise authority of their own and over which Ministers do not have the same direct authority as they have over their own departments.

The new departmentally-related Select Committees were to be given wide powers 'to send for persons and papers' as the Parliamentary phrase has it, in other words to interview whatever witnesses they saw fit to invite and to call for such written evidence as they needed. The Motion also proposed arrangements whereby the Committees could employ staff and hire specialist advisers.

The Government Chief Whip, Michael Jopling, was an enthusiast for procedural reform and he and I worked hard to get the organisation right. The House agreed to the new proposals and the committees were established. Since then some changes have been made following restructuring of Government departments. There are now 16 departmentally-related Select Committees with a membership of 176 MPs, a substantial proportion of the whole House.

The Chairmanships of the Select Committees were allocated between the major political parties by agreement. In early 1980 they started work. I was elected Chairman of the Treasury and Civil Service Affairs Select Committee which had one Liberal MP, four Labour MPs and six Conservatives as its members. They worked hard and the attendance record was almost 100 per cent at every meeting. The cost of servicing each committee turned out to be small. Staffing, printing, even overseas visits, averaged only some £20,000 per committee per year in those early years.

I think I can fairly claim that the Treasury Committee became increasingly authoritative and influential. I was shocked when I received an invitation from Geoffrey Howe, Chancellor of the Exchequer, to meet and discuss working together. I refused it. I am sure it was meant constructively but I regarded the Committee's independence and integrity as paramount. We had to be free to criticise the Government's management of the economy, secure in the knowledge that loyalty to Parliament and to the electorate was more important than loyalty to the Party.

The forces of reaction were not slow to mobilise. I found myself under increasing criticism as Chairman, and retiring members of the Treasury Committee were replaced by others known to be less dispassionate in their view of Government economic policy. I found these manifestations of official displeasure a welcome confirmation that the

Committee's work was effective.

A Liaison Committee of all Select Committee Chairmen was set up, which acted as a co-ordinator, a forum for ventilation of points of concern and an arbiter of methods and procedures. I was elected its Chairman. In December 1982 it published a report to Parliament summarising the first three years' work by the new departmentally-related Select Committees. It chronicled 1,700 meetings of the Committees in this period and the publication of 170 reports. It was commonly said at the time that the new Select Committees had introduced a new dimension into Parliament's work; that a start had been made on tilting the balance of authority back to the legislature and away from the Executive; that as a result of their reports Parliament is better informed and so is the public. There were other, less obvious advantages. For virtually the first time in modern history senior civil servants were given a platform from which to discuss administration and policy; and a new career structure, away from the Party strangleholds, was opened for backbench MPs. Also, the backbencher was given a chance to learn more about the machinery of Government and the decision-making process, and to become involved in it at an earlier stage. He was given an opportunity to question Ministers vastly greater than either debates or question time had ever afforded him. These are all most significant advances.

Few debates in the House took place exclusively on the reports of Select Committees, and some reports were never designed for specific debate. Even so, there have been a number of particular successes (for instance, a report by the Home Affairs Committee on the so-called 'Sus' laws led to their prompt repeal) and there is a multitude of examples to show that as a result of the new Select Committees, Parliamentary debates have become better informed. It is now commonplace for Members to refer in their speeches to facts or conclusions contained in relevant reports.

Another good effect has been to show the public an aspect of Parliament which is far more important than partisan jousting at question time. Most of an MP's constructive work is hidden away, and I was glad when, after a long struggle, Committee sessions began to be broadcast on radio and television, and people could hear and see some of that real work being done.

As Chairman of the Liaison Committee I set myself to focus the attention of my Parliamentary colleagues on the financial aspects of our work. All questions of policy must also involve questions of expenditure, but it seemed to me that until the Select Committees appreciated that

185

control of finance was crucial to influence over policy they would never realise their full authority. We did undoubtedly make some progress. We got agreement that Government would allocate time for three debates each year on specific estimates to be selected by the Liaison Committee. The first debates under this new arrangement took place early in 1983, and the system continues. That backbench MPs choose the subjects for debate is a great advance, a small break in Government's stranglehold over the conduct of Parliamentary business; but these occasions do not yet succeed as they should. Ministers are now obliged to come before Select Committees to justify their policies: so far so good. For a departmentally-related Select Committee to have the opportunity to call a Minister to account before the whole House of Commons in the Chamber is an immense step forward. The trouble is that these special debates are still largely regarded as of interest only to specialists. It is vital that my former backbench colleagues demonstrate how seriously they regard this process. If a Minister at the dispatch box does not convince them of the correctness of his argument they should refuse to vote the necessary finance for the policy under discussion. MPs have the power: they should use it.

In the first of those new debates in March 1983 I put it this way:

> The control of Government is at the heart of Parliament. At the heart of Government is the correct handling of our country's finances . . . We all know the complicated and stately dance through which we go every year, which is designed to see that our constituents' money is not wasted. We also all know that for many decades, this process has been largely unproductive – a charade of concern with nothing much to show for it.

It will not be easy to change matters. Party disciplines are enormously strong and the divisions between parties in the House of Commons are deep crevasses, hard to bridge. It will never be easy to persuade backbench MPs on the Government side to abandon their party loyalties in favour of a patriotic adventure which, if the vote is carried against the Government, must discredit their party. Yet the principle is fundamental: the first duty of MPs is to scrutinise the actions of the Executive. The failure to uphold that principle will render Parliament's proceedings largely meaningless.

In 1981, the year after he had inaugurated the departmentally related Select Committees, Norman St John Stevas was dismissed from the

Government led by the blessed Margaret (as he called her). This gave him the chance to perform a second service to the cause of Parliamentary Reform, this time from the back benches. In November 1982 he won second place in the annual ballot for private Members Bills. I sought him out at once and suggested that he adopt a measure that would complement the work he had done as Leader of the House earlier in the 1979 Parliament, namely to reform the Exchequer and Audit Departments by implementing recommendations made by the Public Accounts Committee. He agreed immediately, and took this measure through Parliament with skill and efficiency. I was his principal, though not his only supporter. We had the powerful backing of the PAC and its Chairman Joel Barnett. A tower of strength was the then C & AG, Sir Gordon Downey, leading the other members of the department. The Government, at first, was suspicious of the Bill and several Ministers were openly hostile to it. Sir Gordon must also have met some opposition from senior civil servants but he never wavered in his support.

St John Stevas explained the purposes of the Bill clearly:

> The first [objective] is to establish that the appointment of the Comptroller and Auditor General should be made by Her Majesty on behalf of the House, and not of the Government . . .
>
> Secondly, the Bill recognises the principle that Parliament has the right to follow public money wherever it goes . . .
>
> Thirdly, the Bill would set up a National Audit Office and bring Parliamentary and other arrangements for audit up to date.

The proposal that public money should be followed 'wherever it goes' at once aroused powerful opposition from vested interests. The CBI objected. Several Chairmen of nationalised industries complained strongly that interference with their right to manage their businesses would be intolerable. There was loud talk of resignations. Even Lord King, the head of British Airways, who should have known better, thundered his objections. Sundry Ministers supported them, as did a number of backbench MPs, obviously briefed by them. This was powerful opposition but we were not put off. We got a closure of the debate on the Bill by 111 votes to nil and an unopposed second reading thereafter.

I regarded the attitude of those in the nationalised industries and elsewhere who opposed us as one of foolish impertinence. Their arguments were not new, of course, but it has never been clear why the nationalised industries in Britain should be exempt from the sort of scrutiny that in most other countries is regarded as normal, in France for example. There was no wish on our part to interfere with the freedom of managers to manage.

The controversy reminded me of the arguments a dozen years previously when the Public Accounts Committee had fought for and won the right to strengthen Parliamentary control over the £200 million block grants given each year to British universities. The PAC wanted to be satisfied that the money was being spent with due regard to efficiency and economy, but education circles complained that detailed accountability to Parliament would interfere with their academic freedom. They started a fearful rumpus. In 1967, the Government accepted the recommendation that the C & AG should inspect the books and records of the universities. This arrangement has worked perfectly satisfactorily, has achieved some measure of efficiency and economy, and the issue of interference with academic freedom has never arisen.

The Government, in view of the quality of the support for Stevas' bill, decided not to oppose it directly, but a number of Ministers did their best to block us by talking it down privately. At the committee stage all the Bill's original clauses were deleted and replaced with clauses drafted by the Government. Inevitably, the scope of the Bill was more limited than we wished. We had some success in defeating our opponents, voting down a proposal to include a Treasury Minister as a Member of the new House of Commons Commission, but we failed to carry the Committee with us in our aim to 'follow public money wherever it goes'. We had worked out a compromise with the Treasury and the nationalised industries to provide for annual audits of economy and effectiveness to be carried out under the auspices of the PAC and the departmental select committees by commercial firms of auditors. This was second best to scrutiny by the C & AG who would clearly have been acting on Parliament's behalf; but in any case the new clause which would have given effect to these proposals was lost on its second reading debate by 10 votes to 7 at the end of April: an unholy alliance of Labour, Liberals and one Conservative MP defeated us. The nationalised industries, I reflected, were a powerful lobby.

On the positive side, the concept of value for money was written into the Bill. The C & AG was given specific responsibility for undertaking value-for-money audits defined in terms of the economy, efficiency and effectiveness with which Government programmes were implemented. This was a large gain.

It was a hard battle to effect so modest a reform. We even had to fight those from whom we had every reason to expect support, and we had to compromise or risk losing the whole Bill, because time was running out.

On 9 May 1983 the Prime Minister announced the forthcoming general election. Now there could not possibly be time for the Bill to complete all its final stages in the Commons, and it had not yet been debated in the Lords. However, Stevas and I used what influence we had behind the scenes. The Government Chief Whip, Michael Jopling, and the Opposition Chief Whip, Michael Cocks, were both helpful. It would have been too bad to have lost the Bill after all the progress we had made. We were lucky to achieve Report and Third Reading in the Commons without debate of any kind, and without objection; and the Bill passed all its stages in the Lords 'on the nod', that is without a single word being spoken. It is now the National Audit Act.

Progress continued. Early in the new Parliament of 1983, as laid down in the National Audit Act, a new All-Party Public Accounts Commission was established to oversee the development of the National Audit Office. I was elected Chairman. We set to work with a will in co-operation with the PAC to do our best to help the National Audit Office operate effectively. We appointed accountants from the private sector to audit its accounts. We made provision to enable it to secure sensible accommodation in London. (It had been operating from no less than twenty-seven offices in London alone. The inconvenience and extra cost of operation which this unnecessary dispersal involved can only be guessed at. We brought all its groups together in a single building.) Salaries had lagged well behind the private sector in the accountancy field and staff losses accelerated as a result. We took action – which was resisted by the Treasury – to put this right, and the NAO was a pioneer in the introduction of performance-related pay in the public sector.

The NAO is big business. Every year its 750 staff audit the accounts of some 750 Government departments, agencies and other public bodies which collect and spend £450 billion annually. Every year it publishes around 50 reports on the results of its value-for-money investigations. It certifies to Parliament that public money is spent on the purposes for which it was voted; it checks and strengthens financial controls in the public sector; it helps departments and other public bodies improve their management and cost-effectiveness. It is not a tiresome critic armed with hindsight: it is a constructive friend of efficiency. In 1992 it recommended more than 200 significant changes in systems and controls and a similar number of changes in the use of public resources – at a total annual saving of a quarter of a billion pounds.

It also has an international role, auditing 50 accounts for 11 major international clients, including part of the UN, some of its specialised agencies and Commonwealth organisations. The NAO earns some £5 million annually from these activities, bringing its net operating cost down to £37 million.

What is sauce for the goose is sauce for the gander. Each year the C & AG must convince the Commons that he is value for money. Since the demonstrable savings from his studies amount to hundreds of millions of pounds, that is normally not difficult.

We can be proud that Britain was the first country to introduce a national auditor, and the modern National Audit Office is a credit to the public sector. I believe that in years to come the introduction of structured programmes of value-for-money audits in the 1970s and the passage of the National Audit Act of 1983 will rank as significant milestones in the history of public financial accountability. Even so, the process of reform is far from complete. The proper ambition 'to follow public money wherever it goes' remains unrealised. Many bodies receive huge subventions from public funds but escape the authority of the National Audit Office. Housing associations annually receive some £1.8 billion. Similar huge sums go to some 280 non-departmental public bodies such as the spendthrift Legal Aid Board. There is a vast area where Parliament votes the cash but has abdicated the right to survey how it is spent. In recent years significant changes have taken place in the way in which Government services and programmes are delivered. Government departments have devolved many of their responsibilities to a wide range of bodies including Executive Agencies, Executive Non-departmental Public Bodies and other organisations such as Housing Associations and Training and Enterprise Councils. Also, private sector contracts are handling an increasing share of the mainstream functions of departments under the Government's 'Competing for Quality' initiative. These new arrangements are revolutionary: they will unquestionably lead to greater efficiency and effectiveness in the provision of public services in Britain, for which Government deserves full credit.

There is, however, an important demerit in the situation. In order for the National Audit Office to fulfil its role to Parliament, it needs access to the records of those organisations which spend money voted by Parliament. Arrangements have been made to enable the NAO to audit or inspect the regularity, propriety and value for money of funds spent by the various bodies and organisations, but there are weaknesses. For

190

example, the Office does not audit all the financial accounts of the Executive Non-departmental Public Bodies, and cannot enforce a general right to inspect the relevant records of organisations or contractors carrying out government functions. Astonishingly, both the European Union's auditors and British local authorities' auditors enjoy a better access in this last respect than does the British Parliament's watchdog, the National Audit Office. The situation needs prompt reform.

The price of freedom, it is rightly said, is eternal vigilance. That is true. The scope for Parliamentary control and surveillance of expenditure also needs careful monitoring: given half a chance the apparatus of Government will curtail it, as it demonstrably has in this changed situation. Obviously, the legislation which governs the Comptroller and Auditor General's activities could not envisage the significant changes introduced in recent years. Contemporary MPs therefore have a duty to see that it is updated and present practices improved to give them, through the National Audit Office, better information and a greater degree of surveillance of public expenditure.

If we root out carelessness in expenditure, we can expect and demand efficiency in its place. Now that the queue for expenditure on deserving projects stretches from Lands End to John o' Groats, and when so many have to be refused for lack of funds, it might be regarded as a criminal offence to waste public money or to set wrong priorities for spending it.

I hope I can reasonably claim that in my time in the House of Commons I did my part in introducing more effective systems of financial control and supervision; the challenge, and the need, is for the present generation of MPs to use them effectively.

CHAPTER 9

THE 1922
COMMITTEE

The following is the job specification for a Member of Parliament, written seventy years ago. The italics are mine.

> Should this letter catch the eye of an honest, broad-minded imperialist, who is prepared to put his country before his Party and to pay his own expenses *[a nice mixture, you will discern, of the philosophical and the practical]* who would scorn to be a mere monkey-on-a-stick to the Central Office of the Conservative Party *[we can all agree about that]* i.e. who has the pluck to refuse merely to raise his hand in voting every time at the imperious dictation of the leaders of the Party in power without due regard to his own conscience or those who he represents *[dangerously radical sentiments these, any Chief Whip would think]* then let him hasten to the Lowestoft Division of Suffolk where an almost certain and safe seat is going 'begging' for the asking.

The advertisement appeared in the *Daily Mail* in 1922 and the successful applicant was a brilliant young man named Gervais Rentoul. He entered Parliament and in 1923 became the first Chairman of the newly formed 1992 Committee.

In 1922 there had been a turbulent dispute within the Conservative Party over whether it should remain in a coalition with Lloyd George's Liberals. In a by-election at Newport the coalition candidate had been soundly defeated by an anti-Lloyd-George Conservative. The Party MPs met in the Carlton Club the next day and, against the advice of most of the leadership, voted overwhelmingly by 137 votes to 87 to leave the coalition. Within hours the Government fell and in the ensuing general election the Tories won a handsome majority. Encouraged by this little history, the newly elected backbench Conservative Members decided that some form of assembly was needed in which they could regularly discuss Party affairs in private. The 1922 Committee was founded and named after the year whose events had brought it into being. The Committee's first secretary was Mr Reginald Clarry MP, the victor at that historic Newport by-election.

Fifty years later, in 1972, I was elected out of six candidates as the Committee's fourteenth Chairman. I held the post for twelve years and became the Committee's longest serving Chairman, and in that time it gave me an inside view of the Party and its leaders that I could not have got in any other way.

The word 'committee' is slightly misleading since it includes all the Party's backbench Members of Parliament. When the Party is in office, Ministers and the Chief Whip are excluded from membership; when the Party is in opposition only the Leader and the Chief Whip are excluded. (In my opinion it would be more sensible when the Party is in Government to include Junior Ministers, who can feel very isolated, and exclude all the Whips who, after all, are the Leadership's intelligence agents.)

The Committee meets every Thursday evening when the House of Commons is in session. Attendance varies from 50 to 250 members, according to the degree of interest in the business going through Parliament. There are also more than twenty satellite committees dealing with different subjects – agriculture, defence, European affairs and so on – and six regional committees, all of which report to the main Committee.

At the beginning of each Parliamentary year the Conservative MPs elect five Officers of the 1922 Committee, including the Chairman, and an Executive of twelve. Whatever the formal minutes of the Committee's proceedings may say, it is generally agreed that the largely unrecorded work of the Executive members has been the foundation of the Committee's success. They are trusted to convey the opinions of their fellow members directly to the Party's leaders, frankly and plainly.

There was an old scurrilous view, known as Walder's Law in memory of a colleague who died some years ago, that the first two or three Members who spoke at the general meetings of the 1922 Committee were invariably mad or drunk. I have never known the latter situation: I have probably experienced the former. However, the Committee does not suffer fools gladly and is unwilling to listen to interventions that are self-serving or unreasonable.

At the end of 1972 I was approached by a number of Conservative

MPs and asked if I would allow my name to go forward as a candidate for the Chairmanship. This was a complete surprise. I had hardly thought of myself as a pillar of the Tory establishment but those who approached me were quite clear what they wanted – someone who would stand up to the Prime Minister, Ted Heath, and ensure he was made aware of Party opinions. They felt that he was ignoring the views of his colleagues in the House. It was the Duke of Wellington who said 'Till I became First Lord of the Treasury I never had a dispute or difference with any body, excepting the scum of the earth.' Heath, my colleagues felt, might equally well have said it too. It was commonly believed that his four years as Chief Whip had given him a healthy contempt for his fellow Members of Parliament in the Conservative Party, while his successes in carrying legislation for the abolition of retail price maintenance though the Commons in the teeth of strong Party misgivings, and in ensuring British signature to the Treaty of Rome against many difficulties at home and abroad had given him a degree of over-confidence in his own abilities and judgement. The Conservative Party in the House of Commons was smouldering.

I was flattered, but refused to commit myself unless those who had approached me could assure me we had an excellent chance of winning an election. I had never courted popularity among my colleagues in the House and I could not be sure what the general reaction would be to my candidature. I privately felt there were others much better qualified for the position than me. On the other hand, not having been included by Heath in his administration, I longed to play a more important part in the senior counsels of our Party. The whole purpose of politics is the search for and use of power to further the views which one holds strongly. A backbencher's life is often frustrating; on occasions he can have some influence on his senior colleagues but its extent is strictly limited and the occasions are few. It is only when he comes together with other colleagues, formally or informally, that he has a real opportunity to influence policies and decisions.

Those who approached me were an attractive group of independent-minded men with disparate views on Party policy. Among them were Jeffrey Archer and Colonel Mitchell, known as 'Mad Mitchell', who had been in command of the Argyll and Sutherland Highlanders in Aden in 1967 and had achieved a reputation for firmness of character at that time. They and a number of others assured me that my chances of success in the Committee's election were good, and I agreed to be a candidate. Somewhat to my surprise I polled more votes than all my several competitors put together. One newspaper, after reminding its readers that Heath had not seen fit to include me in his Government, described my election as an 'elegant irony'.

For the first two years of my chairmanship our Party was in office and the 1922 Committee did quiet, useful work behind the scenes. Then came the general election of February 1974 and that was when the heat was turned on. The possibility of a general election had been discussed at two meetings of the 1922 Committee and the Party was divided about the wisdom of calling one almost eighteen months before the end of the Parliament. Overall, though, there was a groundswell of opinion in favour. There should be a swift election and the issue should be put clearly: who governs Britain, an elected Government or the trade union leadership? Many Tory strategists believed that this would take Labour by surprise and bring us a resounding success. But Heath hesitated. When eventually he called the election, after two or three weeks of public speculation, the element of surprise was lost.

This was the first general election for almost fifty years to be fought in a period of acute economic crisis. The National Union of Mineworkers had some time previously banned overtime working and later called a strike to back a 31 per cent pay claim. The Arab oil-producing States had reduced their production of oil and increased its price fourfold following the six-day war between Egypt, Syria and Israel. In December 1973 a state of emergency was introduced in Britain and on 1 January 1974 Britain began working a three-day week. So serious was the situation that petrol ration coupons were printed and issued, though they were never used.

The miners' strike was a clear challenge to the Government. Enoch Powell, never one to miss the limelight or a chance to discomfit Heath, said he would not stand again for his Wolverhampton seat in 'an essentially fraudulent election'. He was not the only critic: many people asked why the Government did not use its overall majority in the House of Commons and the remaining eighteen months of its term to take firm action and control a dangerous situation. Why have an election now? Why cut and run?

The 1922 Committee got the campaign off to a rousing start. My colleagues agreed that we hold a special meeting to which we invited all the Conservative Parliamentary candidates. We held it not in Committee Room 14 at the House of Commons but in a London hotel. We invited the Leader of our Party to address the meeting and I said a few words in introducing him. To my surprise the five hundred or more Tory candidates present warmly applauded what I had to say. Heath waited in his seat for the applause to continue: that was an act of generosity on his part which touched me. The meeting, the first of its kind in the Party's history, was a success in enabling the Leader to set the scene for the opening of the battle. We repeated the formula at subsequent general elections and later gave Margaret Thatcher the same launching pad that we had arranged for Heath.

As it proceeded, the campaign included a series of happenings which did the Conservative Party no good. The mercurial Enoch Powell recommended the electors to vote Labour. (I remembered the reservations I had felt about him when I first met him in 1950.) It turned out that the Government's figures about the relative pay position of miners compared with other workers were inaccurate. The Director General of the CBI attacked the Government's Trade Union legislation. Half the skill of conducting a successful election campaign is the avoidance of disasters.

Polling took place on 28 February 1974. There were 2,135 candidates for 635 seats, the highest number of candidates in any general election since the War. By comparison with the 1970 election, the number of Conservative MPs elected fell from 330 to 297; the Labour Party increased its number from 287 to 301 and the Liberals from 6 to 14. No party had an overall majority. Heath's gamble had failed. The miners' leadership boasted that they had brought down the Government, as in effect they had. Heath was out.

However, Heath did not immediately resign. Instead he began negotiations with Jeremy Thorpe, the leader of the Liberal Party, to whom he wrote setting out the basis for a possible coalition. He also telephoned me at my home in Somerset 'to ask your advice as Chairman of the 1922 Committee.' I told him two things: first that, as he must know, the Liberals in many parts of the UK and especially in the West Country were the *ancien ennemi* so how could we possible make an alliance with them?; second, that his attempt to cling on to office would be misunderstood in the country. In the event the Liberals refused the offer, demanding a Government of 'national unity'. So on the evening of 4 March, four days after polling day, Heath resigned and within two hours Harold Wilson entered 10 Downing Street as Prime Minister. 'I've got a job to do,' he said as he went in. The first job he actually did was to yield to the miners who had brought about the election and given him his chance of success. The day before the new Parliament was opened by the Queen on 11 March the miners went back to work, having accepted a pay increase of 29 per cent, only marginally below the figure sought. Their strike had been completely successful. A Conservative Prime Minister had been defeated, a lesson Mrs Thatcher no doubt pondered in her Finchley constituency, as we all did. Ten years later she would prove a tougher nut to crack.

In Taunton my majority actually rose from the 8,335 of the 1970 election to 8,440 because the Liberal candidate, who came third in the contest, trebled his vote largely at the expense of the Labour candidate. On the face of it I did well, but Labour and Liberal opponents together polled some 5,000 more votes than I did.

All of us who were Conservative candidates in the general election had learned at the doorstep (and Taunton was no exception) that the Prime Minister was not popular with the rank and file voter. Every one of us was told the same thing many times: 'I have nothing against the Conservative Party but I do not like Mr Heath.' I could remember nothing like this personal criticism of a Conservative leader at any of the eight previous elections I had engaged in.

Labour started from behind and was clearly unprepared, yet the Conservatives lost. It seemed to many of our candidates that the issues were not put powerfully and consistently to the electorate by our Party's leaders. The election was supposed to be fought on the issue of 'Who governs Britain?' but there was a clear lack of confidence at the top that a single issue could be sustained for the whole length of an election campaign and the attempt to do so was not made with conviction – which makes it doubly surprising that the leadership decided to call the election when it did.

These feelings were to fester among Conservative Members of Parliament and they were much discussed privately in the 1922 Committee. My colleagues were angry that our Party was no longer in Government. They felt that the election should not have been lost; many said openly that if the Government had held its nerve, remained in office and seen the crisis through, it would have emerged stronger and with a good chance of winning a general election later. (Those who had given advice at the time in favour of an earlier election – and they were numerous – conveniently forgot they had done so.)

Wilson's Government was in a precarious position without an overall majority. Before long, the battle would have to be fought out again in another general election. At first the Conservatives made no great challenge in the House of Commons, but in the last two months of the summer session Labour was defeated no less than 29 times. Both sides spent much time shaping up for the inevitable general election, publishing policy documents and so on. Parliament was eventually dissolved at the end of September 1974 with polling day fixed for 10 October. It was the first time for sixty years that there had been two general elections in a single year in Britain. The political futures of the Leaders of both the Labour and Conservative parties were obviously at stake.

The result of the election was to confirm Wilson in office. Labour's strength further increased from 301 to 319, the Liberals fell from 14 to 13, and the Conservatives from 297 to 277. Wilson thus now had converted his minority position into an overall majority of 3 over all parties and his lead over the Conservatives was greatly increased.

In the October election the unpopularity of Ted Heath with the electorate became even more marked than it had been in the previous February. My colleagues on the Conservative side returned to Westminster with the clear conviction that with a different leader we might have garnered many more votes, perhaps even have won the election. I personally think this was nonsense but nonetheless that was the strong impression held by an overwhelming majority of Conservative candidates. Furthermore, Heath had done very little to endear himself to members of our Party in the House of Commons. His manner was usually aloof. Although privately a sensitive and generous man, the view that his colleagues in the House had of him was as rather stingy and indifferent to others' views. He had little goodwill to fall back upon when the crisis came.

One particular occasion will serve as an example of this failing. The Officers and Executive Committee of the 1922 Committee had regular meetings with the Prime Minister several times a year. I did my best to ensure that they were harmonious but it was uphill work. Heath would not unbend. The Chief Whip, Humphrey Atkins, who was totally loyal to Heath, worried greatly about this, and he and I tried desperately to improve the situation. Before the first of the 1974 elections. We decided to arrange a meeting with Heath in specially congenial surroundings, so Atkins suggested to him that he invite the Officers and Executive of the 1922 Committee to have a talk over dinner at 10 Downing Street. Heath agreed, but the effort had been wasted. He was in a grumpy mood throughout. I had hoped that good reports of our meeting would have spread through the Parliamentary Party and rebounded to his credit: in the event, the opposite happened. Once again, as so often, I saw Heath lose the goodwill of Party workers. It was a process that in the end would cost him the Leadership of the Conservative Party.

On the day after that disastrous dinner, late in the evening, my wife and I came back by taxi to our house in Lord North Street. We were then living at Number 19, opposite our old home, Number 5, which had been bought by Harold Wilson, still at that time Leader of the Opposition. As we paid off the cab, he was on the doorstep of Number 5 saying goodnight to a visitor.

'Edward,' he said, 'both of you come on over and have a goodnight drink in your old home.'

So we did. We stayed for an hour or more, talking about politics and economics and especially about the situation in Rhodesia. Our old home didn't seem to have changed too much: certainly it still had a happy atmosphere. What an ironic contrast between the attitude of the two leaders, my wife and I remarked when eventually we got home: my political colleague, the leader of my Party, a grumpy and reluctant ally; my political enemy a cheerful friend.

It says much for the practice of democracy in our country that the Chairman of the Parliamentary Conservative Party can be on terms of friendship, if not intimacy, with both the leader of his own Party and the Leader of the Opposition. It is, thank Heaven, the same throughout public life in Britain (except where militants hold sway): political opponents may differ fundamentally over important matters but they can still respect each other. Long may that continue.

Wilson was always an enigma. He was profoundly distrusted by the Conservatives in Parliament, not least because of the company he kept. His repeated visits to Russia aroused suspicion. His liaison with Marcia, later to become Lady Falkender, who exercised immense influence behind the scenes, caused comment ad nauseam. His friendship with certain businessmen cast doubt on his judgement. Even so, I can only speak of the man as I found him. That was by no means the only occasion we spoke privately together. Twice, when Prime Minister, he called me into the Cabinet Room to seek my advice as Chairman of the Select Committee on Public Accounts upon methods by which expenditure might be better supervised in the European Community. Politically I would never have trusted him. Nonetheless I liked him and enjoyed his society.

With the second general election of 1974 lost, the Officers and Executive of the 1922 Committee had to arrange for the election of their successors in the new Parliament, and also the election of the officers of the subsidiary committees. In all more than a hundred positions had to be filled. In the days between a general election and the reassembly of

Parliament the House of Commons is closed to MPs, so we had arranged in advance for the Officers and Executive to meet in my house. After the Party's second defeat in a year, it was obvious to me that my colleagues would be less interested in talking about elections for the officers of Party committees than they would be in holding an inquest, and I was very much afraid that their attention would be mostly concentrated on criticism of the Leader. There was no shelving the meeting, it had been too long arranged, but when it started I seated everyone in a semi-circle in the sitting room and in such an order that if I went round the members in turn, I would be calling first on those most likely to be friendly to Ted Heath. I hoped to avoid a row. It was the only time I ever tried to rig the proceedings.

I deliberately began the meeting by talking about the committee elections and other matters in order to keep the temperature low. All that routine business was settled fairly quickly and I would have liked to end the meeting there, but. discussion of the general election could not be avoided. My colleagues were less concerned with the issues than with the doorstep criticism of Heath they had encountered for the second time within ten months. They were clear and unanimous in what they demanded: Heath should stand down as Leader as soon as possible.

Having heard them out I gave them my own opinion as forcefully as I could. I said that they would be most unwise to come to any final conclusion so soon after the general election; they should allow the heat of the campaign to die away and give time for mature reflection. The present mood might well be one of disappointment with the present Leader, but this could change during the coming months; whereas prompt public execution would discredit the Party. Heath had rendered long service; it would be unseemly to appear revengeful and ungrateful.

My colleagues would have none of it. I was instructed to see the Leader of the Party, the Chief Whip and the Chairman of the Party that day and to give them all the same message: in the unanimous opinion of the Officers and Executive of the 1922 Committee, Heath should resign at once. I again told them that while I would do as I was instructed their view was not mine and I thought they were making a mistake. The Committee still said that they expected me to deliver those messages and to meet them the following day to tell them what the reaction had been.

Looking out of the window of my house as the meeting broke up we could see that journalists and photographers had gathered outside. We agreed that none of us would talk to the press, except to say that we had been discussing matters of administrative concern and that our meeting had been prearranged and was purely routine in character. We would not under any circumstances discuss the subject of the leadership with third parties. However there was a problem: where should we meet the following day so that I could make my report? The House of Commons was still closed to us and it appeared that my own house was likely to be watched by the press. I therefore proposed that we should meet at the City office of Keysers, of which at that time I was Chairman, and I would make the boardroom available. This struck them all as an admirable idea. It would surely allow us to have our next talk together completely in private.

Meantime I did as I was told. I first saw the Chief Whip, Humphrey Atkins, and told him the unanimous view of the Officers and Executive of the 1922 Committee. He, to do him credit, thought of nothing but his natural loyalty to the Leader of the Party. He wanted to argue the matter with me but of course that was not possible. He was upset at the news but I dare say he was not surprised.

I then went to see Heath. He was not alone. I reported to him the discussion at the 1922 meeting exactly as it had occurred.

'Don't they realise what they are doing to our Party?' he asked. I said I was quite sure that none of my colleagues wanted to make life difficult for our Party but he should appreciate that he had now been Leader for ten years. That was a fair stretch of time. It was not unreasonable that Conservative Members of Parliament should wish to review the position after the loss of two successive general elections and decide whether or not they wanted to elect a new Leader.

I then put to him an idea of my own. The new method for electing the Leader of the Conservative Party, approved by the 1922 Committee in Alec Douglas Home's time, had one important omission. The rules did not provide for a challenge to be made to an existing Leader. The moment of the Leader's retirement was left entirely to his own discretion and nobody could force an election before he decided to go. That omission was deliberate. It had always been thought that it was unlikely that the Conservative Party would have an insensitive Leader. Those of us who put the rules together were judging Sir Alec's successors in advance by his high standards. I therefore suggested to Heath that, in order to gain time, the sensible thing would be for him to announce that he would re-establish the committee which had devised the original election procedure and get its members to introduce a new proposal for an election to be held if required as a matter of routine at the beginning of each new Parliament.

Heath promised to think this over. I told him that I thought that the time gained would give him an opportunity to rally support. He was in no way convinced. However, my colleagues' message had been faithfully delivered and I thought that in making my proposal I had hit on a way of giving the existing Leader the best chance of success in the election that was bound to follow.

I saw the Chairman of the Party, William Whitelaw, at dinner in my house. He spent a little time telling me that he thought I had been badly treated by the Party in the past, but it was not the purpose of the dinner to talk about me; it was to talk about the Leadership, and again I delivered my message. He was unsurprised.

I found it all very disagreeable but it had to be done and it was done. As the Duke of Wellington used to say, it is the best practice to do the business of the day in the day. It was all done in half a day.

The next day the Officers and Executive of the 1922 Committee met at my City offices in Milk Street as planned. None of them had any difficulty and their entry into the building was unobserved. Sitting round the boardroom table I reported my conversations and in particular I told the meeting about the suggestion I had made to Ted Heath. The Executive endorsed the proposal and instructed me to write a letter to Heath saying so and confirming our original view that he should step down.

It was when we came to leave the Keyser's offices that we had difficulties. Representatives of the *Daily Express* and the *Evening Standard* had turned up with photographers and were waiting for us at the front entrance. It later appeared that one of the Officers of the 1922 Committee had mentioned the meeting to his wife who had been acting as Heath's personal assistant during the general election. She was a great enthusiast for Heath personally and wanted to help him. She told him that the 1922 Executive was having a further meeting and said where it was to take place. There was no reason, I suppose, why she should not have done so, but as it happened it was a fearful indiscretion. The conversation was overheard by a member of Heath's staff, a press liaison man employed by Conservative Central Office. He promptly telephoned the *Daily Express* or the *Evening Standard* or both, no doubt in an attempt to discredit the 1922 Executive.

We all left the Keyser's premises as best we could but the damage was done. A piece appeared in the afternoon editions of the *Evening Standard* and was given considerable prominence. The Officers and Executive of the 1922 Committee were referred to as the 'Milk Street

Mafia'. After consulting my colleagues I immediately issued a writ for libel against the *Evening Standard* in order to stop the further use of that damaging and insulting phrase. The story had appeared under the name of Robert Carvel, the paper's respected Lobby Correspondent. I made it clear to him privately that nothing personal was intended and exactly what my intentions were. He understood the point.

It was clear that henceforward there would be a determined attempt to discredit the Officers and Executive of the 1922 Committee. A battle was on. Further mischievous pieces appeared in the newspapers. There was an article in the *Sunday Telegraph* which was unpleasant about me personally. It was a surprising newspaper, one might think, to mount a personal attack. A friend of mine later questioned the author. He replied that he was merely repaying a debt; in other words, he had had information in the past from the Heath camp which he had found useful and he was doing them a favour in turn. No wonder the general public is cynical about much that they read in the papers.

It was an unpleasant time. I do not suggest that Heath was involved directly but some of his supporters were in the business right up to their dirty necks and I cannot believe that he was unaware of this; after all, he read the newspapers daily as we all did. He could easily have stopped the campaign to denigrate the Parliamentary Party's elected representatives and their Chairman in particular – as easily as Attlee stopped the Labour Party's warmongering attack in Walthamstow in 1951. The campaign did not succeed, of course; in fact it had precisely the opposite effect. Conservative Members of Parliament are sophisticated politicians. They knew what was happening and they disliked it. When the elections for the 1922 Committee took place in November every member of the old Executive and all the previous officers were elected unopposed.

After Parliament reassembled there was a crowded meeting of the 1922 Committee. I shall not forget the prolonged applause that greeted the announcement made by the Chief Whip that I had been re-elected Chairman unopposed. It lasted from the moment of the announcement while I walked through that large room, the largest committee room in the Palace of Westminster, to my place in the Chair under the tapestry showing the English fleet off the West country coastline forming up to repel the Spanish Armada.

So the battle was won and Heath accepted my advice. The rules of the election process were rewritten so that there would be an opportunity to hold an election for the Leadership of the Party immediately after every general election. This process of rewriting the rules did not take very long, and then the Leadership election campaign began.

It was clear that Heath would be a candidate. To my astonishment he asked me to join his Shadow Cabinet. Whether this was because he felt that I genuinely had something to contribute or whether he sought to neutralise me, I have no idea. It was in any case an offer I could not possibly accept. I was the umpire in the contest to come. When the new procedures for the election of the Leader of the Conservative Party were adopted I would have the responsibility for supervising the process as Chairman of the 1922 Committee.

After consultation with Heath and others I announced that nominations would close on 30 January and the election would be held on 4 February. Heath had a full three months to consolidate his position, but he did not use the time well and those who tried to help him again achieved results opposite to those they sought.

The next meeting of the 1922 Committee after the election of the Officers and Executive was attended by a large number of backbench MPs and the future of the Leader was immediately raised. Kenneth Lewis, MP for Rutland and Stamford, spoke a telling phrase describing the position of Leader of the Conservative Party as a leasehold, not a freehold. It suited the mood of the meeting exactly. Inevitably the discussion was reported in the next day's newspapers, the general tone of it unfriendly to Ted Heath.

Most of the following Sunday's newspapers then carried a story, obviously inspired by the Heath camp, that I had selected to speak at the meeting only those Members I knew to be opposed to Heath. This was a travesty of what actually occurred, as some 210 Conservative MPs present at the meeting could testify. I had held firmly to my habitual custom of calling Members to speak in the strict order in which they caught my eye. The attempt to discredit me failed with the Parliamentary Party, of course, but what did the non-Parliamentary members of the Party think? I was not left in doubt for long. My telephone rang with repeated calls from senior Conservatives in the constituencies critical of the clumsy attempts by Heath's supporters to influence opinion. Once again his supporters' intrigues had backfired.

I was embarrassed to find my own name mentioned as a possible candidate for the Leadership. I did nothing whatever to encourage this, but just before Christmas I received a formal letter signed by fifteen Conservative MPs. It read as follows:

Now that the procedure for electing a new leader has been devised, we feel that it is not only important that there should be an election fairly soon, but that the Party should have the opportunity of choosing from those best able to shoulder this burden.

For some time it has been increasingly obvious to a number of us that you have the qualities which are required in a new leader: your warmth, your ability to present our case forcefully and sympathetically, your skill as chairman and, above all, the affection in which you are held by your colleagues, make it essential, as we see it, that you should offer yourself for the leadership of our Party. Indeed, we consider it is your duty to do so.

We know that it has not been your wish to stand for election, but during the space for reflection that the Christmas recess will bring, we ask you to consider your position and what we have said, and we earnestly hope that you will feel able to allow your name to go forward on the first ballot when nominations are made.

It was a generous letter, delivered to me by Nigel Fisher, the MP for Surbiton and distinguished author. The ad hoc group which had met and decided that it should be sent was twenty-five strong, almost exactly one-tenth of the strength of the Conservative Party in the House of Commons if Shadow Cabinet members were excluded. It was a strong power base from which to develop a campaign. In addition I was sought out by a number of other Conservative MPs who assured me of their support. Even if one discounted some of these personal assurances it was clear that a bandwagon was ready to roll. A number of Members told me privately that I would have an even better chance of success than I had had when I stood for election as Chairman of the 1922 Committee two years earlier, and I had won that contest convincingly enough. Having canvassed opinion widely, they also said they had no doubt that I would have a better chance of being elected than any other probable contender.

It is difficult even now, two decades later, to write about these events without feeling. There is no sweeter trust than the confidence of one's peers, openly expressed. I should have enjoyed being Leader. I do not believe I would have found it difficult to communicate with the Conservative Party generally or with the public through the media and I have always been wholly at home in the House of Commons. And if I had gone on to become Prime Minister I certainly would have known exactly what to do with power; that would have been the least of my problems. Nor, at the end, unlike more than one of my predecessors, would I have outstayed my welcome.

The pressures on me to stand were persistent. When I showed reluctance it was suggested that I stand for election on the understanding that if I were successful I would act as caretaker for one year only, thereby giving my colleagues more time to make a considered choice. I rejected the idea at once: a year of indecision would hardly improve our standing with the electorate. Also I had only just been re-elected as Chairman of the 1922 Committee and if I became a candidate for the leadership it would be suggested that I had engineered criticism of Heath in order to push my own chances.

Now there was a good deal of confusion among Conservative MPs. There seemed to be no obvious successor to Ted Heath. Sir Keith Joseph vacillated, then made a speech which put him in an unsympathetic light and his chance of success – if he had wanted it, and I suspect he did not – was lost. Most other potential candidates seemed minor figures. But then Margaret Thatcher began to emerge as a possible contender and I regarded her as the most attractive candidate by far in every way. I had known her for twenty-five years since we were both candidates for Parliament in 1950 in constituencies to the east of London, she in Dartford, I in West Walthamstow. I remembered our first meeting when she was a member of the Conservative Candidates Association, of which my late, good friend Airey Neave was Secretary. She was strikingly attractive, obviously intelligent, a goer. She was often the first in any meeting to get to her feet to ask a question. Most of her fellow candidates found this habit off-putting: they thought her too keen by far, too pushy. On the other hand, when she once came as a Minister to my Taunton constituency to open an old peoples' home, my constituents had liked her.

It would be a coup for the Conservative Party to have a woman leader, the first woman in history to lead a political Party – since Boadicea, the wags said. A bronze Boadicea rides her chariot with its scythed wheels at the end of the Embankment on the other side of the road from Big Ben. Why not bring her indoors?

The more I considered the matter, the more I believed that Margaret Thatcher would be the best candidate. I certainly thought she would be superior to me. I asked her to come to see me in my house in Lord North Street and I told her so. I think she was surprised, but she was careful not to say so. She and her husband Denis sat together on a sofa: the meeting was more of a formal interview than a friendly discussion. Until that moment I think the summit of her ambition was to be Chancellor of the

Exchequer, and I am sure she would have been successful at that. But it was my honest opinion that she would be the best possible Leader at that time and so it proved to be. She held the Party together in long years of opposition, and as Leader she won three elections triumphantly, more than any other, remarkable achievements by any standard.

The rules for the election of the Leader provide that account must be taken both of the views of Conservative Peers in receipt of the Whip and of the rank and file membership of the Party in the constituencies. Among the Peers, and also among the party activists in the country, support for Heath was overwhelming. (Loyalty, it is said, is the Tories' secret weapon.) The Officers and Executive of the 1922 Committee faithfully relayed this intelligence to the Conservative Members of Parliament in the House of Commons, but it made little if any difference to their intentions. Conservative Members of Parliament regarded themselves, like those attending the annual conference of the Conservative Party, as representatives, not delegates.

I duly presided over the election, and it was successfully concluded. Airey Neave conducted a careful and skilled campaign for Margaret: Ted Heath's campaign, by comparison, was lacking in conviction. One sad aspect of the election contest was the series of personal attacks made on Margaret, I guess provoked by some of Heath's supporters. When they thought I would be a candidate they first of all went for me. They went for Keith Joseph when he seemed to be a runner: 'unbalanced' was one epithet, 'the mad monk' another. Then the dirty tricks brigade concentrated on Margaret and their attacks were fierce. If she was hurt, and she must have been, she had the inner strength not to show it by so much as an eyebrow's twitch.

There were two ballots before the election was concluded. In the first, Margaret Thatcher and Sir Hugh Fraser were the only two candidates to challenge Heath, who remained favourite to win. The result was: Hugh Fraser 16 votes; Edward Heath 119; Margaret Thatcher 130.

HOUSE OF COMMONS
LONDON SW1A 0AA

<u>ELECTION OF A LEADER OF THE CONSERVATIVE PARTY</u>

The votes for each candidate in the First Ballot were as follows:

Hugh Fraser	*16*
Edward Heath	*119*
Margaret Thatcher	*130*

Scrutineers

Since the conditions in the procedure have not been fulfilled, there will be a Second Ballot. Nominations made for the First Ballot are void.

New nominations for the Second Ballot must be lodged not later than noon on Thursday, 6th February. The Second Ballot will take place in Committee Room 14 on Tuesday, 11th February between noon and 3.30 p.m.

Chairman, 1922 Committee
4th February, 1975

I announced the result to a large number of Conservative backbench Members of Parliament in Room 14. It was received with some surprise, and then warm cheers. More than half the Parliamentary Party had voted against their Leader. Heath resigned immediately and with dignity.

A second ballot had now to be held because under the rules the minimum number of votes required for a victory was 50 per cent of the electorate plus one vote, and Margaret had fallen just short of that. The second ballot took place a week later. This time five candidates offered themselves for election. The fact that there were so many caused irritation among Conservative Members of Parliament. I spoke to each one: none would withdraw. All told me the same tale: they had been pressed by their friends to stand and they could not let them down. I said I was not convinced, but I did not say so too loudly.

The Chairman of the 1922 Committee with an admiring audience.

The contest, I felt, was a non-event. By her courage in challenging and defeating Heath in the first ballot Margaret Thatcher had put the matter beyond doubt. Only William Whitelaw polled an appreciable vote and by comparison it was hardly a serious challenge. The actual figures which I announced after the poll were: Geoffrey Howe 19 votes; John Peyton 11; James Prior 19; Margaret Thatcher 146; William Whitelaw 79. Margaret had comfortably exceeded the minimum needed to win.

The general election of 1979 in which she was to lead the Conservative Party to a notable victory was four years away. Much hard work lay ahead, but that is something she has never been afraid of. My duty was to support the new Leader and to keep the Parliamentary Party behind her. In opposition that was a difficult task, never consistently plain sailing, always requiring careful watchfulness. Not every Member of the Parliamentary Party appreciated her style of leadership nor its direction, but she commanded respect. There was never an overt challenge, but much muttering and on occasion some serious questioning.

Goodwill paid off hugely. The dinner given by Ted Heath for the Officers and Executive of the 1922 Committee in 1974 had in that respect been a failure. In 1979, the year of the general election, I gave a lunch for Margaret Thatcher which was a splendid success. We subscribed for a brooch of gold, a Tudor rose, with the figures 1922 inscribed at its centre. She usually wore it afterwards when she met the Committee. We had a happy, close bond with her then, and the Party did better in its work inside and outside Parliament in consequence. It became as united a group as any such organisation of opinionated people can be.

I admired her abilities and her dedication greatly, and above all I admired her courage. She also had another quality, of which her friends are well aware but which her detractors prefer not to discuss, her solicitude for her associates and their families and for those who worked for her. Despite the 'Iron Lady' image it was genuine in those days.

I greatly enjoyed our meetings during the time I was Chairman of the 1922 Committee. If I ever wanted to see her, I was given an immediate appointment. She has a reputation for hectoring some of her private audiences, but whatever I had to say to her on my colleagues' behalf was always listened to with patience and careful attention. She did not invariably agree but she took notes, and mostly the advice I gave – either my own or the recommendations of my colleagues – was accepted and acted upon. There were occasions, it is true, when I took the Officers and Executive of the 1922 Committee to see her and she talked too much and listened too little; but I would send a message afterwards and it would be different the next time. I like to think that I was able to help and support her. I always told her the truth. I am not sure that all her advisers invariably did the same.

General Election 1979

Lunch given to the leader of the Conservative Party
by the officers and executive of the 1922 Committee on 5th.April.

One recurring problem was that I found it impossible to persuade her to work less intensely, to pace herself more steadily, to delegate responsibility to a greater extent. Anxieties were frequently expressed among Conservative Members of Parliament on all these accounts. We would ask her to allow herself more leisure to plan matters of economic and political strategy: she would listen politely, smile, and so far as we could see pay little or no attention to our advice. Months later we would repeat our request, again it would be heard most courteously and again nothing would appear to change.

Margaret Thatcher is a close person, with few confidants. I learned that early on, first when she and I met to discuss which of us should stand for the leadership in 1975 and then, surprisingly in a talk with Airey Neave shortly before his wretched death at the hands of Irish terrorists. Airey and I used to meet often: he was very helpful in keeping lines of communication open between Margaret and the Party, and particularly

211

with the Executive of the 1922 Committee of which he had been a member while I was Chairman. Airey had the reputation of being a particularly close confidant of Margaret's, but even he told me that he was not as close to her as he would wish and so could not help her as much as he would like. I was astounded.

Leaders must make their own rules of conduct, and pick their own trusted friends to help them. A little impatience or intolerance in a leader is not unreasonable. Churchill, in wartime, was a hard taskmaster, as friends who were close to him have told me. 'Forgive me,' he said to Alanbrooke, 'if I have been a little unkind this day, but pray remember the burdens I bear.' Ted Heath was invariably unreasonable; Alec Home, never; Macmillan, unusually. Margaret at first was all reasonableness and consideration, never deviating in her convictions or her purpose but also always ready to work with the grain of her colleagues' opinion. In the early days of her leadership she went to endless lengths to keep in touch with opinion in the Conservative Party and outside; she has always enjoyed discussion with informed and intelligent people and she has always been ready, in my own experience, to take advice. I never knew her to be anything but courteous and friendly in those early years, even in circumstances that would try the patience of a saint.

Over the years she changed. She could bully senior colleagues shockingly, and more than once I have been embarrassed at her lecturing of Keith Joseph when he was Secretary of State for Trade and Industry, Peter Thorneycroft when he was Party Chairman, and Geoffrey Howe when he was Chancellor of the Exchequer. In such a mood she was hard to respond to. Her victims seemed to find it impossible to do so, except that Geoffrey, in his resignation speech in the House of Commons, at last allowed his bile to overflow in public view; as did Nigel Lawson's to a lesser extent but no less damagingly. As time went on she became less tolerant of others' opinions, less grateful for the automatic loyalty of colleagues, more reliant on her own empire at Number 10, more impatient and more dogmatic; and perhaps she had fewer candid friends with the authority and experience to guide her.

When in 1983 we celebrated the sixtieth anniversary of the 1922 Committee with a dinner at the Carlton Club Margaret was our guest. When she left to go back to Downing Street I went with her to the car. She turned to say goodnight and I kissed her. 'You're the first Prime Minister I've ever kissed,' I said. She has, alas, not much sense of humour.

When she came to form her first Cabinet in 1979 I was not included. The reason turned out to be an extraordinary one. Returning home one evening I found a message inviting me to telephone the Chief Whip, Humphrey Atkins. He was difficult to reach on the telephone and when I did speak to him he was obviously tired and not anxious for a lengthy conversation. He was not entirely clear as to what he wanted to say to me but I gathered that the Prime Minister had asked him to tell me that there was shortly to be published a report by the Board of Trade inspector who had enquired into the affairs of a company to which Keysers had lent money in the days when I was Chairman. I was mentioned in two paragraphs: he could not recall exactly what was said. There was no criticism of me personally but I was reported as saying that Keysers had been irresponsible in lending the money. It proved to have been a mistake to have been so truthful.

Some days later the full report was published and although it was true that I was not criticised the *Evening Standard* started a chorus to the effect that the 'du Cann bank' (which Keysers certainly was not) had made an imprudent loan. They must have been woefully short of news that day, or short of judgement, or both. I hope they were not getting their revenge for our little disagreement over the 'Milk Street Mafia' affair. If you do have a row with a newspaper they usually get their own back on you sooner or later. The *Daily Telegraph* and the *Guardian*, I remember, were particularly sensational, though as the BBC commentator pointed out in the Today programme, there was precious little of substance in their reports and he could hardly understand the reason for mentioning my name so prominently, if at all.

I called an immediate meeting of the Officers and Executive of the 1922 Committee. An election for the chairmanship was due: should I withdraw my name? Nobody said I should and in the event I was re-elected with a comfortable majority. So I continued in the post and it was from that position that I witnessed the first five years of Margaret Thatcher's premiership.

The fact is probably best forgotten, but it was no easier keeping the Parliamentary Party behind the Leader after she became Prime Minister than it had been in the four years while she was Leader of the Opposition. There was never an overt challenge to her but the mutinous mutterings and openly critical conservations were a content concern to me. It was a point well made in a leading article in the *Times* in 1995, sixteen years after her first general election was won:

> People forget how vulnerable Mrs Thatcher was in her first few years
> in office. Thatcherism was vigorously opposed by many backbenchers,
> senior Cabinet Ministers and much of the Party. True believers were in
> a minority.

Keeping my fellow MPs on side was hard labour.

My most vivid memories go back to the time of the Falklands War. When the Argentines invaded there was an emergency debate in the House of Commons. I remembered the Suez affair and dreaded seeing the Conservative Party drawn into the same agonising doubts and indecision. The difference was that this time I was sure we were right and I meant to do all I could to help hold the Party together behind a determined Leader. The debate was opened by the Secretary of State for Defence, John Nott. He spoke to a tense, crowded House but his speech seemed to lack conviction. He was followed by Michael Foot as Leader of the Opposition and then I rose, the first MP to speak from the back benches. I strongly supported the action to liberate the Falklands.

By the end of the debate opinion in our Party was far from reassured. There seemed to be a lack of clear purpose among Ministers, echoes of the indecisiveness that had led the Argentines to believe it would be safe to invade. We had to get the Party together as soon as possible to pledge support for the Government. Accordingly I arranged for a satellite committee of the 1922 Committee, the Defence Committee chaired by a former Navy Minister and a member of the Executive of the 1922 Committee, Sir Anthony Buck, to meet immediately after the emergency debate had finished. Lord Carrington, the Foreign Secretary, spoke to it and he had a cynical audience to address. The Foreign Office did not seem to have managed the events that led up to the Argentine invasion at all competently, and it has to be said that many Conservatives have a low opinion of the FO in general. They regard it as a rather woolly-minded organisation, too self-contained, too often self-satisfied, and not as zealous as it should be in promoting Britain's interests. They see it appointing ambassadors of noted left-wing views to Communist countries such as China, and at its worst they remember how it retained Philby, Burgess and Maclean in important and sensitive positions, unreprimanded and even promoted despite flagrantly bad personal conduct that would have got them dismissed from any other organisation.

Nevertheless the atmosphere on that April Saturday when the Defence Committee met was anxious rather than angry. The room was full, with something over a hundred Tory backbench Members present.

The discussion was on the whole reasonable, but Carrington appeared uncomfortable. He thought, so I now understand, that the meeting was a rough one. Perhaps that misjudgement was easily made by a man without House of Commons experience. Tony Buck and I several times discussed the events of those days in the years since. It was undoubtedly, as meetings in the House of Commons go, a placid one. It would not have been difficult for Carrington to bring it on to his side, but he seemed unwilling to try. He preferred to answer questions rather than make a speech and that was a mistake. His reticence and his rather withdrawn attitude were seen not as modesty but, wrongly, as arrogance.

I left the meeting a few minutes before its end to catch my train back to Taunton. The Parliamentary journalists, the Lobby, were present in the corridor outside in some force to discover what had happened in the meeting. I was surrounded and questioned. For the first and only time in my life I was guilty of misinforming them. I was asked about the atmosphere of the meeting and I represented it as calmer than it was. That was quite deliberate: I cannot apologise, at a time when our country was technically engaging in war, for trying to give an impression of calm and resolution. Among other things, I was asked by several journalists if there would be any resignations from the Government among Foreign Office ministers. I replied that I was quite sure that there would not be: that I genuinely believed to be the truth. The Lobby was shrewder than I was. Lord Carrington and a number of his colleagues, including the Foreign Office spokesman in the House of Commons, Humphrey Atkins, resigned their offices over the weekend. Peter Carrington's demeanour at that Committee meeting was the clue: he felt responsible for the Falklands debacle and believed he had no alternative but to resign. Colleagues, notably Lord Whitelaw, spent the weekend trying to dissuade him but he was adamant. Few of us in the Parliamentary Party foresaw his resignation on that Saturday.

Honourable as his conduct was, I believe he was wrong. His resignation left the Prime Minister a lonely figure at a time when she most needed support. Peter Carrington was a Foreign Secretary of particular qualities, highly experienced, greatly respected. That he and his colleagues, overnight, were no longer at the Prime Minister's side to advise her, to conduct difficult negotiations at the United Nations, with our partners in the European Community and with our friends in the Commonwealth, was an immediate and severe handicap to her and to the Government. She had to face two enemies, not only the obvious enemy overseas, but a second enemy at home: the critics, lying in wait, invidious, vigilant, ready at any moment to carp and even to destroy. True, she had her Party in Parliament with her – she had strong backing, in fact, in all parts of the House – and she had overwhelming support in the country. But public opinion is a fickle thing: if world opinion were to be anything worse than neutral, the attacks on our national purpose would start. There would be articles in the press and snide pieces from the commentators on television and radio. Then the critical speeches in Parliament would begin. In a short time the pressure could become irresistible.

It was at that moment of decision that her friends at the Foreign Office left her side. Fortunately the new Foreign Secretary, Francis Pym, Ted Heath's old Chief Whip, was a skilled negotiator, wise in the ways of men and of Governments. He and the Foreign and Commonwealth Office deserve the highest praise for ensuring that overseas opinion remained overwhelmingly neutral in the conflict and that the United Nations remained committed to a Resolution which justified Britain's strong response to the invasion.

Pym was removed as Foreign Secretary in 1983; some would say, as soon after the conflict as possible. The story goes that Margaret regarded him as less than staunch in his support of her while the British expeditionary force was at sea, en route for the Falklands; he was in favour of pursuing peace proposals which seemed to her to be impractical.

I had some personal evidence of this. During the conflict she allowed me to bring an emissary from the President of Mexico to see her privately at 10 Downing Street. The diplomat described to her the President's conversations with General Galtieri, the Argentine dictator. Galtieri, he said, wished to negotiate a settlement and was willing to meet Mrs Thatcher on neutral ground, perhaps in Mexico. The President of Mexico saw his country as something of a halfway house between South America and the Anglo-Saxon world, situated as it is geographically neither in South America nor in the United States, committed to the point of view of neither camp and a friend of both. The Prime Minister listened politely but nothing came of the Mexicans' friendly initiative.

No political leader who has experienced war can willingly order a later generation into action if there are alternatives available. I know I would not find it easy. If that was Francis Pym's position it was an honourable one. Yet the Prime Minister was probably right to be impatient of the various peace negotiations, including the so-called Peruvian peace initiative. They were unlikely, any of them, to produce a solution acceptable to British opinion. Talks there would have been in plenty and, as the talks continued, the Argentine occupation would have been increasingly a *fait accompli*. The British resolve might well have weakened in the face of mounting criticisms from the ever-active anti-colonialists in the United Nations and elsewhere. The Government's policy was to talk in the hope of finding an acceptable solution, while preparing and sending the expeditionary force to retake the islands without delay. It was the correct policy and it succeeded brilliantly. It depended for its success on the Prime Minister's own resolve more than on any other factor. It also depended on speed. Delay in accomplishing an invasion was one reason why the Suez campaign failed. It seemed we had learned that lesson.

Throughout the conflict over the Falklands, the 1922 Committee gave the Prime Minister its full and unquestioning support. I was determined to avoid the mistakes the Conservative Party in the House of Commons had made at the time of Suez. During that time there were almost daily meetings of one Party Committee or another, including the 1922 Committee. There was thus an atmosphere of continuous drama. It was a serious error to allow this to happen. I was anxious above all that we should preserve an atmosphere of calm and I am gratified that we succeeded. There were doubts, of course. When British warships were sunk there was a sense of shock, if not outrage. But the Prime Minister's own steadfastness found its equal in the Conservative Party in Parliament and I am proud to have had the chance to exert some influence over it at that critical time.

That was a moment of crisis and for a while the work of the 1922 Committee was publicly noticed. For most of the time the work of the Chairman of the 1922 Committee is done in private; passing a word of warning to a Minister, acting as a continuous listening post, giving advice to a colleague with problems, subtly exercising discipline in the general interest. The Chairman's ideal physical characteristics are the same today as they were in 1923 – a long nose to sniff out impending trouble, the oversized ears of a ready listener, a firm hand to deal with the problematical and a boot to apply to the recalcitrant.

Private advice sometimes inadvertently becomes public knowledge. One day in 1984 we heard that Brian Walden's influential Sunday lunchtime programme was to attack the Prime Minister. The Executive of the 1922 Committee pressed me to take on her defence and thereby to keep others off the programme and I did so gladly. One line of attack was that as Prime Minister Margaret Thatcher took too much onto herself, acting less as a conductor of the Cabinet orchestra and more like a one-woman band. While supporting her strongly I agreed with my questioner that the appointment of a deputy to whom she could delegate much day-to-day responsibility might be a sensible proposal. This was reported prominently in the newspapers the next day as being my original idea and much featured by caricaturists.

'What else is Edward du Cann saying about me?'

I did not find it difficult to give clear advice at the time of the bombing of the Grand Hotel at Brighton in 1984. The Metropole Hotel where I was staying, next door to the Grand, was owned by Lonrho. We immediately made its facilities available and I put up the leading members of the

National Union in my sitting room. I insisted that the conference continue and my advice was immediately accepted. Over the years I have lost too many good friends to Irish extremist assassins: Mrs Wakeham, the wife of the Government Chief Whip, and Tony Berry MP at Brighton, Lord Mountbatten and Airey Neave MP in 1979 and Ian Gow MP in 1990. The bomb that exploded outside the House of Commons a few years earlier might have killed my devoted secretary. As it was, all my personal records were destroyed. Extremists, in demonstrating their contempt for our democratic system, fortify our resolution to defend it.

Sadly, it was necessary on several occasions to voice anxiety about the business affairs of the Prime Minister's son Mark. First, there was doubt about his associates, then about his activities. Matters first came to a head in 1983/84 when the newspapers were pursuing a story that he had been paid a substantial commission by the Cementation company for facilitating a construction project in Oman and that his mother had in effect assisted with the enterprise. My friend David Wickins persuaded him to leave the country and for the moment pressure was relieved; but it recurred constantly.

Mark exploited his mother's position quite unashamedly, trading on her name, demanding services from Britain's overseas representatives and using 10 Downing Street for personal purposes. It was hard to say whether the warnings and representations tactfully made to the Prime Minister were heeded or not. In contrast, he was tactless: in conversation he could be openly disparaging about various of her Parliamentary colleagues, and often was. Alas, that carelessness was bound to result in unnecessary enmity towards her when it was reported to those of whom he spoke critically. Mark Thatcher displayed an arrogance which was as aggressive as it was on occasions absurd. In a restaurant in Detroit with my friend Wickins he boasted to a waitress with whose slow service he was unimpressed, 'I am Mark Thatcher.' Replied the waitress, 'I don't care if you are Mark Twain, you take your turn like everybody else.' To be fair, he relates the story against himself. Nonetheless, while Margaret was Prime Minister, Mark was an Achilles' heel.

I often thought it right informally to instruct newly elected colleagues about procedures, or behaviour. I wish the same service had been available to me when I was a new boy in the House. Clear instruction is patently needed in many cases today. It is better to avoid accidents than to have the messy job of clearing up after them.

During my twelve-year Chairmanship of the 1922 Committee I was re-elected each year, and some years when there were general elections and new Parliaments began I had to stand for election more than once. Altogether I fought and won seventeen elections, in only three of which I was unopposed. In 1984 I had four opponents and (I suppose understandably, since no one else had been in the post so long) they campaigned on the slogan 'Time for a change'. The *Daily Telegraph* ran true to form and attacked me in a leading article on that theme. I refused to have an organised campaign run in my support, though I suspect my opponents did not have the same scruples.

The election was held under a system of proportional representation, which my colleagues had insisted on introducing after the 1979 general election. I led on the first ballot and lost on the last. I have always hated PR.

A number of my friends came to my room in the House to commiserate and we went out to dinner together. When I got home at about ten o'clock I found, waiting for me on the mat, a letter from Margaret Thatcher covering three pages of foolscap and written in her own hand expressing her gratitude for my period of service, saying that she would recommend me in accordance with precedent to be made a peer in due course and that in the meantime I would be offered a knighthood. To have taken the time to write a personal letter so promptly and not a typewritten stereotype the morning after was just one instance of her thoughtfulness and generosity, even if she later forgot her promise about the peerage.

She had her blind spots: she was insensitive about MPs' pay and conditions. The last time I had a private talk with Margaret Thatcher in the House of Commons was the day before I told my friends in Taunton that I would not stand for Parliament again. 'I made a mistake,' I said, 'in staying too long as Chairman of the 1992 Committee until eventually I was voted out. It's better to resign too soon than to stay in office too long. I hope you won't follow my example.' She was not pleased, but I still think it was good advice and I wish she had taken it. Today she would be twice the heroine she deservedly is. At least I took my own advice. I miss Taunton; I miss my friends there – I can never forget their loyalty and generous support over the years – we started with a majority of 650 and we ended with a majority of more than 12,000; I miss the political and constituency work and the political life.

I was certainly sorry when I stepped down as Chairman of the 1922 Committee. I had enjoyed my time. I had missed only two meetings out of some four hundred and that was when I was asked to lead the Inter-Parliamentary Union delegation to China, the first in history to make the visit. If my work was useful it was largely because whatever my personal feelings I tried to avoid being entangled in disputes within the Party and associated myself with neither the right nor the left of the political spectrum. I disliked the increasing polarisation of views within the Party and did my best to moderate it, but in recent years I have watched with dismay as it has become more obvious, and more eagerly publicised in the media. Those who are responsible in the 1922 Committee are foolishly irresponsible. The impression of disunity is doing irreparable damage to the Party's electoral chances.

When my time came to go I congratulated my successor in front of the whole Committee and wished him well. It is a good rule, if you have to lose, to do so with dignity. Don't spend the next years nursing your bitterness, sniping at your successor, and cherishing the ridiculous idea that you thereby get people's sympathy. All the same, there is one way in which I confess to being un-English. I cannot understand the idea that there is something rather noble about losing, and I do not share our national preference for dwelling on defeats as if they were something to be specially proud of. Why do we remember the evacuation at Dunkirk more often than the splendid victory at El Alamein? For myself, if I have to lose I like to be a good loser, but I vastly prefer to be a winner.

CHAPTER 10

LONRHO *versus the* GOVERNMENT

If you live, as I have done, in the two realms of business and politics you must expect sometimes to get caught up in a frontier war. Having, as it were, dual citizenship and owing loyalties to both sides can be a painful experience. It can also be quite disillusioning. In Britain today we do not manage the relationship between Government and industry as well as some complacent folk in high places think we do.

As well as the occasional skirmish, I have been involved in two frontier wars. The first occurred when I was launching the unit trust industry in the teeth of Government indifference and cynicism, and the second while I was a director, and then Chairman of Lonrho. This latter culminated in the sad and baffling affair of Lonrho's attempt to take over the House of Fraser. It was baffling because I could not understand why the Government not only failed to help an important British company develop its legitimate business but actively intervened to oppose it and in the end forced it to back off in favour of foreign adventurers. Ministers and officials accepted a whole series of lies with astonishing credulity, and when those lies were exposed they spent their energies not on putting their blunders right but on seeing that as little as possible of the truth was published. It was particularly sad for me because it was a Conservative Government that behaved so badly.

Governments in France, Germany, Japan and in many other countries see it as their duty to foster their nation's business interests. In Britain, if there is a conflict between political advantage and industrial logic and efficiency, politics will be all too likely to win.

This has been an important aspect of what the Government's White Paper of 1994 on competitiveness described as 'over one hundred years of relative decline'. When my father was born, British exports of manufactured goods amounted to the equivalent of one third of the world's eleven main industrial countries. Today that figure is well under 10 per cent. Britain is rapidly on the way to becoming a third-rate commercial power. In recent years our good luck in having a supply of oil under the North Sea has helped to mask our failures, but that windfall is finite and when it runs out we have little in the way of strategy to cope.

Outside Government, too, there is a frightening complacency among the people who should be giving a lead – in the universities, in the Civil Service, in the professions, even in the City of London. They neither diagnose the disease nor try to cure it. They prefer to live in a comfortable make-believe world where Britain still wields an international power and influence which in reality was lost many years ago, and at home can rely upon unlimited Government largesse. John Peyton, my neighbour as MP for Yeovil, put it well: 'This country cherishes the belief that the sounding alarm is only the dinner gong signalling second helpings.'

It is true that for a long time we were held back by the intransigence and restrictive practices of the trade unions. Margaret Thatcher's great triumph was to break that stranglehold and to encourage a greater economic realism, but to suppose that the unions were the sole root of all our problems is only another symptom of our complacency. There are many other reasons for our failure. We should look for some of these reasons at the top, among the people who govern us. The story of my time at Lonrho is worth telling if only for the clear, harsh light it throws on this situation.

One of the things I learned when I joined Lonrho was that Tiny Rowland's activities as a negotiator and peacemaker in Africa were not appreciated by the British establishment. Our own diplomats' relationships with African leaders were often less close and a good deal less cordial than his. They were jealous of him and jealousy led to retaliation. Lonrho's representatives would be denied invitations to official receptions when African leaders visited London. The protests that I and others made were sometimes effective, more often not. During my twenty years as a director, including eight years as Chairman when I succeeded Lord Duncan Sandys in 1984, I received only two official invitations. One was to a banquet at Buckingham Palace given by the Queen in honour of the visit of the President of Mexico which Tiny Rowland attended: we were, after all, representatives of one of the UK's largest investors in that country. The other was when Tiny Rowland and I lunched at 10 Downing Street on the occasion of the visit to the UK of President

Machel of Mozambique.

I had earlier recommended to the Prime Minister that if we planned to give financial aid to Mozambique the amount should be generous.

'Edward,' she said, 'you do know Machel is a Communist.'

No, I told her, in reality he was anything but a Communist. The trouble was that, like many African leaders, he had met too few non-Socialist political leaders in the West. He could easily be influenced in favour of the free world and its ideas, and he was already becoming disillusioned with his Soviet and other allies whose economic aid had been of such doubtful practical use. His visit would give us a chance to begin to convert a potential enemy into a friend. Margaret heard me out, signified neither approval nor disapproval, but did as I suggested.

At the Downing Street lunch for Machel, Tiny Rowland was seated next to Geoffrey Howe, then Foreign Secretary. The table included the Mozambique Foreign Secretary, in front of whom Geoffrey started asking Tiny questions about Lonrho's investments in South Africa, then under a pro-apartheid Government. No doubt he meant no harm; probably his questions were asked out of a genuine interest; but Tiny, who had little regard for Geoffrey's supposed knowledge of African affairs, rightly regarded such a probe in the presence of a black African Minister as, at best, tactless and, at worst, offensive.

I had urged Margaret Thatcher to meet Tiny Rowland privately and she had agreed. We met at Chequers for lunch one Sunday – wives and· husbands – six of us in all. Tiny was at his most charming and his ability to charm is legendary. I had told Margaret that no one knew Africa better than he did, and on more than one occasion I had retailed to her his constructive work for peace in Angola and Mozambique, and his friendship and personal influence with African leaders in Malawi, Zimbabwe, the Congo and other countries. I had urged her to learn from him. After lunch they sat together on a sofa in the long gallery while the rest of us toured the house. It appeared to me that they got on famously together but although I suggested further meetings, none took place.

A major cause of friction between Lonrho and the British Government was the suggestion that Lonrho had been guilty of breaking the sanctions imposed on Rhodesia after Ian Smith's unilateral declaration of independence in 1965. Twelve years later an enquiry chaired by Thomas Bingham QC (now a Lord of Appeal) looked into this and found (what we all knew) that some British companies had indeed been supplying oil to Rhodesia through their South African subsidiaries. It was these oil supplies that prevented the Smith regime from collapsing within a matter of weeks after UDI but, amazingly, the enquiry exonerated these great oil companies from all blame on the absurd ground that they could not be held responsible for the actions of their own subsidiaries. By contrast, Lonrho, which was always strongly opposed to UDI, had closed the pipeline it had constructed to carry oil from the Mozambique coast to Umtali on the Rhodesian border. This meant a great pecuniary loss for Lonrho, while the oil companies continued to draw large profits from their fortunately 'uncontrollable' subsidiaries. Yet it was Lonrho, not Shell or BP, that was often smeared as a sanctions buster. Oil men are powerful propagandists.

Time and again when dealing with Lonrho's affairs I ran up against official obstruction and the apparent indifference of Government to the success or failure of British enterprises. A minor example of this derived form Lonrho's ownership of a small cargo-carrying airline. I discovered that British aid to overseas countries, paid for by the British taxpayer, was being carried by foreign airlines in preference to British. This was, we understood, no cost advantage. Naturally I complained and when private representations failed I made my criticisms public in a debate I initiated in the House of Commons. What possible justification could there be for allowing foreign carriers to carry aid financed by the British taxpayer? I asked. Had nobody understood that the recipients of this aid, seeing it arrive in foreign aircraft, would naturally assume that it came from non-British sources? The Minister who replied to the debate, briefed by the officials who naturally were reluctant to confess their error, gave no credible reply. Why are British officials so reluctant, too, to support their compatriots?

A bigger conflict with Government arose over its policy for the steel industry. In 1977 Lonrho purchased Hadfields, a group of steel-making companies based in Sheffield, which produced high quality heat-resisting steels used in the manufacture of axles, crankshafts and the like. They had a leading position in UK alloy steel markets and employed well over five thousand people. The company had a proud tradition and a record of success.

By the summer of 1980 Britain was in deep recession and the steel industry was badly affected. Hadfields took urgent action. The business was rationalised and concentrated on two sites at Sheffield, and the workforce was reduced by almost half to 2,700. Despite that the company maintained a similar steelmaking capacity to that of 1977, increasing productivity by 220 per cent.

In the winter of 1980 there was a strike lasting three months in the nationalised sector of the steel industry. Hadfields' workers refused to join it. Our premises were subjected to mass picketing for many weeks. There were ugly scenes outside the factory gates, violence and intimidation by the pickets and noisy crowds. On 14th February 1980, St Valentine's day, there were 3,000 pickets outside Hadfields' works, 650 of whom were members of the National Union of Mineworkers, who had been paid by their union to be present. The Deputy Chief Constable advised Hadfields' management that the Sheffield police could not prevent a break-in nor could he guarantee the safety of our workforce. I telephoned the Home Secretary, William Whitelaw, to protest. He took my call and heard me out but refused to intervene directly. It was only the resolution of Hadfields' management and its workforce that prevented anarchy. The police were criticised at the time for being too soft in the face of a violent crowd. They learned from their experience. Their tactics were to change in later confrontations.

With the advantage of hindsight one can see that the attack on Hadfields was a rehearsal for other strikes to come, notably in the coal industry. It was significant that Arthur Scargill, President of the NUM, was prominent among those involved. I met Scargill only once, when we appeared together in an 'Any Questions' radio broadcast. David Jacobs, the Chairman, gave me a word of warning before the programme began. 'Watch him,' he said, 'he doesn't behave like a normal panellist.' And he did not. He had not come to the pre-programme dinner. He arrived at the church in Putney where the programme took place only a couple of minutes before its start and barely acknowledged the polite greetings of his fellow panellists. During the programme he made no effort to debate: he stuck to his party line throughout. The BBC were filming for a TV documentary during the programme – a day in the life of Arthur Scargill. The bright lights were switched on when he spoke and went off when he was silent. The effect was weird, a blaze of blinding light on Scargill, comparative darkness for the rest of us. The programme over, Scargill departed at once with his minders and hardly a goodbye.

The 1980 steelworkers' strike involved 150,000 workers, and almost nine million working days were lost. Hadfields' workforce and management were at one in their determination to continue working and by and large they succeeded. They deserved some recognition for their refusal to give in to intimidation, but they did not get it. They were to be carelessly betrayed and the fatal weapon was not in the hands of some aggressive union baron. It was wielded by a Conservative Government.

Private steel producers in the UK at that time had to compete with

226

the nationalised British Steel Corporation. They would have done so easily enough but for one vital fact: BSC collected massive subsidies from the Exchequer while the private companies had to find their own funds and return a profit on them. Over the five years after Lonrho bought Hadfields, BSC received £3,823 million from the Government: most of it went to cover the corporation's continuing losses which in 1980/81 alone were over £1 billion.

At that time production of engineering steels was divided almost 50/50 between four private-sector steel works and the BSC. The private sector was producing 2 million tonnes a year; BSC slightly more. All were losing money, BSC more than the private companies combined. In the background loomed the horrific over-production of steel in the European Community. In practice the UK was no longer free to protect her own domestic interests in this field, though the full implications of this would only become clear some years later.

The solution to this crisis, devised by the Conservative Government and code-named Phoenix II, was to rationalise and privatise this sector of the steel industry. The route the Government chose was to allow most of the private sector companies to go bankrupt while simultaneously maintaining the State sector at the public expense. Government money poured into BSC at an alarming rate with the result that the BSC management was able to dictate the market by selling its steel at low, uneconomic prices. The private sector simply could not compete.

Protests went unheeded. So did the representations I made, as Chairman of Hadfields, to the responsible Minister (Keith Joseph was Margaret Thatcher's first Secretary of State for Industry – his term was twenty-five months) and even to the Prime Minister, Margaret Thatcher.

'I know you are right,' said one junior Minister to our representatives, 'but there is nothing I can do.'

'I could explain our strategy to you,' Keith Joseph told me, 'but you'll not agree and it will take too long.'

It would have been more honourable if the policy had been openly declared in advance; but in England that is not the way in which Governments always work. The Department responsible for sponsoring our industry refused to give a fair hearing to the private companies: it was too deeply involved with the State sector. For example, one of the senior civil servants in the Department of Industry, to whom the directors of Hadfields were making their representations for fair treatment, was also a director of BSC. I complained to the Prime Minister: to her credit she had this man's responsibilities rearranged, and in my presence she bawled out

Keith Joseph. It was a charade: the overall policy remained in place.

All four private sector companies went under. All were bought by BSC for sums well below their true worth. Almost before the ink was dry on the contracts of sale BSC shut them down. Now British Steel has a monopoly and the only alternative source of supply for British customers is imported steel.

My own position as I watched the destruction of Hadfields was an uncomfortable one. As a Tory MP I owed my support to the Government, but as Chairman of Hadfields I was also bound to do all I could to save our company from undeserved ruin. That necessarily included using my contacts with Ministers to persuade them that we had justice on our side. A conflict of loyalties, certainly, but a conflict of interest? Not, I believed, in any improper sense. If my analysis that British Governments fail to understand and help British companies is right, then it was both my public and my private duty to press for a different policy, as I did in the House and at meetings with Ministers, and my commercial interest was always declared.

The same was true – even more uncomfortably true – over my involvement in the attempted takeover by Lonrho of the House of Fraser. The story began in 1977, when Lonrho acquired a share interest in Fraser, and it came to an end sixteen years later in 1993 when the new Board of Lonrho decided to abandon its campaign to buy Fraser and peace seemed to break out between Tiny Rowland and Mohammed Fayed.

By July 1977 Lonrho held about 30 per cent of the issued share capital of a Scottish company, Scottish and Universal Investments Limited, founded by the late Lord Fraser – usually called SUITS for short. Among other investments SUITS owned just over 10 per cent of the issued share capital of the House of Fraser, which in turn owned Harrods and over a hundred provincial stores, mostly, like Harrods, household names. At that time Fraser was said to be the largest department store group in Europe. In September 1977 Lonrho acquired a 20 per cent stake in Fraser, in addition to its 30 per cent share in SUITS, and in the spring of 1978 we made a public offer for the remainder of the issued share capital of SUITS. It made good commercial sense to do so, but the bid had to lapse when the Labour Secretary of State, Roy Hattersley, referred it to the Monopolies and Mergers Commission (MMC)

This was the first of a number of enquiries we were to undergo. It lasted nine months. All aspects of Lonrho's affairs which could possibly be relevant to its bid for SUITS were considered and at the end of the day the MMC concluded that the Lonrho merger, both with SUITS and with

Fraser, would not be expected to operate against the public interest. Not only did the MMC approve the two mergers, but it also concluded that Lonrho was a 'dynamic organisation' and it appeared more than satisfied with its management, praising Tiny Rowland's contribution in particular. Lonrho therefore renewed its bid for SUITS. The bid was successful and SUITS became our wholly owned subsidiary in June 1979. As a result, Lonrho's direct shareholding in House of Fraser was increased to just under 30 per cent and our bid for the whole of that company was now in serious prospect. Tiny Rowland joined Fraser's Board as Deputy Chairman, and Lord Duncan Sandys, Chairman of Lonrho, also became a director.

The logic of a bid for Fraser was compelling. We could reduce our dependence on our African businesses, increase our asset base and acquire the financial muscle that the ownership of a substantial business in the consumer goods sector would give us. We could also make a market in Fraser's stores for produce from the underdeveloped countries in Africa. Fraser had only a moderate financial record. We believed that we could improve it substantially. The MMC clearly agreed with us; the 1979 report referred to the 'contribution which the directors nominated by Lonrho could make' and to 'the entrepreneurial drive of Lonrho and its wide industrial and commercial experience'.

One might have expected a welcome for their new shareholders from the Board of Fraser, whose objective should surely have been the improvement of the business and the financial benefit for its shareholders. It was not to be. On 4 August 1980 Tiny Rowland received a letter saying that on the following day he was to be replaced as Deputy Chairman by a new outside director, Professor Roland Smith, who was also to chair a new executive committee of the Board. Lonrho, Fraser's largest shareholder, was denied any representation on that committee. Professor Smith and another new director, Ernest Sharp, had been nominated by Warburgs, the merchant bank who let Lonrho down so badly a few years earlier, now appointed financial advisers to Fraser. Smith was a professor of marketing at the Manchester Business School. He lacked heavyweight commercial experience, but he was a forthright, combative man, chosen chiefly (no doubt) for the strength of his personality. The intention was clear – keep Lonrho out at all costs.

Professor Smith's comments were reported in the national press the following weekend:

They [the two Lonrho directors] are not on the committee that is going

229

to run the company. They will have no influence on it. Term time in Manchester starts in October. I would like to see Lonrho off by then.

An anti-Lonrho agitation was engineered. House of Fraser engaged a Conservative Member of Parliament, Peter Hordern, as a lobbyist; at lunches at the Savoy he impressed Parliamentary colleagues with an anti-Lonrho point of view and he published an anti-Lonrho article in *The Times*. (His paid-for loyalty was not declared: the newspaper printed his article as if it were disinterested comment.) Every opportunity was taken to lobby for Government intervention, another enquiry, anything to delay or prevent Fraser shareholders receiving the benefit of an offer from Lonrho. Warburg's defensive tactics included orchestrated share dealings by institutions friendly with Fraser's Board or with Warburg, and attempts to buy out Fraser shareholders who were Lonrho supporters.

Lonrho's position was now impossible. Our investment in Fraser was performing badly. Fraser's management was unable to turn the company's fortunes around yet we were allowed no influence on its affairs and every constructive proposal we made for the better management of the business was rejected. For example, when Fraser completed a controversial sale and lease-back of the D. H. Evans department store site in Oxford Street we criticised the proposal as commercially disastrous, but our views were ignored. Immediately afterwards the Board turned on its own Chairman, Sir Hugh Fraser, the son of the business's founder, because of his friendliness with us, and deposed him in favour of Professor Smith.

Lonrho's choice was simple: we either had to sell our shares or bid for the whole company. We chose the latter course and offered Fraser shareholders 150p in cash, a premium of almost 30 per cent over the market price. We felt confident that this bid would resolve our problems, for we knew we could substantially improve the profitability of the business. A referral of our bid to the Monopolies and Mergers Commission seemed most unlikely for two reasons: first, the businesses of Lonrho and House of Fraser were complementary and no one could imagine any real issues of competition arising; second, the MMC report on our acquisition of SUITS had considered our bona fides and our competence as managers of businesses and concluded clearly in our favour.

But the powerful Fraser/Warburg lobbying machine was hard at work. In February 1981, a month after our offer was announced, we were shocked to learn that we had once again been referred to the Monopolies and Mergers Commission by the Secretary of State for Trade, John Biffen (the third man to hold that post under Margaret Thatcher, his term lasting only fifteen months). So, two years after concluding their previous enquiry, the MMC set to work for another nine months to consider every possible implication of our bid for Fraser.

Enquiry Number Two covered much the same ground as the first, but this time the Commission was inundated with orchestrated complaints about the potential effects of a Lonrho takeover. The directors of Fraser threatened to resign en masse. A large number of groups and individuals, including Fraser suppliers and MPs with Fraser stores in their constituencies, were persuaded to lobby the MMC against our bid. MPs too often act as mass post-boxes, passing on correspondence or complaints without the least attempt to evaluate either. It is a lazy procedure. Fraser's advisers certainly earned their substantial fees. On 5 December 1981 the MMC, bowing to this pressure and in stark contrast to its 1979 report, concluded (though not unanimously) that the proposed merger 'might be expected to operate against the public interest.'

Entering Tiny Rowland's office early that morning I found I was the last director to arrive. 'They've found against us, Edward,' he said. I couldn't believe what I heard.

The astonishing verdict was endorsed by the Secretary of State for Trade who showed, for the second time, an uncharacteristic lack of courage in failing to overrule such a muddle-headed report. Lonrho was required to give a written undertaking that it would not seek to increase its shareholding in Fraser beyond 30 per cent. Lonrho's Chairman, Lord Duncan Sandys, complied.

It was small consolation to us at Lonrho that the MMC report was universally criticised in the press. The MMC (or rather a majority of its members, few of whom had any significant commercial experience) had based its report on 'management efficiency', and yet the one management consultant on the panel (Mr H. Hunt, a past president of the Institute of Management Consultants) rejected the majority decision and concluded, as had the MMC enquiry into our takeover of SUITS, that 'Lonrho's wide business experience with House of Fraser's retailing competence could well result in enhanced performance from House of Fraser.'

Encouraged by the almost universal view that the report was mistaken, we were hopeful that Lonrho would in time be able to negotiate a release from our undertaking and would be allowed to bid again for the rest of Fraser's shares. Throughout the spring and summer of 1982 we and our advisers were in close contact with the Office of Fair Trading and the Department of Trade and Industry, but it soon became clear that the political will to release us was not there. The decision had been made, however flawed the MMC report; the outcry had died down and no official was going to upset the status quo.

We had to reconsider the future of our investment in Fraser. The company's performance continued to be miserable. The management was entrenched. However, the more we looked at Fraser the more clearly we saw the root of its problems. Most of its hundred-plus department stores around the country were performing badly and a number were losing money. On the other hand, the Harrods business in Knightsbridge showed a remarkable return on capital invested and an improving performance. The Board of Fraser was using Harrods as a milch cow: its substantial profits were being dissipated in propping up the rest of the group, while nothing was being done to improve the performance of the provincial stores.

What could we do? We could not bid for Fraser, but Lonrho was not a quitter. For the good health of our business we needed a substantial UK asset and we meant to have it. The answer was to propose the demerger of Harrods from the other Fraser stores.

The logic was impeccable, not only for Lonrho but for all Fraser shareholders. Harrods would be free to develop independently, while the management problems of the other stores would at last have to be dealt with – and not before time. In financial terms, demerger was even more attractive. Separate shares in Harrods would be issued to all Fraser shareholders and a new quotation for Harrods' shares obtained on the Stock Exchange. Harrods, with its excellent financial record and international reputation, would surely attract a premium rating, while the rest of the Fraser business had a basic net asset value which would act as a floor for the share price. The demerger would thus produce a handsome overall re-rating of the two sections of the business and a significant profit for Fraser's shareholders.

The proposal was first put to the shareholders of Fraser in November 1982. Fraser's directors promised to consider the proposal but then came up with every conceivable objection and delay. Fraser shareholders were sent circulars from its Board which spoke of the legal difficulties, the tax complications, the accounting problems and the requirements of the Stock Exchange. It became clear that the Board was determined to stop its shareholders accepting the proposal, and if its tactic was confusion it certainly succeeded in achieving delay.

We were resolved not to give up. We canvassed opinion among the investing institutions, explaining the good sense of the demerger proposal, and we sought to put the proposal directly to Fraser's shareholders. In May 1993 they voted in support of the Board on a confidence motion linked to the proposed demerger, but only by 65.6 million votes to 63.9 million, a narrow majority. Two months later, in July, they voted in support of the demerger by a majority of 4.7 million votes.

The Fraser directors refused to accept the majority view, but before the demerger issue could be resolved on its merits events took a sinister turn. Following its defeat by shareholders the Fraser Board was clearly vulnerable. It could not risk another reference to the MMC. So, instead, Fraser and its advisers alleged that Lonrho had acted in concert with other shareholders to evade the undertakings given in 1981 not to increase its shareholding. These allegations were delivered to the Department of Trade and Industry in secret in support of a demand for an investigation under the Companies Act. On 23 August 1983 the then Secretary of State (Cecil Parkinson, the sixth Secretary of State for Trade and/or Industry to be appointed in Mrs Thatcher's four-year-old administration: his term lasted only five months) appointed an Inspector to enquire into the allegations, none of which had been put to us beforehand. Enquiry Number 3 had begun.

The appointment of a lone Inspector was an unsatisfactory way to proceed. The complexity of the issues required a tribunal of at least two, as was usual in company enquiries. (The same complaint was rightly made about the constitution of the Scott Enquiry into the export of arms to Iraq in 1994.) The Inspector who was chosen, John Griffiths, was patently unsuitable. Not only was he lacking in experience in the relevant field but while serving as Attorney General in Hong Kong he had been under heavy criticism for 'errors of judgement' and a 'grossly misleading . . . statement'. The terms of reference given to him were vague. He conducted his enquiry in a covert manner. During it he accepted a brief to appear, as a barrister, for the National Coal Board pension fund, a supporter of Fraser and Warburgs, from whose representative he had already taken evidence during this enquiry, thereby risking his impartiality. The enquiry was a bizarre affair, established for inadequate reasons, sloppily constituted and conducted by an unsatisfactory Inspector in a questionable way. One year later (and at further cost to public funds) the Inspector found that the allegations of a concert party were unproved.

Fraser's advisers had certainly learned the recipe for exploiting the machinery of Government to frustrate commercial activities: create a little fuss, whisper a few suspicions in Ministerial ears, and hey presto! out of the departmental hat comes an enquiry and a year's delay at least. Most commercial company managements, frustrated by the prospect of a tedious enquiry conducted on the whole by laymen, abandon their takeover ambitions. The amount of senior management time and the huge expense (especially the lawyers' fees) make even a good cause hardly worth the fuss. However, giving up a good cause is no part of Lonrho's style. If we could not get our proposal accepted in one way we would try another. Twice we had been frustrated; third time lucky perhaps?

Still excluded from participation in Fraser's management decisions, still convinced that Fraser was earning a smaller return on its assets than an abler and more skilled direction would obtain, Lonrho proposed resolutions at Fraser's 1984 Annual General Meeting for the appointment of a number of distinguished outsiders plus a number of Lonrho directors to the Board of Fraser. The purpose of the proposed appointments was to ensure that the issue of demerger was properly considered by a board which would be more concerned to make a disinterested assessment of the merits of the proposal than the existing directors, who had so clearly shown themselves to be prejudiced against Lonrho, their major shareholder.

However, before Fraser shareholders had the opportunity to vote, the new Secretary of State for Trade and Industry (Norman Tebbit, Mrs Thatcher's seventh appointment to the office, whose term last twenty-three months) referred the matter on 31 May 1984 to the MMC. So began Enquiry Number 4.

Only a month later, the same Secretary of State announced in the House of Commons that his merger policy had been, and would continue to be, to make referrals primarily on grounds of competition. Quite how the prospect of the shareholders of Fraser appointing additional directors to their Board constituted a threat to competition mystified everybody. Surely, we reasoned, if his policy had changed, the Minister should be releasing Lonrho from its undertakings not to bid for House of Fraser rather than initiating yet another enquiry. It was as if an amnesty had been declared and the warders forgot to release the prisoner.

The confusions didn't stop there. At the first hearing which we attended before the MMC it became clear that the Commission had not decided what it was supposed to be considering. Was it the appointment of additional directors, or was it to consider yet again the implications of a Lonrho bid? After protracted legal argument the Commission was forced to say that it would have to reserve its position until the end of the enquiry. Put bluntly, it would wait until the enquiry was over before deciding what it was supposed to be enquiring into.

For Lonrho this meant that we were locked into another gruelling and expensive investigation and it was difficult to see how it could go in our favour. How could the MMC, still under the same Chairman, Godfrey le Quesne, now admit that it had been mistaken in its 1981 report, as a result of which we had been refused permission to bid for Fraser? Matters dragged on and, to make things worse, the Chairman of MMC got the Secretary of State to extend the time allowed for the enquiry from nine months to a year. (Later we heard that another member of the Commission was surprised by this request and thought the delay unnecessary.) The four enquiries into Lonrho/Fraser were to take, in total, some four years. At Lonrho we recalled Tiny Rowland's comment about le Quesne. Sitting before him Tiny observed a hole in the sole of his shoe. 'I wondered,' said Tiny, 'how a man could be expected to organise the MMC when he couldn't even organise his own shoe repairs.'

Immediately, we faced a most serious situation. The stock market would take the extension of the enquiry as a signal that Lonrho would not be allowed to bid for the 70 per cent of the share capital in Fraser that we did not already own, and the quoted price of Fraser shares would undoubtedly fall, perhaps substantially. If it fell by £1 per share we would lose £44 million on our investment. Our own shareholders, the 60,000 owners of the Lonrho business, many of them small shareholders and dependent upon Lonrho's management to safeguard their capital and their income, would be unhappy. We could not take the risk.

At one meeting with the MMC its Chairman had asked me why we continued to hold on to our investment in Fraser shares. We took this as a strong hint that a sale would constitute the new circumstances which the Commission seemed to consider so important and afford its members an excuse to overturn their previous decision. So we decided to sell. Our Board was unanimous. There were several potential bidders and in November 1984 we sold at an excellent price to a then little known Egyptian, Mohammed Fayed, one of Lonrho's shareholders. We realised £138 million in cash, a profit of over £70 million on our original investment. We were to be criticised for making the sale; even Ministers were to be critical; but if we were not to risk losing money we had no alternative.

However, to signal our continuing interest in Fraser, we acquired a much smaller but significant shareholding (6.3 per cent) by buying shares in the market. In that way we had removed the huge downside risk of losing money on our investment while retaining a platform from which to bid for Fraser, if allowed to do so. The small shareholding would also act as a deterrent to any other outsider contemplating an offer. Tiny Rowland and Lord Duncan Sandys remained on Fraser's Board to show our commitment but they were both to be forced off it by the other Fraser directors at the end of the year.

In mid February 1985, the MMC completed its report on Lonrho and Fraser and delivered it to the Secretary of State at the Department of Trade and Industry, Norman Tebbit. The Department, however, made no announcement as to the Commission's findings. Meanwhile, it again refused our continuing request to be released from our undertakings not to bid for Fraser.

Then, on 4 March, to our astonishment at Lonrho, Mohammed Fayed and his two brothers announced a full takeover bid for House of Fraser. We knew Fayed did not have the funds. He had earlier approached Lonrho asking us to take over his interest in the Trade Centre in Dubai. He said he was afraid that the ruling family was about to expropriate it and he also pleaded an urgent need for cash. The suggested price was some $8 million. We sent one of Lonrho's directors, Robin Whitten, out to Dubai to make an inspection and subsequently rejected the deal. Now, suddenly, Fayed was in a position to acquire the entire shareholding of House of Fraser at a cost of almost £600 million. Where had the money come from? In the whole world there are very few people who have money on that scale and their names are known.

Even more astonishing to us, the bid was immediately recommended for acceptance by Professor Smith and Fraser's Board. (Professor Smith, whose professed intention it had been during the past five years to maintain the independence of the Fraser company, accepted from the bidders a substantial increase in his salary. For some reason which is not altogether clear to me this coincidence largely escaped newspaper comment, I presume because it was only coincidence.)

Articles began to appear in such national newspapers as the *Financial Times*, the *Daily Mail*, the *Sunday Telegraph* and *The Sunday Times*, all favourable and highly flattering to the Fayeds, all making claims of huge resources on their behalf: they came from an old-established Egyptian family with a history of successful and profitable trading with Britain; they had a fleet of ships, a vast unencumbered empire. The Fayeds' merchant bankers, Kleinwort Benson, peddled the same line on television. As we suspected – and as we were soon to confirm – it was bogus: a massive confidence trick engineered by the Fayeds' public relations advisers.

I now freely admit a serious misjudgement: I believed that the

Fayeds' bid would be referred to the MMC. I believed that others would express the same doubts about them and their resources as we at Lonrho had. Lonrho directors had two meetings at the Department with Tebbit and his deputy, Fletcher. The meeting with Tebbit did not go well: it seemed to me that he had already made up his mind not to make an MMC reference. Tiny Rowland made it clear that the financing for the offer from Fraser could not have come from the Fayeds' own resources, but I was astonished to see that Tebbit was indifferent to its source.

We wrote to the Department and the Office of Fair Trading urging an MMC referral and offering strong evidence to back our counter claims concerning the Fayeds' wealth. Ministers, quick to establish an enquiry into the allegations against Lonrho, were deaf to our representations. We were ignored.

On 7 March, three days after the announcement of the Fayeds' bid, the Department of Trade and Industry published the MMC report into our own bid. In a complete *volte-face* on its previous conclusion, and in the knowledge that we had sold our 30 per cent stake, the MMC gave us the go-ahead to bid. So far so good. Even so, the Secretary of State, inexplicably, still refused Lonrho's demand for an immediate release from the undertaking not to bid given by Lord Sandys some three years earlier. For the next few vital days Lonrho was held back while the Fayeds were left free to proceed and to buy Fraser's shares in the Stock Market. By 11 March they had acquired over 50 per cent, and so gained control of the company. Three days later the Secretary of State announced that he would not be referring the Fayed offer to the MMC. Only then, and on the same day, did he release Lonrho from its undertaking not to bid.

And so the ownership of an immense British retail company, the largest department store group in Europe, with stores in virtually every major British city, employing many thousands of people, providing a service for millions of British customers and work for many hundreds of British manufacturing companies, with immense buying power and influence, was taken over by unknown Egyptian brothers with no management record in the United Kingdom and no record of retailing experience anywhere in the world, with sources of finance that lay outside the knowledge of the public, and who were accountable, it would seem, to no one. Further, the Fayeds exercised their ownership though a Liechtenstein company, the shares of which are in bearer form and so can be transferred at will to anyone without a word of enquiry.

It is impossible not to believe that the Secretary of State was purposefully obstructing Lonrho in order to leave the way open for the

Fayeds. The MMC report had concluded that there was no reason (and it follows that there never had been any reason) why Lonrho should not buy Fraser. Despite that, the ban on our bidding was deliberately kept in force until the Fayeds were securely in control: only then was it lifted.

What possible motive could a British Government have for so blatantly favouring dubious foreigners over a reputable and established British company? If Lonrho had to be investigated so thoroughly, why did the Government go out of its way to see that there should be no revealing enquiries into the Fayeds?

One answer lies in the nature of bureaucracies. The Department of Trade and Industry was up against the fact that, if the MMC was right in its previous report, the Department had for years been imposing a wholly unjustified restraint on Lonrho. Bureaucracies will do a great deal to avoid that kind of admission. Then there was the prejudice against Lonrho, and against Tiny Rowland in particular. But behind it all was the fact that Government was not really worrying about commercial considerations. It was playing a hidden political game.

At Lonrho we started to learn some new and startling facts. Years before Mohammed Fayed had left the Island of Haiti in doubtful circumstances. A day or so before the bid was cleared he had lunch at 10 Downing Street at Margaret Thatcher's party for the visiting Egyptian Prime Minister. I asked Margaret why he was invited, and I told her: 'He is not the sort of man you should receive in your house.' That put it mildly: I had the gravest doubts about the man, his motives and his character. I believed he lied about himself, his background, his history and his wealth. Events would later prove me right. Margaret Thatcher said she supposed the Egyptian Embassy in London had suggested his name. We discovered Fayed had not visited Egypt in years: the Egyptian Embassy in London said he was unknown to them. We also discovered that Gordon Reece, a public relations consultant, worked both for the Prime Minister and for the Fayeds, another coincidence no doubt. (Reece was subsequently knighted on the Prime Minister's recommendation.)

More significant, we discovered that Mohammed Fayed had earlier been to Number 10 in company with the Sultan of Brunei. Did the cash used by the Fayeds to buy Fraser come from the Sultan? The answer is undoubtedly that it did – we were later to uncover evidence that the Sultan of Brunei had given Fayed a power of attorney. Was the British Prime Minister misled into believing that on this occasion Fayed was purchasing House of Fraser on the Sultan's behalf? Quite certainly.

Was this why Lonrho was unfairly denied House of Fraser? There had to be some reason and indeed there was. Money and oil. The Sultan is reputedly the richest man in the world with a personal fortune estimated by *The Sunday Times* at \$24.7 billion. More importantly, the State of Brunei is rich in oil, and sources of energy outside the Arabian Gulf have an obvious strategic value. Never mind that the Sultan, the despot of Brunei, rules illegally in defiance of a United Nations resolution of 1975 and agreements with Britain; never mind that democratic representation in Brunei is denied and dissenting citizens are imprisoned without trial. There is no criticism from Britain; we help supply troops to keep the Sultan in power.

The circumstantial evidence concerning the Sultan's involvement appears conclusive. The Sultan did not respond to communications Lonrho published: perhaps, like the British Government, he preferred not to admit he had been used. Twice Lonrho published pamphlets about the Sultan's relations with Fayed, and on neither occasion did we receive any complaint from the Sultan or his professional advisers; no writs for libel, no solicitors' warning letters. I regarded this at the time as confirmation of their accuracy. I still do.

*Before the discussions begin Mrs Thatcher will give
us her rendition of 'I'm just wild about Harrods'.*

At Lonrho, the injustice to our shareholders rankled. It became a crusade to see that justice prevailed and that the Fayeds' lies were exposed. We continued our pressure and we continued our personal investigation into the Fayeds' true origins, the findings of which we later published in a book entitled *A Hero From Zero*. Tiny Rowland himself was in touch with the Prime Minister, the Secretary of State for Trade and Industry (both Norman Tebbit and his successor, Leon Brittan) and the Director General of Fair Trading no less than fifteen times between June 1985 and March 1986.

At last the tide began to turn. The *Financial Times* published an article questioning the Fayeds' claims. Immediately afterwards it published an apology. Fayed, like Maxwell, knew how to muzzle the potential critics. Then another journalist, Peter Wickman, revealed facts about the Fayeds' origins in an article in the *Observer*. Unusually, the Fayeds did not issue a writ for libel. This was significant, like the dog that did not bark in the night: it indicated that Wickman's article was accurate. At that time the *Observer* was owned by Lonrho which had purchased it from its American owners, the Atlantic Richfield Oil Company, in 1981. Of course we were only able to buy the paper after an official enquiry which cleared us to bid, the fifth enquiry we suffered in those years.

'I'm putting you on the Lonrho inquiry, Hammersley
– an excellent career with a substantial pension.'

The Government had rightly insisted that Lonrho should not influence the *Observer's* editorial policy and had appointed independent directors of the paper to ensure that we did not. Even so, I was later told that various Conservatives blamed Tiny Rowland and myself for Wickman's article, and even Mrs Thatcher blamed us for subsequent pieces that were to appear in the *Observer*, including those questioning the origins of Mark Thatcher's wealth.

On 9 April 1987 Paul Channon (the ninth Trade and Industry Secretary since Margaret Thatcher came to power in 1979: he was in office for seventeen months) announced an enquiry into the circumstances of the Fayeds' purchase of shares in Fraser in 1984 and 1985. Now, I thought, the truth will out and we will be vindicated. The Inspectors were a distinguished leading counsel and a senior chartered accountant. That was to be the sixth enquiry, but the only one for which it can truthfully be said there was a compelling *raison d'être*.

Fayed continuously vented his spleen on Lonrho. His lawyers and other associates tried to disrupt our shareholders' meetings and to discredit our Board, our accounts and our professional advisers and accountants. They made complaints to the Stock Exchange and the Institute of Chartered Accountants. After enquiries lasting some months, both bodies flatly rejected them. Tiny Rowland was attacked in circulars. Fayed's insinuations were foul and deeply offensive; if Tiny Rowland was hurt by them, and he must have been, he was too big a man to show it. In one circular he was accused of being a Nazi. I said I hoped he'd sue the authors. He reminded me of the late D. K. Ludwig's vulgar but realistic advice: 'Never get in a pissing match with a skunk.'

The Inspectors' report was delivered to the Secretary of State (Lord Young, the tenth holder of that office since 1979: he held the post for two years and one month) at the end of July 1988. Almost two months went by. Then Lord Young told Lonrho's directors, at a meeting at his Department in September, that he would publish it. He did not. The excuse, we later heard, was that the Serious Fraud Office suggested that publication would prejudice any criminal proceedings. That seemed surprising: we were not aware of any precedent for this inaction; but even when the SFO's enquiries were completed the report remained unpublished. None of us at Lonrho knew what it contained.

At the end of November 1988 Lord Young announced publicly that he would not publish the Inspectors' report nor would he refer the Fayeds' takeover of House of Fraser to the MMC. Following this, Young and I both received invitations to be interviewed on the 'Today' programme on Radio 4. Always avid for publicity, Young accepted the invitation. I consented also to appear if I could be interviewed second. I heard his interview on my car radio parked in Portland Place outside the BBC while I waited to enter the building. He admitted that the report disclosed 'wrongdoing'. I dashed inside: 'He's given the game away,' I said on air in reply to Brian Redhead, and again demanded that the Department publish the report. The *Evening Standard* gave that exchange huge headlines on its front page – bigger than the Milk Street Mafia spread that had infuriated the 1922 Committee some years earlier.

'It was horrible Sir Edward. I was just taking dictation when a mummy rushed in and laid a curse on Mr Rowland.'

We took Lord Young to court, and won a direction that he should both publish and make a Monopolies Commission reference. On appeal the case was lost – I am not the only one in recent years to have expressed nervousness at the judiciary's reluctance to quarrel with or question the Executive's decisions. We lost our case again in the House of Lords, though I recall with admiration the moral courage of one judge, Lord Justice Watkins VC, who declared that no responsible Minister could have reached the decision arrived at by Young: it was 'irrational' and the suggestion made by the SFO that publication of the report would interfere with their collection of evidence was 'fanciful'.

Mohammed Fayed maintained his scurrilous personal attacks on us. For a long time he employed a sad lady to distribute letters and pamphlets mostly attacking Tiny Rowland and sometimes myself. She paraded outside our City offices and our shareholders' meetings. Eventually she realised that she had been exploited and called at our offices to confess her regret. She gave a detailed statement to our solicitors with a full account of her dealings with Fayed and the cash payments she had received.

I must record that not all the world was sympathetic to our complaint or to our attempt to see villains exposed. Attacks on Lonrho were made in the House of Commons, two of them coming from a Tory MP, Tim Smith, who did not disclose that he was an indirect beneficiary of the Fayeds' charitable largesse. He was to get his comeuppance in 1994.

Ted Heath and Lord Chalfont both attacked Tiny Rowland for being critical of the Sultan of Brunei. We replied to them in circulars to which we gave a wide circulation, but the predominant reaction from the establishment was, at best, 'What's done is done, so stop boring us.' The English, of course, hate being involved in embarrassing situations, and I found that, however hard I tried to stand up for what I knew to be right, to be involved in a dispute of this kind can make one a suspect character. When Princess Margaret visited my constituency the Lord Lieutenant of Somerset invited me to lunch with her. At her request the invitation was withdrawn 'because of the Fayed row.' It sickened me that a close member of the Sovereign's family should ostracise me because of my attempt to defend the right and expose villainy.

Other unhappy circumstances came to light. A fulsome testimonial for the Fayeds was written by a member of the Sunley construction family and sent to the Inspectors: it was false. Sunley was known to have connections with Lord Young and Denis Thatcher. It was even rumoured that Mark Thatcher had visited Brunei in 1954 and had been in touch with the Fayeds.

The Inspectors' report might have remained buried in departmental files if it had not been for an extraordinary event. There was a substantial undercurrent of public indignation at the treatment of Lonrho and at officialdom's cover-up, and one day this took unexpected practical shape. Just before Easter 1989 an unknown person delivered a duplicated copy of the Inspectors' report to Lonrho's city office in a carrier bag. Someone was apparently keen to see justice done.

I read the report in full on my return to the office after the Easter holiday. It was a devastating indictment of the Fayeds for their blatant lies about themselves, their family history and their sources of funds. It was an indictment of Kleinworts, their merchant bankers, and Herbert Smith, their solicitors, for their acceptance of the Fayeds' self-valuations without adequate scrutiny. It was an indictment, too, of the newspaper editors who similarly accepted the public relations blurbs about the Fayeds without careful verification. It itemised the numerous occasions on which we at Lonrho had drawn the attention of officials, the Office of Fair Trading and Ministers – Tebbit and his deputy Fletcher – to the facts about the Fayeds. The report stopped short of criticising Ministers – as events were to prove, if the report was published the commentators would certainly not be so kind – but the implication was clear as crystal. The Government was the victim of a confidence trick. An injustice had been done. Ministers and the Department of Trade and Industry were to blame. No wonder Lord Young had decided not to publish the report: no wonder officials had advised him to suppress it. The Department was already under strong public criticism for failing to heed warnings about dishonesty in a company called Barlow Clowes which collapsed owing over £100 million and whose investors had been defrauded. The warnings given to officials and to Ministers about the Fayeds were more numerous, more frequent and more specific and detailed than had been the case over Barlow Clowes.

The question for Lonrho was how to bring the report out into the open, how to force publication? The photocopy delivered to us was patently genuine. We had waited so long for the truth to be revealed. Now we had it in our hands the truth about the Fayeds' misrepresentations clearly stated by impeccable authority. Of the Government's two appointed Inspectors one, Henry Brooke, was a leading QC, shortly to be knighted and made a judge. The second, Hugh Aldous, was a chartered accountant, one of the senior partners in a leading British practice. Their integrity was undoubted. At last, at last! Now we could surely settle this matter once and for all; force the Fayeds to divest themselves of House of Fraser; produce for our shareholders the result we had so keenly sought for so long. All that expense, all that travail, all the attacks we had borne, none had been in vain. It was a great moment.

But the practical question remained – how to bring the report out into the open?

Donald Trelford, Editor of the *Observer* was told that we had a copy of the report. Immediately after the Easter weekend, Trelford, a number of Lonrho directors and I met Tiny Rowland in the garden of his home in Chester Square. Trelford, like us, was excited by the report. Melvyn Marckus, the *Observer's* respected and successful City Editor, had been indefatigable in his questioning about the Fraser affair, and in that respect he was almost a lone voice in Fleet Street. The *Observer* had been attacked by its sister newspapers for its support of Lonrho's continued battle for justice and we were delighted to find that in their report the Inspectors paid its editor and its writers a justified tribute. 'The paper had been virtually alone among national newspapers,' they wrote, 'in being willing to put at issue the honesty and bona fides of the Fayeds.' Furthermore they saw no reasons to contradict the judgement of the *Observer's* independent directors that there had been no improper interference by the proprietor in this respect. They confirmed the editorial integrity of the paper and gave the lie to Mohammed Fayed and others who had complained that the *Observer* was no more than Lonrho's mouthpiece.

There were immediate practical problems for the Board of Lonrho to face in dealing with the report. The Annual General Meeting of Lonrho's shareholders would take place in London, in the Great Room of the Grosvenor House Hotel, in three days' time. The Lonrho AGM was invariably one of the best attended company meetings in the UK with up to 1,500 people present, and the Great Room would again be full to overflowing. At these meetings it was the usual practice for me to conduct the meeting, make a speech about our Company's progress and subsequently to answer all the questions from shareholders, a heavy responsibility but one I enjoyed and felt at home with.

At a meeting of shareholders the previous year I had referred to the Inspectors' report, as I was bound to do, urging that it should be published. Now, a year later, we knew its content. We had in our hands the justification for all we had said in past years. Our shareholders had paid dearly for this history. They had every right to know the truth. The problem was how to present it to them.

There was much discussion among us and in the end it was Trelford who volunteered the solution. The *Observer* would produce a special edition. It would be on the news-stands on the Thursday morning, the morning of our shareholders' meeting, and a copy would be placed on every chair in the Great Room.

Trelford produced a strong, hard hitting document of sixteen pages, retailing at 25p a copy. Headlined *Exposed: The Phoney Pharaoh*, it contained extracts from the report and stated of Lord Young that he had not 'acted in good faith' and was a 'party to a cover up'.

By the time the AGM of Lonrho's shareholders started at 11.45 a.m. a quarter of a million copies of the *Observer's* supplement had been printed and distributed. Every shareholder had a copy. I took the chair at the meeting and spoke for longer than usual, to a packed hall. I rehearsed the basic facts of the long dispute and then came to the Inspectors' Report which had so completely vindicated us. I told the meeting how Lord Young had met members of our Board and had undertaken to publish the Report but had later reneged on that undertaking. I also read out part of the Report, which included the following damning judgements:

> The Fayeds dishonestly misrepresented their origins, their wealth, their business interests and their resources . . .
>
> We received evidence from the Fayeds, under solemn affirmation and in written memoranda, which was false and which the Fayeds knew to be false . . . The evidence before us . . . indicates that it is likely that the Fayeds used their association with the Sultan of Brunei and the opportunities afforded to them by the wide powers of attorney from the Sultan of Brunei to enable them to acquire those funds [for the acquisition].
>
> The lies which the Fayeds were telling about themselves and their resources have been given a credibility they would not otherwise have attained when they were repeated by their very reputable advisers. Their advisers accepted at face value what they were told by the Fayeds. In our opinion they did not take sufficient steps to check the accuracy of what they were told.

Apart from applause and occasional gales of laughter, I was heard without interruption or dissent of any kind. 'A shoplifter at Harrods would be prosecuted,' I said. 'These people have pinched the whole shop – they should not be allowed to get away with it.'

Prompt action by the Department of Trade and Industry's lawyers followed. At Lonrho we had discussed among ourselves the possibility that the Government would obtain an injunction to stop publication of the Report. Nothing had happened so far as we were aware before the shareholders' meeting began but while I was speaking I was conscious of much activity behind the scenes. Telephones were ringing in the Great Hall. Messages were being passed to the platform. The lawyers seated behind me got up and left the platform and then returned. Well accustomed as I was to open-air political meetings with constant interruptions (not to mention loutish behaviour indoors in the House of Commons) I found it possible to get on with my speech and at the same time take in some of what was happening around me.

A note was put in front of me: I knew what it said without reading it. The Government had gone to Court to get an injunction to stop distribution of the *Observer* and to stop me disclosing the report's contents. I had no intention of slowing down, let alone stopping. I had, I believed, in the interests of good Government and of Lonrho's shareholders, to tell the truth and that is what I did.

Young did not restrain his fury. He made a statement in the House of Lords. It came in response to a question by Labour's front bench spokesman, Lord Williams, and it was full of sanctimonious humbug. Young gave an account of events designed to put Lonrho and the *Observer* in a poor light and to represent himself as a pillar of rectitude and sensible conduct. It was, he said his 'dearest wish' to publish the report; however, his hands were tied. The matters disclosed in the report were of 'such a nature' that he had 'no choice but to refer the report to the Serious Fraud Office and the Director of Public Prosecutions,' and of course that made publication impossible. Strange, then, that when, seven months earlier, he had given his undertaking to Lonrho's directors that he would publish the report he did not mention the SFO or the DPP.

He went on to say that there were 'no public interest grounds for a reference to the Monopolies and Mergers Commission.' It is hard to see how that could be the case if the matters disclosed in the report were so serious as to warrant a reference to the authorities responsible for criminal investigations.

'I greatly deplore,' he said, 'the *Observer's* action in publishing this special edition . . . I also greatly deplore Lonrho's use of the special edition at their annual general meeting.' He went on to allege that I had refused to return the copies of the report or to give him voluntarily an affidavit saying how the copies had come into Lonrho's possession. In both these respects he came close to misleading the House. All the copies of the Report which we had made were returned and I had no reason not to say that a copy had been delivered anonymously to Lonrho's city offices.

The Labour spokesman, Lord Williams, was good enough to 'regret the use of this House for personal attacks on persons who are not members of the House'. Quite rightly, he suggested that there was an element of absurdity in the Government's refusal to publish the Report when its contents were now widely known, a copy of the *Observer's* special edition being available in the library of the House of Lords. Four of Young's subsequent questioners complained that if the criminal investigating authorities had received the report as long ago as the 26 July 1988, it was absurd that on the 3 April 1989, almost nine months later, no decision had yet been made about any prosecution.

Throughout the thirty-minute debate Lord Young maintained the posture of an injured innocent. He had obtained an injunction to stop any future publication of the *Observer's* special issue, he said, yet he acknowledged that its circulation to date would not prejudice a trial if there was one. He posed as a defender of the law, although the effect of his actions – and his inaction – was to be that wrongdoers escaped the law.

Rereading the exchanges after the passage of time I have no reason to doubt the opinion I formed when I first read them. Young's conduct of the affair was a scandal.

Now I was guilty of another misjudgement. I expected that other newspapers and also some Members of Parliament, concerned to see the best practices in corporate affairs and the sensible regulation of them, would feature the report and its conclusions, demand redress, insist that what the Fayeds had gained by deceit they should be forced to surrender, call for better practices in the City, more effective safeguards to protect British shareholders and the like. Not a bit of it. MPs were silent. The newspapers, proved to be gullible, were unwilling to admit their errors: they preferred to attack the *Observer* for being, they alleged, in thrall to Lonrho and Tiny Rowland. The police sent two officers on a fruitless and ridiculed visit to Cairo, but otherwise did nothing. There was a conspiracy of silence and inaction.

Lonrho and four of its directors were to be the victims of further embarrassment. Over a period of time we had sent a multitude of circulars giving our point of view to opinion-formers – company directors, Members of both Houses of Parliament, lawyers, accountants, professional people and the like – as any individual or group of citizens in our free society has a right to do. In a case heard by the Appellate Committee of the House of Lords in March 1987 the presiding judge, Lord Keith of Kinkel, had complained that some of these had been received by judges. There were other similar complaints and Lonrho was advised by its solicitors not to send such literature in future to judges and especially to Lords of Appeal. Unfortunately the clear instruction given by the member of Lonrho's Board responsible for such matters was, through an administrative mistake, not acted on by the mailing clerks; some more circulars, including the special edition of the *Observer,* were sent to judges.

I only learned of this when, together with Tiny Rowland, two other directors of Lonrho, the Editor of the *Observer,* a partner of our solicitors and a young barrister who had acted for us – seven of us in all – I found myself hauled before a tribunal of Law Lords accused of contempt of court. It would have been foolish to argue. We did as we were advised and made handsome apologies. Lord Keith and his colleagues were unforgiving: the trial for contempt must proceed, they ruled.

Our advisers told us, jokingly perhaps, that the last action of this kind had taken place more than a hundred years ago, and that the lady accused of contempt was found guilty and hanged. We hoped that history was apocryphal, but it cast a cloud of gloom over us when we attended the House of Lords to defend ourselves. We also felt extremely impatient. I repeated to myself the familiar French aphorism, '*Cet animal est très méchant. Quand on l'attaque il se défend.*'

We had learned of Lord Keith's complaint in early April 1989. The hearing of the case began in the House of Lords on 23 May and the final judgement was received on 27 July. Thus the proceedings occupied our attention for four months and we spent some four weeks, off and on, in the Moses Room in the House of Lords, used by their Lordships as a courtroom.

The trial was an example of our country's legal incompetence at its worst. Five Law Lords sat at one end of the room, as far from the defendants as possible, but on the same level so that it was impossible to see them. When they spoke, they did so in low voices and much of the proceedings were inaudible.

I felt I was at the Mad Hatter's tea party. How could it be that we who were advocates of truth and justice found ourselves arraigned before five of the most senior judges in the land at the whim of an elderly man whose chief motive appeared to be spite? Nonetheless I looked forward to addressing their Lordships from the witness chair when my turn came. I was determined to have my say and to expose the business for the idiotic and contemptible farce that I thought it was.

But in the event the tribunal recused itself (meaning that it resigned from the case) and so justified the complaint made by our counsel that they might be thought to be biased against us. Three other Law Lords were appointed in their stead, and this new and smaller tribunal quickly dismissed the case without even calling upon the defence witnesses to give evidence. Pleased as I was with the result, I admit to more than a twinge of disappointment that I had lost the chance to make my case from the witness chair.

The case of contempt should never have been brought. It wasted much time and it cost us many hundreds of thousands of pounds in legal expenses to defend our company and ourselves. There was no recourse against Lord Keith.

The Inspectors' Report was eventually published by Lord Young's successor, Nicholas Ridley (Margaret Thatcher's eleventh Secretary of State since 1979 who was to be in office for only a year) in March 1990. In a short statement in the House of Commons, lasting under two minutes, he announced that there would be no prosecution against the Fayeds. It was not, he said, in the public interest even to disqualify the Fayeds from acting as directors. Disqualification was 'not a punishment'. Harrods was not to be deprived of its Royal Warrants.

The House of Commons gave Ridley a hard time. He was questioned by no less than sixteen MPs and his response was to shift responsibility onto others. He said that it was for the Attorney General to decide whether the Fayeds should be prosecuted for perjury or for giving false evidence; it was for the Law Society and the Bank of England or others to decide whether the Fayeds' advisers, their merchant bankers and solicitors, should have any action taken against them.

Labour's front bench spokesman asked perhaps the most pertinent question: why had Tebbit cleared the Fayeds' bid for Fraser in only ten days although allegations about their unfitness, now known to be true, were known to him and had been made with vigour? Sir Teddy Taylor made the same point. Many MPs used strong language. Ridley stonewalled. Perhaps the truth was that his hands were tied by a decision which had been made by Prime Minister Thatcher and Norman Tebbit in 1985. However, that decision was now conclusively shown to be wrong, and nothing can excuse the Government's failure to take action against the Fayeds in the light of the clear conclusions of the report.

The All-Party Select Committee on Trade and Industry under the Chairmanship of Sir Kenneth Warren MP had meantime been conducting an enquiry into company investigations. It took evidence widely, from the Department, the Bank of England and the Law Society, among others. I had earlier sent the Committee a memorandum giving my own view of the way in which Ministers and the Department had mishandled the takeover of Fraser.

The Committee reported to the House of Commons two months after Ridley's statement. The Report was scathing. It attacked three Secretaries of State for their handling of the Fraser affair. Sir Leon Brittan was criticised for failing to appoint Inspectors (as Lonrho had recommended). Ridley was criticised for not having allowed the courts to decide whether or not the Fayeds should be disqualified as company directors (as Lonrho had recommended). Lord Young was criticised for not referring the Fraser takeover to the Monopolies and Mergers Commission (as Lonrho had recommended). Thereby, said the Committee, Lord Young 'deprived himself of the most potent weapon available to him to respond to a manifest breach of the UK regulatory system'.

Still no significant action followed. Lonrho did begin litigation, notably against the two Secretaries of State, Ridley and Tebbit, but litigation in Britain is a long and expensive business and in 1993, after Bock became the controlling influence at Lonrho, the last suit was dropped. Tiny Rowland and Mohammed Fayed were photographed together in apparent camaraderie.

The ironies continue. Harrods has been demerged from the rest of the Fraser stores (as Lonrho had earlier recommended). The sale of the provincial Fraser stores realised over £400 million for the Fayeds. That sum, when earlier sales of some thirty stores in the original group and capital additions are taken into account, roughly equates to what the Fayeds had paid for the whole Fraser group. Harrods (and its not inconsiderable other assets) which one can value at at least £750 million has therefore cost the Fayeds nothing. Who says that misrepresentation does not pay?

I have often heard people say, Who cares who owns Harrods? What does it matter? I care, and I care deeply. Officials and Ministers have been deceived; lies and perjury have gone unpunished. Their perpetrators now own a substantial British company and have made themselves rich. All who care about truth and justice and commercial probity should share my concern.

The extent of the Fayeds' malign influence continues to be exposed. Neil Hamilton was accused of accepting hospitality from Mohammed Fayed at the Ritz Hotel in Paris. He denied the allegations and the Select Committee concerned decided that he had breached no rules. Yet he was forced to resign as a Minister and one might well ask why he was consorting with such people at all.

Tim Smith, a junior Northern Ireland Minister, was also obliged to resign his position in late 1994. He admitted not declaring his links with

Fayed, although Lonrho had criticised him in an open letter as long ago as January 1989 when, in the House of Commons, he attacked our exposure of Mohammed Fayed.

It is clear that the Fayeds have been free with their largesse, not least to journalists, and they would not be human if they did not expect favours in return.

A further example of their methods was when Mohammed Fayed's pique at the scathing denunciation of his conduct by the Inspectors in 1994 apparently led him to send an emissary to see the Prime Minister in an attempt to get the report withdrawn. The Prime Minister rightly sent a full account to the Director of Public Prosecutions. Since this coincided with an attempt in conjunction with the *Guardian* to blacken the good name of at least one Member of the Cabinet it is unsurprising that one backbench MP suggested that a blackmail attempt had been made. Unusually, the authorities completed their enquiries with despatch but recommended that no action be taken against Fayed.

Today's emphasis is on formal rules for the conduct of MPs (in Mr Hamilton's case, for example, on whether the letter of old obligations was obeyed). It has been too easily forgotten that the spirit is more significant than the letter. The institution in the House of Commons of a register of Members' interests has been a useful step but it has not terminated abuses. Sadly, it is clear that the standard of Members' behaviour since its introduction has fallen, not risen. The public expects Conservative politicians to conduct themselves properly: it is a shame that a larger number than used to be the case fail to do so.

Quite apart from the question of corruption (and it has been suggested that the Fayeds were handsome contributors to Tory Party funds), Norman Tebbit asked a staggering question when Lonrho's Board went to meet him in March 1985: 'What does it matter who brings in the money providing it's brought in?' Tiny Rowland asked him, 'What if it came from the IRA?' He got no answer but the point is a valid one. What if the money for a company takeover comes from the Mafia or one of the other huge criminal syndicates which control resources worth millions of pounds, and which are eager to invest in legitimate businesses? Of course it matters and responsible Government has a duty to be concerned, to investigate sources of finance and to bar criminals from commercial activity.

Who cares who gets Harrods? Who cares if a foreigner owns *The Times* or the *Daily Telegraph*? Does it matter if BMW buys up Rover and the last British large-scale car manufacturer passes into foreign ownership?

I care, is my answer. It does matter. If Ministers do not care, they should.

British commerce is increasingly owned by foreigners – even Lonrho. I have found it sad to contemplate the company's recent history. Thanks to Tiny Rowland's excellent German connections and his understanding of the German scene, we developed successful partnerships with several important German enterprises over the years: we handled the distribution of Audi and Volkswagen cars in the UK; we owned a half share in Kuhne and Nagel, one of the largest firms of freight forwarders in the world; and a co-operative venture in the development arm of Krupp. In the context of Germany's remarkable industrial and economic advance since the War these were far-sighted moves: they made Lonrho one of Germany's largest foreign investors. Then, for the first time in thirty years, Tiny Rowland sold shares in Lonrho to a foreigner – Dieter Bock, a German property developer – taking him in effect as a partner.

Judged by an outsider (so far as that is possible), it seems that Mr Bock is hardly a man of his word. In 1994 Tiny Rowland surprisingly announced his decision to retire as joint Chief Executive. It was announced that he would become the Company's President. In a remarkable *volte-face* Bock allowed the defeat of this proposal at Lonrho's annual general meeting of shareholders in early 1995: the smaller shareholders at the meeting voted overwhelmingly in favour of Tiny, the institutions lodged proxy votes against.

The City of London, its critics rightly argue, likes a short-term profit: the prospect of a few extra pennies on a share price often outweighs all other long-term considerations. Institutional shareholders believed apparently that the constituent parts of Lonrho are more valuable than the whole. It is sad to see useful or profitable parts of the Lonrho portfolio of investments sold off. The *Observer* was sold at a good profit, the announcement being made on the day Bock joined Lonrho. The latest disposal was the Krupp holding, surely a mistake since the potential for profitable work in the former Soviet empire must be huge.

The break up of a great British enterprise is to be regretted; so is the insensitivity of those who acquiesced in the ousting and humiliation of its founder, not least those who owed their positions to him; so, last, but by no means least, is the dismissal of so many employees in junior positions in the UK and Africa to whom Lonrho was not just an employer but also a way of life. It is an anti-climax to a marvellous and romantic success story.

For the first time in my life I have some sympathy with the Labour Party that the commanding heights of the British economy should be in British hands – not in state hands of course, but British owned. British owners of British businesses can, in general, be trusted to manage them in the British interest: foreign owners cannot. In the case of Harrods, the Trade Union of Shopworkers, USDAW, has, in a seven month period at the end of 1994, and early 1995, won twenty-five tribunal cases against Harrods on behalf of workers who had been unfairly sacked or victims of racial discrimination.

Whoever owns British newspapers (or TV stations or publishers) will mould British opinion; whoever owns British retail outlets will patronise the suppliers he favours, British or foreign; whoever controls a British car manufacturer will wield vast purchasing power and decide whether the components are manufactured in Birmingham or Dusseldorf – or Nagasaki. Besides manufacturers and newspaper owners, the controllers of banks and insurance companies and the managers of pension funds now wield vast economic power. Perhaps we should not attempt too much control or influence over these natural forces; but the least we can do, surely, is to ensure that this power is never used against the British interest. We cannot afford to delegate any future influence in our country to those who may not put British interests first: we have already surrendered too much.

Over recent decades we have watched ourselves ousted from our own market in various industries, such as consumer electronics and shipbuilding – two examples out of many that readily occur. How much further has this process to go? This is a question that merits a high place on the current political agenda. The Conservative Political Centre would do well to promote discussion papers on subjects of such fundamental importance.

Ministers say, and rightly, that the UK economy can benefit from foreign competition: a little competition will sharpen us all up, make us keener. So it may, but to allow the Japanese or other foreign producers to destroy large areas of British industry, as they have, is sheer folly. During my lifetime whole industries have disappeared. Of course, some industries come and go as technology advances, but that does not mean that we should lose control of economic or industrial development in our own country. Foreign ownership of British businesses has gone too far for comfort.

One example will suffice. In 1984 I founded the All-Party Parliamentary Maritime Affairs Group in the House of Commons. I got Jim

Callaghan, who had been a wartime naval petty officer, from the Labour Party and David Owen from the Centre Party to join me. I had been shocked at the decline of the British merchant fleet. In 1900 UK registered shipping (ships of 100 gross tonnes and over) represented 51.5 per cent of world tonnage; by 1970 the figure had fallen to 6.4 per cent; by 1990 it was less than 2 per cent. As I said in the House, it would be impossible now to mount another Falklands operation. The UK does not have the ships. Apart from defence considerations, there are many good reasons, economic and social, for wanting an expanded UK fleet: to develop Britain's excellent maritime services, chartering, insurance and the like; to provide a greater number of ships available to Government in times of crisis; and by no means least, to provide revenue and employment, direct and indirect. Through Government indifference an important British industry has been hugely reduced and what makes it still more inexcusable is that the reasons for the decline in the British merchant fleet are easily remediable by the adoption of favourable fiscal measures and more aggressive Government action in the European Community.

This is true more generally. The wholesale takeover of British business could easily be influenced and even reversed by a Government that had the will to do it. But the will is lacking, and the reason for that lies in a more general failing. In all my commercial experience, and especially as the Fraser affair ground on its way, one fact was borne in on me time and again. The Government and the Civil Service do not understand business and neither greatly cares for it. There is too little contact between the two worlds, and what contact there is is often of the wrong kind. The means some lobbies use to pursue their ends can be dubious, to say the least, and because senior civil servants have no commercial experience they too often lack the judgement to distinguish between a good case badly presented and a poor case presented well or to realise when they are being misled.

There is also the danger of a so-called political adviser using his position of influence within Government to advance a private cause. This demands an important reform. Whenever people from outside the Civil Service are appointed to a ministerial private office they should be obliged to include in a public register all their past and present commercial interests, including the names of the companies for which they have worked, as Members of Parliament have to do.

There is no doubt that powerful lobbies, even without recourse to illegitimate means, are able to influence Government policy to favour their interests. Perhaps the most notorious example of this is the way the whole of European agriculture has been distorted by the EU's Common Agricultural Policy for the benefit of French or German farmers and at immense cost to the rest of us. Net producer subsidy equivalents now exceed 40 per cent of the value of total farm production, equal to almost $80 billion, and the figure and the proportion has grown markedly in recent years. Faced with such abuses, it is easy to plead for a complete divorce of Government from business, but in my view that would be a serious mistake. The less Governments understand commercial realities the easier it will be for the unscrupulous to manipulate them while legitimate businesses will go on suffering from lack of enthusiastic support on the part of Ministers or civil servants.

Much of the problem lies within the civil service. The overwhelming majority of senior civil servants have not had and never will have any commercial experience whatever, while the number of industrial managers who have had any first-hand experience of civil service work is equally infinitesimal. People from commerce who suddenly find themselves involved with ministries at a senior level, as my colleagues in the steel industry in Lonrho did, are often appalled at the seeming lack of commercial understanding on the part of the officials with whom they are dealing; and, it has to be admitted, their occasional indifference.

The secondments for two or three years of managers in commerce or industry to civil service work (or vice versa) are excellent (and the President of the Board of Trade boasted of some ninety secondees in his department in 1994) but they are too few to change the general ethos. More interchange between commercial and Governmental bodies, with rigorous safeguards against improper influence, should be fostered in Britain. Something far more radical than the Government's proposals of 1994 is required.

The problem starts in the field of education. My friend Sir John Templeton, an American and a Rhodes scholar at Oxford before the War, was so shocked by the uninterested attitude of the university authorities towards business that a few years ago he generously endowed Templeton College as a business centre. I was pleased to help him achieve this. His example deserves to be more widely followed. Oxford University and various of its colleges are now appealing to business for funds to be subscribed on a massive scale. They want business to support them but it seems that in other ways they prefer to keep their distance from it. My old college, St Johns, for example, numbers not a single businessman on its list of some twenty honorary fellows.

Many of our MPs, too, are surprisingly ignorant about what goes on

256

in the industrial and financial worlds. It is the aim of bodies such as the Industry and Parliament Trust to enable MPs, officers of both Houses of Parliament and MEPs to widen their experience and knowledge of industry, and also to help business managers understand the problems of Parliament in dealing with matters affecting industry. In any year some sixty MPs and MEPs are involved in courses. This is excellent but the body is underfunded and no part-time academic experience can possibly be a substitute for full-time managerial involvement.

Perhaps the exposure of the Fayeds' duplicity had one satisfactory result, the refusal in 1994 by the Home Secretary to grant UK citizenship to two of the brothers. Other tasks remain.

Something must be done to see that professionals such as lawyers and accountants take greater care to investigate the bona fides of the companies that employ them. In the Fraser affair it was the naiveté and amateurishness of the solicitors and bankers involved that allowed the Fayeds' lies about themselves and their resources to go unchallenged by anyone except Lonrho. Those solicitors and bankers were among the most prominent in their fields and it was upon their support of their clients that Government chiefly relied. There have been several other notorious cases in the last few years where it is clear that the professionals involved have been similarly naive, to put it at its kindest.

Something – perhaps a great deal – could be achieved by insistence on greater openness in Government. The Americans may have gone too far in this but quite certainly we have not gone far enough. If it had not been for the anonymous caller with the plastic bag the Inspectors' report on the Lonrho/Fraser affair could have been buried for ever, as officials obviously wanted. It should never be the case that those whose misdeeds and incompetence are to be exposed are the same people who decide whether that exposure shall be made. Unless there is a genuine threat to national security or some other vital interest (which does not include giving officials or Ministers a comfortable life) it should be mandatory for reports to be published and published promptly.

Along with this goes a need for greater protection of private people from allegations made against them by Governmental or quasi-Governmental bodies without their having an adequate right of reply. Ironically, this point is now being made, of all people, by the Fayeds themselves. They have opened a campaign alleging that they were treated unfairly and that 'the British system of enquiries is out of step with other nations' (reported in the *Evening Standard* in April 1994). Now of course it is true that anyone familiar with the Fayeds and their behaviour must find it richly comic that they should be the ones to complain of unfair treatment, especially since the criticisms made of them by the Inspectors would assuredly have been put directly to them and their advisers and they would have had every opportunity to reply, but nevertheless the general point is a valid one. It is possible for someone to be investigated by a board of enquiry of whose accusations he is not informed, and to which he is given no right of reply or even an opportunity to question the evidence.

I found this out to my cost some time after the Fraser affair was over, and I realised then how prescient Donald Trelford's editorial in the *Observer* supplement had been. He wrote:

> The report makes it clear and we modestly admit, that the only people not led up the garden path were Lonrho, the *Observer* and the Poirot-like inspectors themselves. By publishing today we are ensuring that the public is not led up the same path. The Government, of course, may not take this charitable view of our public contribution. It is hard to forgive people for being so completely right and they will doubtless try to find ways to make us pay for it.

Two years later officials at the Department of Trade found an opportunity to revenge themselves on the Chairman of Lonrho. They seized it eagerly.

BATTLING
ON

I was still Chairman of Lonrho when in August 1991 I was told out of the blue that the Government was to take action against me. The outcome of this has been personal catastrophe. One result was that I lost my home, which is ironical because I had been helping other people to buy their own houses. But I must not anticipate: a social issue as important as housing deserves some background. Also, my own crash may best be interpreted as the result of failures in Government policy: first, that a historically distorted housing market has been reformed only by fits and starts; second, that no Government has seriously tried to rectify the wrongs inherent in the public enquiry system, which continues to be a shameful anomaly. It is these two failures rather than a desire to complain about my personal problems that have prompted me to write this chapter.

Housing in Britain, throughout my lifetime and much of my father's, has been the subject of social engineering on a grand scale. It started during the First World War when, in 1915, Parliament passed an Act giving tenants a new security and limiting increases in mortgage costs. It was meant to be a temporary wartime measure but in fact rent restrictions have continued as a permanency, with more than fifteen Acts of Parliament following that first 'temporary' measure.

In 1914 only about 10 per cent of homes were owner-occupied; the rest were rented from private landlords. Between the wars council housing, which also began at about that period, became increasingly important and by the outbreak of the Second World War it accounted for 10 per cent of the 11½ million dwellings in England and Wales. The number of owner-occupied homes had risen to about a third of the total while the number of those privately rented had fallen to under 60 per cent.

Under the Socialist Government elected in 1945 a doctrinaire approach prevailed. New house building was almost entirely by public authorities for rent. Rent controls in the private rented sector were fiercely maintained and that sector continued to shrink. The choice for families became increasingly between owner-occupation and a tenancy from the public authorities. By 1951, when the Conservatives were again elected to office, owner-occupation accounted for 31 per cent of the housing stock and the public rented sector had grown to almost 20 per cent. Even under Conservative Governments the increase in local authority ownership continued. By 1978 Britain's housing stock had hugely increased to more than 20 million homes, with public sector tenants occupying almost one third of them.

Reflecting on events since I became involved in politics, I cannot understand why it took the Conservative Party so long to press hard, as a policy objective, the proposal to sell council-owned houses and flats to sitting tenants. We continuously boasted that we supported home ownership as a concept, and we adopted various fiscal measures to facilitate it. For example, as I have recorded, in the Budget of 1963, during my time as a Treasury Minister, we abolished the much disliked Schedule A tax (an extra impost on home owners). We halved the rate of Stamp Duty on conveyances to 1 per cent and abolished it altogether on smaller transactions. So far so good: we could and should have done so much more, and years earlier.

The imaginative phrase about a property-owning democracy was first heard in the 1920s but it was Anthony Eden who gave it emphasis in his speech to the Conservative Party conference in Blackpool in 1946. This excited much attention. The idea had universal appeal and it combined the best of two worlds: it was emotive and it was also realistic – it could be done. Yet it was not followed up in a practical way to any appreciable extent even during the long period of Conservative administration between 1951 and 1964. We were slow to practise what we preached. During those thirteen years of Conservative Government the proportion of owner-occupied dwellings did increase to 49 per cent but even so it was well below the totals in other English-speaking countries such as Australia, Canada, New Zealand and the US, where the proportion ranged between 62 and 70 per cent. During those years the number of council house tenants also grew rapidly, but that we did not advertise. We preferred not to admit to the huge misuse of public money and power that kept so many of our fellow citizens in thrall to local authorities, some five million families.

There was well documented evidence that most people would be happier as home owners than as Council tenants. Conservative Party literature stressed that 'home ownership gives people independence and buttresses a family's freedom'. It also made the important point that helping people to become home owners represented a bargain for the taxpayer, since the average subsidy on a newly built council house added up to more than four times the tax relief available on an average new mortgage. Thus the political, social and economic arguments in favour of selling council houses to sitting tenants were overwhelming, but it was not until 1957, the year I started Unicorn, that a tentative start was made by the Conservative Government to encourage council house sales. Under the Housing Act of 1957 local authorities were given the power to sell council houses. A number of Conservative-controlled councils took prompt advantage of this, but even so the results were unimpressive. By 1964 only 25,000 houses had been sold to tenants by local authorities, out of a stock of some five million.

Thus the story was one of small steps forward by Conservatives, large steps backward under Labour until under Margaret Thatcher's leadership the Conservative Party came out wholeheartedly in favour of the sale of council houses to sitting tenants who wished to purchase them. The election manifesto of 1979, which, as I have said, I had a hand in drafting, stated: 'In the first session of the next Parliament, we shall . . . give council and new town tenants the legal right to buy their homes.'

The promise was kept. Under the 1980 Housing Act the majority of public sector tenants were given the right to purchase the homes they lived in at a discount which rose with the total length of time they had been tenants and could be as high as 50 per cent. They were also given the right to a mortgage from their local authority landlord.

That Act brought about a major transformation in housing tenure. As a Department of the Environment report of 1988 stated, 'In less than ten years over one million public sector houses have been sold of which nearly three quarters were right to buy sales to sitting tenants.'

The Labour Party lagged far behind popular thinking. In the general election of 1983 it was fighting a rearguard action against the sale of council houses, with threats to take away a tenant's right to buy his council house, to prevent Councils selling (even voluntarily) at a discount and to force any former tenant who wanted to sell his house to sell it back to the Council. Labour paid the price for this backwardness. As I noted earlier, the popularity of council house sales was an important factor in the Party's defeat in the 1983 and 1987 general elections.

The advance in house prices and house values over the years since I was first elected MP for Taunton had been striking. In the year of my election, 1956, the average price of a new house was £2,280. By 1985 it had risen to £37,000. Inflation must be taken into account and so must the increase in wages and salaries over the years; even so, the rise in house prices in real terms was huge. People who had borrowed money from building societies and other lenders to buy their own homes had seen their value grow, and of course that was particularly true of those who had bought them from their local councils at a discount. They were the subject of envious gossip among their neighbours who were still tenants on the council estates. The newly purchased ex-council houses stood out clearly. Walking down a road which ran through a council estate in any town in England, the houses with the new front doors and the double glazing were immediately noticeable, obvious signs of ownership and of pride in possession, a daily reminder to neighbouring rent-paying tenants that the house purchasers had been more prudent and successful than they had been.

Nonetheless, by 1989 the volume of council house sales was declining. My own constituency experience even before this time was that a substantial deterrent was the tenants' lack of financial sophistication. Many simply did not know how to set about making a purchase: they found the formalities and procedures a huge difficulty. Problem areas included dealing with the local authority over the initial application to purchase, arranging a survey and a mortgage, and obtaining legal representation and advice. Many potential purchasers just gave up. I was not alone in reflecting that if all the responsibilities involved in house purchase were undertaken by a single body on behalf of the tenant, many more families would be encouraged to go through the process.

I became directly involved when, early in 1988, I was asked to become a non-executive director of a newly formed company called Homes Assured Corporation. The idea behind HAC, which had started trading when I joined it, was that it would take on responsibility on behalf of council tenants who wanted to buy their homes from local authorities. It would provide them with finance through building societies, negotiate the necessary life insurance cover, commission property surveys, and last but not least, arrange conveyancing at lower than market rates. If a tenant wished, as many did, HAC would also arrange finance for home improvements.

The idea was excellent. It was a one-stop operation. The intending council house purchaser found it highly convenient and efficient to deal with the representative of a single company rather than with a number of different and – to many tenants – intimidating and sometimes supercilious bodies. It is not easy for anyone to get time off work to attend meetings and negotiate with half a dozen different representatives of various authorities, firms and institutions at different times, on different days. HAC took over negotiations with local authorities, which were often a protracted affair – and not only with dogmatic left-wing councils. Some Conservative councils were no less obstructive as the number of council tenancies fell and councillors saw their empires disappearing. Resentment led to obstruction, and sometimes it could take as long as six months for councils to do their paperwork.

HAC was established under excellent auspices. The Chairman had enjoyed a most successful career, ending as General Manager and a director of the Commercial Union, one of Britain's largest insurance companies. HAC's Finance Director was the former Finance Director of British Telecom. Its auditors and solicitors were leading firms. Its original shareholders included a leading financial institution, the Bank of Boston in partnership with others, which carried out a painstaking due-diligence investigation of the company, its financial projections and its personnel before advancing some £500,000 as an initial investment. Other financial institutions flocked to offer support, including building societies and insurance companies. The prospects for success seemed excellent, and HAC did have some success. During its short lifespan it dealt with thousands of applications. Not all resulted in sales but the company did help around 1,500 tenants to purchase their properties.

Increasingly, as time went on, conditions became more difficult. Long delays on the part of many councils in processing applications to buy houses led to much frustration and unnecessary expense. General economic circumstances, too, often made difficulties for intending house purchasers. Interest rates increased from the 8 per cent ruling when HAC started to 14 per cent. As the economy slowed down, personal incomes fell: there was less overtime working. Unemployment was increasing. These factors, but chiefly the delays on the part of the councils, led to many understandable cancellations of undertakings to purchase.

Buying a house is the biggest financial undertaking in the lives of most families and it has to mean careful financial calculation. Most family budgets allow little to spare after essentials are provided for, especially in families with growing children. A few extra pounds a week to pay out unexpectedly and the household budget is thrown completely out of kilter: what originally looked like an affordable cost soon goes beyond the family's capability. At that point the potential capital gain from buying a house at a substantial discount goes to the back of an intending purchaser's mind: what counts is the immediate question of how many quid a week it is going to cost now.

All of this inevitably affected HAC's position. The large number of cancellations by people who had applied to buy their houses but felt unable to go through with the purchase was particularly costly. The insurance companies with which HAC was working did not supply the company with up to date and accurate statistics for cancellations. For that reason the full time executives in HAC continued to give the Board forecasts of profitable trading. Like any non-executive director of any company I did not have responsibility for day-to-day management; my chief function was to give the Board political and general guidance. That I did in many ways. I helped to organise the original funding for the company and I met and negotiated with these and other funders from time to time. I introduced the company to headhunters which led to the appointment of its full time Managing Director. While the Housing Bill of 1988 was passing through Parliament, I represented HAC in an interview with the Housing Minister. We discussed evidence that HAC had given the Minister about the delays to which certain local authorities had subjected potential house-buyers in processing their right-to-buy applications; as a result, the law was tightened up. In short, I carried out the usual functions of a non-executive director in what I hoped was a constructive way; but I always made it clear that my responsibilities as Chairman of Lonrho would preclude me from playing any part in the management of HAC. As a non-executive director I worked for HAC at arm's length, and knew no more about the details of the company's affairs than what the full-time directors told me.

By the spring of 1989 it seemed to me that I had done what I set out to do, which was to help the company in its initial stages and to set it on its course. I was going to be heavily involved in Lonrho's contempt case in the House of Lords and would have little time for anything else. I told the Chairman of HAC that I wanted to resign my directorship. He begged me to stay – 'We'd like to feel we can still call on your advice' – and somewhat reluctantly I agreed. That loyalty was to prove a huge and costly mistake.

HAC, I now know, was going through a testing time, but the full-time, qualified executives of the company were confident that it would soon be a highly profitable company. At times like that what matters is to have the company's backers stand by it, giving it the credit it needs in the short run in the expectation that in the long run they will profit. Throughout the time that I was a director this was true of HAC. It was being supported financially by its shareholders who put a total of £2 million into the company, and by its bankers who allowed it an overdraft of £250,000. The Legal and General insurance company, with which HAC was in partnership, and another insurance company too, also advanced hundreds of thousands of pounds for HAC's use in promoting its business. All these were sophisticated, experienced and careful people. They had all done their detailed examinations of HAC's affairs and prospects. In addition to all this there were consistent reports to the Board of additional finance being offered by other leading financial institutions.

So confident of HAC's potential for profitability was the company's chief financial backer, a chartered accountant and experienced businessman, that following a financial report on HAC by a finance committee consisting of another two chartered accountants and a well qualified banker he offered to buy out the majority shareholder for £1.6 million. The offer was refused, no doubt because the majority shareholder thought it was lower than the value he could achieve for his shares in due course.

Financial support for HAC was still in place from its bankers, the insurance company with which it was effectively in partnership and from its minority shareholder, and the shareholders had continuously said that it would be continued, when I notified the Chairman in July 1989 that despite his earlier plea I would now resign as a director. Some weeks later, in late August, despite their pledges, the shareholders refused further funding. Barring a rescue scheme the company was bound to go into liquidation.

That, I thought rather sadly, was the end of that. I was wrong. In August 1991, two years after the Company's failure, I was told, without prior warning, that the Official Receiver was bringing a civil action to disqualify me from acting as a director of companies, mainly on the grounds that I knew, or should have known, that HAC was insolvent. At no time in the previous two years had any criticisms been put to me by the authorities. My solicitors at once asked to be given particulars of any complaints against me. The Treasury solicitor, acting for the Official Receiver, refused in writing to do this. My solicitors asked for a meeting. This too was refused.

On learning that the Official Receiver was to proceed against me I resigned my Chairmanship of Lonrho, a position I had held for eight

265

years. Clearly I could not continue to head one of Britain's largest companies, often negotiating with Ministers, Heads of State and the most senior representatives of some of the world's most important corporations, while the proceedings lasted. It was effectively the end of my business career. I was advised by my solicitors that the ongoing cost of defending the action against me would be at least £300,000. That was a substantial underestimate. In March 1992 the solicitors concerned bankrupted me since I was unable to pay the fees that they had so far demanded. Ironically, I remain a creditor of HAC.

I suppose some people would say that this is a private calamity and I should endure it in a proper British fashion without making a fuss in public. (Never complain, never explain.) They would be wrong. Apart from its devastating effect on me personally the affair raises general issues that are of considerable public importance. They fall under three headings: the role of non-executive directors, the judgement of the authorities in instigating prosecutions, and the justice or injustice of the process of enquiry.

There is a considerable drive to recruit non-executive directors to the boards of prominent British companies. An organisation for this purpose has been established, supported by the Bank of England, the clearing and merchant banks among others – all the great and the good. As a result of my experience I am firmly of the view that anyone who is or has been prominent in public life, an MP for example, would be unwise indeed to accept an appointment as a non-executive director even of the most attractive and apparently responsible companies, as Polly Peck or BCCI or Barings were once held up to be.

In real life, whatever may be the official view of a non-executive director's responsibility, he inevitably relies on the executive directors and senior management to present him with an accurate picture of the company's affairs. It is simply not practicable for him to investigate them in detail for himself – that would take far more time than he can give. He is usually invited to join a company, as I was, for the sake of his knowledge of the wider world and his contacts in it. This means that he is likely to be engaged in a number of other matters: he will be a busy man, and that 'busy-ness' is a large part of his usefulness to the company. A sensible law would recognise this fact and discriminate between the areas a non-executive director can be held responsible for and those that must rest on his executive colleagues. Our law is not sensible. It makes no such differentiation, so that if executive directors make mistakes or fail to supply a non-executive director with full and

266

accurate information he is still held accountable and is as guilty in law as they may be.

The public importance of this lies not only in the injustices that can be done to individuals, although it is true that if my case becomes a precedent and is generally followed hundreds if not thousands of non-executive directors of companies that fail could face proceedings for disqualification. The law as it stands is already leading to able people refusing to serve as non-executive directors for fear that executive directors might commit acts or omissions of which they were unaware, and could not possibly be aware, but for which they could be held fully responsible. Inevitably the courts will construe the law strictly, as is their duty. I can only say, on the basis of the civil proceedings brought against me in the HAC case, that every director of every company in Britain which is making trading losses but which is being supported financially from time to time by its bankers and its shareholders is at risk of disqualification action – and that must apply, I am sure, to most of the companies owning teams in the Football League. The situation is absurd; but that is the law. The law needs review.

As to the second question, the judgement of the authorities in deciding who and who not to pursue in disqualification actions – well, judgement is hardly the word. Their frequent capriciousness has become a recurring scandal. When HAC went into liquidation three people had criminal charges levied against them for fraudulent trading. Two of them, the Managing Director and a man who had served for only one month as Finance Director, were acquitted on these charges, the latter on appeal. The case of the third man merits a Zola to plead his cause. He was the founder of the company but was not a director at the material time contained in the indictment. During his trial it was accepted by the Crown that he ceased to be a director whilst the company was still believed to be solvent. The proceedings were bizarre: every obstacle was put in the way of the defence, including the withdrawal of legal aid. His only remedy now will be at the option of the European Commission for Human Rights. The implications of the decision in his case are extremely serious: his conviction rests on the fact that he had admitted responsibility for raising finance for the company. On this basis any merchant banker arranging financing for a company, if he eventually fails, may be liable for a prison sentence.

The evidence on which the Official Receiver is relying in the civil disqualification against me is the same as that produced in the criminal trial – in which I was in no way involved. The criminal proceedings marked the first time that this evidence had been tried in cross-examination and it was – largely – found wanting. If the full-time Managing Director was acquitted of the charge of allowing the company to trade while insolvent I find it hard to see how I – a non-executive director – could be found culpable on the same evidence.

The civil proceedings seeking a disqualification order against others and myself indicated an extraordinary capriciousness on the part of the Official Receiver. As a sometime non-executive director of HAC who was not a director when the company crashed I face a disqualification action: the Chairman of the company, who was its Chairman from its inception to its demise, was not proceeded against. Nor was the chartered accountant who was the full-time Finance Director until a month before it went into liquidation. Nor, most significant of all, has the Official Receiver proceeded against HAC's controller, the chartered accountant and experienced businessman who was backing HAC financially and had promised continuing finance, to whom the Managing Director and Finance Director reported and under whose direction they were accustomed to act; indeed, who was so much in charge of the company that he even signed cheques to pay its bills. Why not, one must ask?

Despite my repeated requests I have not been offered any explanation of this curious pattern of charges. How, one wonders, do the authorities decide which directors, and particularly which non-executive directors, to proceed against? What are the criteria?

The Comptroller and Auditor General published a report into the Insolvency Service in late 1993. This states:

> Since the introduction of the [Company Directors Disqualification] Act [in 1986] there have been around 153,000 corporate insolvencies in Great Britain. Elements of unfit conduct by directors have been identified to the Agency in around 28,000. By 31 March 1993, some 2,900 applications for disqualification have been made of which 1,700 have resulted in disqualification orders.

At the very best therefore this is a success rate of only some 6 per cent. It follows that the Directors Disqualification Act is not giving the public the protection which Parliament intended. The C & AG's report goes on to say:

> There are large variations between Official Receiver offices in the recording of unfit conduct, the selection and pursuit of cases, and the

time taken to deal with them. These variations might suggest that, nationally, not all cases of director unfit conduct are being processed and selected for court proceedings on a consistent basis.

The case of HAC exactly bears out this statement, and looking at the operation of the Directors Disqualification Act in general, it is manifest that it is being applied in a thoroughly haphazard fashion. There are a number of cases of people prominent in public and commercial life who have been non-executive directors of companies that have experienced financial difficulties or even failed but against whom the Official Receiver has not proceeded: notable examples are those concerned in Polly Peck, Queen's Moat, British and Commonwealth, BCCI and Blue Arrow.

The case of Polly Peck International is a particular scandal. In nine years the company achieved a market capitalisation of £1.5 billion: in 1990 its share price peaked at 462p, a staggering increase on the price per share of 9p at which Asil Nadir took control of it a decade earlier. Within six months the Stock Exchange quotation was suspended and the shares were apparently valueless. Nadir, its Chairman, seems for the time being to have escaped justice by fleeing to Northern Cyprus while on charges of theft and false accounting after his company collapsed with debts of over £1 billion. The non-executive directors of Polly Peck, under whose noses, it is alleged by the authorities, fraud and deception took place on a massive scale are apparently not to be proceeded against. Why not?

Inconsistencies also abound in the treatment by the authorities of fraud cases. One example will suffice. It is incomprehensible that after being convicted in a fraud involving no less than £34 million Mr Levitt escapes with a trivial penalty of one hundred and eighty days community service. As I write these words there is a man in Ford open prison who, I am told, sold his business to Mr Levitt and was never paid: waiting for payment he helped himself to his clients' funds. This of course he should not have done, but it is a sad irony that the penalty he deservedly paid should have been so much heavier than that paid by the man whose victim he was and whose massively greater fraud drove him to commit his crime.

LAUTRO, at the time the regulator for life insurance, unit trust companies and friendly societies, levied fines on companies that broke its rules. It had to fine some of the best known names in the City of London: examples picked at random from a long list include the Commercial Union, Legal and General, Scottish Widows, J. Rothschild Assurance and Norwich Union. The breaches included such complaints as inadequate monitoring and control of sales forces and issuing misleading advertisements. In 1993 these fines totalled £840,000, and in 1994 £1.8 million. The fact of their being levied on established companies handling huge amounts of money, mostly subscribed by members of the public in comparatively small amounts, indicates corporate carelessness on a grand scale. So far as I am aware not a single director of any of these companies has paid a penny piece towards these fines out of his own pocket: none has been held personally culpable by the authorities. Why not?

Now even the mighty Prudential, which was such a fairweather friend to Keysers during my chairmanship, is under investigation for its pension-selling practices, the subject of complaint by a large trade union. The Prudential is only one of many companies in the industry setting aside sums to pay possible compensation. Yet none of the Prudential's directors is held to be culpable.

The mis-selling of pensions by the life insurance industry represents a scandal on a massive scale. It is said that life officers will have to examine at least 350,000 cases to identify people who were wrongly advised to opt out of company and occupational pension schemes and to transfer into personal pension plans. Nearly one million more cases could demand a similar review from their pension provider. *The Times* has estimated that the pensions industry faces a bill in compensation and costs that could top £3 billion. No wonder that the Chief Executive of the Personal Investment Authority, the regulator responsible for policing firms that sell investments direct to the public, says: 'There is potentially a big problem here.' That seems like an understatement.

From HAC's history and other contemporary cases, as well as from the C & AG's report, it is clear that the system designed by Parliament to protect the public against misfeasance by a minority of company directors is largely failing to do so. The capricious application of the law requires review by Ministers.

The third issue raised by HAC's treatment is the justice or injustice of the process of enquiry. There are now too many cases where individuals have been judged culpable after secret enquiries, then publicly denounced by statements to the media and their lives broken in consequence – without having been given the chance to defend themselves.

It is the most basic principle of justice that the accused should be told what he is accused of, precisely and in detail, and that he should be allowed to confront his accusers over the charge. If you are the subject of an enquiry by the Official Receiver or various other Government bodies that principle can be completely ignored. My own case was regrettably typical. I was obliged to attend the Official Receiver's office twice, for two hours on each occasion. I was required to answer prepared questions about HAC, my answers being laboriously recorded in longhand. Evidence was collected from other witnesses in secret proceedings and was then publicised by the Official Receiver. I was not allowed to confront or cross-examine any of them or even to know who they were. Their evidence was therefore not tested in any way: it was of a kind that would probably not be admissible in a court of law but on the strength of it the Assistant Official Receiver prepared his report which forms the civil case against me to disqualify me from acting as a director in future.

The decision to bring the case and the initial proceedings attracted massive publicity. Thus my reputation, such as it is, was sullied. The cardinal principle of English law, the presumption of innocence, was violated. The mere notice of proceedings has effectively prevented me from earning my living since it was issued in August 1991, because it is impossible to act as a director of important companies in the context of an allegation by Government of unfitness to do so. It ruined me. I have had no opportunity to challenge those who framed the proposal, nor to defend myself before a court of law. The procedure is patently unfair and oppressive.

If I had been brought before a court and had been facing a small fine, the court, by process of law, would have pronounced me guilty or not guilty, and if guilty I would have paid up. But I do not face a court, and my fine has already been paid. I have lost everything I possessed. The Official Receiver made quite sure that I lost my reputation by publishing his findings to the world with massive publicity. I was the target of many hurtful and damaging reports in the press: people who knew nothing else about me thought they knew I must have done something shady to be attacked in that way. In a court of law I could have cleared my name, but even now, years later, I am still without access to a court and to the chance to recover my reputation. I have been told that the civil case against me is unlikely to be heard until January 1996, some four and a half years after I was given notice of the proceedings and some six and a half years after the failure of the company.

Prima facie the situation is a breach of Article 6 of the European Commission on Human Rights which provides: 'In the determination of his civil rights and obligations . . . everyone is entitled to a . . . hearing within a reasonable time.' What is a reasonable time? Is it a year, two years, three? Perhaps it is easier to say what is an unreasonable time. In my view six and a half years is wholly unreasonable. In all my life I have never anticipated that British legal procedures would be inferior to any other. Now it seems, ironically, that although an opponent of European Union I may get a fairer and prompter hearing from the European Commission than I have had from my own compatriots. I deeply regret that. No wonder there is pressure from leading members of the English judiciary to write into English law the safeguards which the European Commission regards as normal: there has been a plethora of cases where the European Court of Justice has found our processes open to serious criticism, an unacceptable, shaming situation.

If the proceedings against me have been protracted and unjust they have also been ludicrously extravagant. The cost to the taxpayer of the HAC case so far is estimated at some £10 million, and there will be further heavy costs to come. Similar extravagance has characterised many other cases. The public is usually flabbergasted when it learns how much has been spent on prosecuting an alleged fraud, often unsuccessfully. Parliament needs to look hard at the methods now being used to see if they really offer anything like value for money, and there is one very obvious possibility of abuse which ought to be investigated. To a layman it appears that in many instances accountants and lawyers alike have a vested interest in perpetuating expenditure on a massive scale without an equal benefit to the public.

Moreover, the rules of procedure in criminal cases, whilst effective in normal criminal trials, are usually wholly unsuited to trials involving commercial and corporate fraud. Such cases are massively expensive and a whole new procedure is needed for testing the evidence in them. Incredibly, it was announced in March 1995 that a criminal trial of several defendants in Newport involving some millions of pounds in an alleged mortgage fraud would be abandoned because the case was too complicated to be understood by a jury – this after immense expenditure including, it is said, over £100,000 to construct a new court room to accommodate the proceedings. Either the system is at fault or the prosecuting authorities deserve censure for not having presented a more comprehensible case, perhaps both.

As Chairman of the Public Accounts Committee at the time when the concept of value for money was developed in the process of public audit, I now urgently recommend Ministers and Parliament to investigate the undoubted and substantial scope for effecting large savings of public money in this field. In the context of the many failures to sustain a successful prosecution – witness the collapse of the second Guinness trial, the failure of the year-long Blue Arrow fraud trial and the farcically lenient sentence on Mr Levitt – a thoroughgoing review of the effectiveness of such bodies as the Serious Fraud Office and the Crown Prosecution Service is essential.

Faulty procedures, unjustified expense and poor discrimination are serious enough matters, but in my own case I suspect a still more serious failing. I have naturally pondered long and hard on why I was picked out and proceeded against when others, more directly responsible for HAC's affairs, were not. I have been reluctant to draw the obvious conclusion. The way in which some in the Lord Chancellor's department appeared to regard the criminal proceedings was demonstrated when the Parliamentary Secretary to the Lord Chancellor's department, John Taylor MP, entered the court one day while the trial proceeded. 'Is this the du Cann trial?' he asked the QC acting for one of the defendants. The language used seemed to confirm clearly enough the way in which the trial was regarded. I was not in the dock, not even in the witness box, but I was the focus of their attention.

We like to think we have a scrupulous and unbiased civil service which will always act in the public interest and it is always painful when facts emerge to shake that faith, as a number have done recently. My own faith was shaken to the point of destruction by my experience in the Lonrho/Fayed affair. In that, not just politicians but civil servants, too, acted to protect their own positions and to cover their own mistakes, and they gave that process a higher priority than the pursuit of the public good. I greatly offended some of them by obstinately persisting in the struggle to get justice for Lonrho, dragging their discreetly concealed blunders out into the crude light of day. I made myself particularly unpopular in the Department of Trade and Industry, of which the Official Receiver's department is a part, and I return to Donald Trelford's prescient warning about what was likely to come of that. For a long time I attempted to persuade myself that such things had nothing to do with the decision to single me out in the HAC case, but I have given up that attempt. The facts seem to me too strong.

At any rate, it is on the evidence of those facts that I am ready to be judged.

and NOW . . . ?

'Histories,' wrote Francis Bacon, 'make men wise.'

Whether my own history has made me wise is something best left to others to decide upon, but certainly my two lives have given me many opportunities to observe the workings of men and institutions, and to draw lessons therefrom.

In the light of that experience I look to the future with a mixture of hope and concern, alas with more of the latter; and yet, given the right policies, there should be every reason for hope. The lessons I have learnt find me convinced on two counts.

The first is that our times are critical. The decisions made for Britain now will have profound effects for many years to come. They must be the right decisions. We must beat a path to both Houses of Parliament that will attract our most able people. Everyone knows that we are failing to do so. This failure is inexcusable: the fault is our own. We need, therefore, to involve more people in the democratic process.

The second is that we are not helpless. Despite the current national mood of disillusionment, we need not be reduced to puppets at the mercy of forces beyond our control. Karl Marx observed that men do make their own histories, but not out of the whole cloth. That is a fair statement of Britain's position today. We work within severe constraints but we have enough room for manoeuvre to choose between a disappointing future and a fulfilling one. A better future is within our reach. It is up to us.

When, many years ago now, Dean Acheson made his famous remark that Britain had lost an empire but not yet found a role, the anger he aroused was all the greater because what he said was true. It remains true today.

Not only has our country's influence in world affairs diminished but our economic performance overall since the War has been profoundly disappointing: in consequence our people are less well off than many of our competitors. Out of more than two hundred countries measured by GNP per head we are only twentieth: ten European countries enjoy a standard of living higher than does Britain. This too is inexcusable.

It is time we found – or rather made – an international role for ourselves. What should it be?

Britain's unique strength is that we are a part of Europe, but not only that. Our imperial past may now be well behind us yet the Commonwealth remains a valuable association of free peoples with traditions and standards held in common with us. World-wide links of trade and goodwill are still there. We should revive and strengthen them, building on the work of men like Tiny Rowland and remembering that trade on fair terms is among the greatest benefits we can bring to developing countries.

Europe has no monopoly of economic prosperity: indeed, as many of us who refused to support Britain's signature to the Treaty of Rome foresaw, there are many other areas in the world such as the Far East and South America where developing standards of life are easily eclipsing our own growth rates and which offer us vast potential markets. There are other areas such as Africa and Russia which will do so. The prospect is an exciting one, in contrast to the boredom, if not resentment, which is the dominant emotion most British people feel towards our European partnership. Britain's aim must be to maximise development of the Community as a trading bloc, leaving individual members free to negotiate their own trading arrangements with countries outside the Community. Britain's oyster should be the world; the Common Market a springboard, not a restrictive prison.

Nevertheless, however much we develop our contacts in the wider world outside Europe, we still have to make something of our position within the European Union. Unless we are prepared to leave it – and I do not know many people who now think that is a possibility – then we must find a constructive role within it. It seems to me quite possible to do so, incidentally in a way which would put an end to the quarrels on this issue among Conservatives which divide the Party and have gone a long way towards destroying its electoral changes.

We should acknowledge publicly that there are some decisions that need not be taken. There is no immediate prospect of a European super-state – I hope there never will be. The European Union is a long way from becoming a single political entity. Its failure to exercise even the least constructive influence for peace in the appalling conflict in Yugoslavia is an instance of its political impotence and lack of cohesion: that situation will not change for a long time to come. Nor do we need to tear ourselves apart over the issue of a single European currency. It will be some years before the conditions for it exist. When the time comes we shall have to reach a decision. Our immediate strategy should be to increase the number of members of the Community. As the classicists say: 'tot homines quot sententiae.' More agricultural nations at the EU's negotiating table must mean the death of the CAP as presently constituted. The more voices at the table the better the prospect, too, of leading the Community away from federalism and towards our ideal of a free trade area – and the better our chance of associating our own country independently with areas of the world where political and economic influence can be enhanced. Meanwhile there are practical matters in Europe that need our immediate attention.

The abuses that are becoming entrenched in Europe are in many ways similar to those we face in Britain. They raise the common question, Who rules the rulers? Europe groans under the dictate of an over-mighty executive, which exercises power through an inadequately controlled bureaucracy. In theory the principle of 'subsidiarity' means that centralised power should be confined to what is necessary. In practice the Maastricht Treaty is hopelessly vague as to what is strictly necessary. Inevitably, in the absence of guidelines or instructions, the centralising authorities will define the extent of their own powers. They are continuously seeking the widest direction: all the pressures, not least in the European Parliament, are for greater authority, secrecy for the decision-making process and less accountability.

The constitution of the United States of America clearly sets out the boundaries between State and Federal power. Before Europe steps further towards integration it urgently needs to work out a similar constitutional framework, reserving maximum authority for national Parliaments.

Most people are well aware of the excessive power of European institutions when it impinges on them in small but irritating ways. They do not know whether to laugh or cry when Brussels dictates the shape and size of the vegetables we shall be allowed to eat. They are angry when small businesses are forced to close by so-called health and safety regulations whose real value in terms of anyone's health is questionable. And they are right to feel that such things are symptoms of a growing non-accountable power which ought to be checked.

Control of the purse is fundamental. Fraud and corruption in Europe, involving billions of pounds, are an open scandal. The Common Agricultural Policy is costing every family in Britain well over £1,000 a year for doubtful advantage to the UK consumer – or farmer. Payments by the British Exchequer to the European Union are on a sharply rising curve, and by 1996/97 the gross payments after taking into account the rebate negotiated by Margaret Thatcher at Fontainebleau in 1984 will be no less than £8 billion. We surely need a public debate on why it is that Britain, with one of the lowest standards of living in the EU, should still be one of the largest net contributors to EU finances – second only to Germany.

The British Parliament has every right to insist on strict criteria for Community spending, and British MPs in our British Parliament must do so. One billion pounds saved out of the UK's contribution to Brussels would be enough to give every British OAP, myself included, another two pounds a week. Extravagance in Brussels has become the norm. Eurocrats are paid far higher salaries than British civil servants. Currently every Commission employee costs £150,000 a year in administration costs. The European Parliament rents five buildings in Strasbourg, five in Luxembourg and seven in Brussels. The cost is £47 million per annum. Yet another building is under construction in Strasbourg. The total costs of the Parliament are over £550 million a year, almost £1 million a year for each MEP, more than three times the cost of a British MP.

Extravagance and fraud are both controllable. All it takes is the will to control them. When I was Chairman of the Select Committee on Public Accounts I strongly recommended on more than one occasion to Harold Wilson, then Prime Minister, that the Court of Auditors in the EU should operate on the lines of the PAC in the House of Commons. He agreed. He was a strong supporter of the PAC of which he had been Chairman before me. Nothing was done. I made the same recommendation to Margaret Thatcher when she became Prime Minister. Still nothing has been done.

In short, in Europe as in Britain, we should give our rulers the powers and the money they need to carry out efficiently and economically the tasks with which we entrust them – and no more. And in Europe we should put Britain, our country and the interests of our people first.

If our own country is passing through a difficult time, so most certainly is the Conservative Party. Some of our problems are temporary, the result of the recession from which we are now emerging; for example the problem of negative equity which traps many people in homes that are worth less than the outstanding mortgages on them. Other problems arise from the deep structural changes taking place in our society. Perhaps the most important of these is the widespread insecurity caused by the transition from a time when having a job for life was a normal pattern to a time when young people know that they may well have to change jobs several times and when more and more workers in full-time jobs are being replaced by part-timers. Paternalism in business is dead. The fear of redundancy and unemployment is spreading even among middle and working class people who previously thought themselves comfortably secure.

However much Conservatives rely upon the market to resolve economic problems there are a vast number of significant issues that have to be addressed politically. The structure of the benefit system, priorities in Government spending, the provision of training, the reform of the nation's schools which continue to send a horrifying number of young people out into the world illiterate and innumerate, the effectiveness or otherwise of shareholder democracy, the growing economic power of institutional investors, the structure of Parliament and its effectiveness, the scope of local democracy, the relationship between central and local Government – the list is endless and all these are matters that should be the subject of a ferment of debate such as took place in the Conservative Party in the sixties and seventies. How much is the Party encouraging that debate, at the grassroots of the Party, in the institutions and academic circles, at every point where new ideas might spring up or a consensus develop? Very little, I fear. Ministers seem now to be permanently on the defensive against many vociferous lobbies which are quick to exploit public sympathy while the Government's policies, often constructive and sensible, go largely unexplained and uncomprehended. Why has Government handed news management over to its opponents? Why is it not seen to be working with the grain of informed opinion?

Crime is another area in which the Party is increasingly challenged. It is unsurprising that people are deeply concerned about crime. In my lifetime the number of murders a year has doubled. That single statistic is fearful enough. The figures for the recorded increases in lesser offences are horrendous: woundings have increased from under 1,500 a year to over 170,000; robberies from some 200 to 36,000; burglaries from under 10,000 to over 500,000; rapes from 130 to 3,400 and thefts from 110,000 to over 2¼ million.

Crime is, of course, a symptom of a deeper malaise. Happy and cohesive societies do not have high crime rates. John Major has proclaimed his intention of trying to forge a nation at ease with itself and that is a noble aim, but again we need a creative debate on how it is to be achieved. How do we make the problem families on run-down council estates feel themselves to be a part of society, with responsibilities, not alienated from it? How do we close what is now a growing gap between the poorest members of society and the average worker – let alone the very rich – without imposing restrictions that will stifle initiative and in the end make everyone less well off? Because they believed that would be the effect of the European Social Chapter the British Government rightly opted out of it. But what is to be the Conservative solution to the problems of low wages and bad conditions of work which still exist despite the undoubted improvements in output, productivity and efficiency that have taken place since 1979?

Rising prosperity, to which Conservative policies have contributed so much over the last sixteen years, the development of unit trusts, widespread share-ownership of privatised utilities and the move from council-owned to family-owned houses have done much to improve the lot of people in modest circumstances and to enable many to share in growing national prosperity. The task now is to extend the process to take in those who have not yet benefited from it.

Every responsible citizen in Britain today well knows so many of the problems which our nation faces. The chief reason, I am sure, why the Conservative Party has forfeited trust on such a wide scale, and especially among committed Conservatives, is that there are few who believe that there is any meaningful effort to think their problems through with a view to finding a solution to them. Reform of the Second Chamber is an obvious example: for sixteen years of Conservative administration the question has been shelved. Now Labour comes out with its own proposals. Imperfect they may be, but the Conservative Party, supposedly the constitutional party, still has nothing to say. No wonder its supporters are unhappy.

One obvious symptom of failing social cohesion can be seen in the decreasing respect that so many of our institutions command. This is true of Parliament, of the Church and (thanks largely to the irresponsibility shown by some of its minor members) of the Royal Family. It is certainly true of politicians and too often that is their own fault. Whether a Minister or an official ought to resign if it turns out that he has a mistress as well as a wife is something on which people of different views may disagree. There should be no possible disagreement that anyone found taking bribes (which is what accepting favours comes to) or being in any way subject to improper influence should be forced to resign instantly. A generation ago that would have been automatic. Now it is not. There have even been two instances in recent years of senior Ministers found by the courts to have broken the law by their actions as Ministers. Neither offered his resignation.

These are all problems that Governments of any political colour would have had to face. There are others that are more particularly the province of the Conservatives.

The Party needs to understand the difference between giving a clear lead and being dogmatic. It was the failure to do so in her last years that brought down Margaret Thatcher, and a slavish adherence to Thatcherite proposals now threatens both the Party's unity and its electoral chances. It was certainly necessary to privatise British Airways, British Telecom or water, to take three successful examples, but the logic of privatising the Post Office or breaking up the railways escapes even the Party's most committed adherence, chiefly, perhaps, through lack of explanation. The Party has a tradition of pragmatism, of having clear principles but interpreting them day by day in the light of events. It must shun dogma and recover that tradition.

By doing so it will make it easier to maintain the unity within the Party that is so obviously lacking at the moment. Some Cabinet Ministers promoting their view through the media give the impression that the Party is fundamentally divided about its aims. That is not true. Even on so contentious an issue as Europe there is a large area of common ground, quite enough, I believe, to make it possible to devise a programme of action – for example the one I outlined earlier – on which everyone could unite. But it has to be just that, a programme of *action*, responsive to events. The attempt to produce a rigid ideology is alien to the Conservative cast of mind and in the end it will always fail.

The change of style must start at the top. We must reverse the move towards a presidential style of premiership which was the bad side of Margaret Thatcher's strong leadership; and we must remember the disastrous results of Ted Heath's distancing himself not just from colleagues but still more from the ordinary members of the Party who work so loyally for it and on whom in the end its success depends. Somehow we must recover the sense, which my colleagues and I strove so hard to foster during my chairmanship of the Party, that everyone matters, that everyone is free to contribute ideas and that they will be listened to.

Along with that we must urgently set to work to restore our position in local government. It makes me sad to see that the commanding position we built up in the 1960s has been changed for one which, over large parts of our country, Scotland especially, Conservatives have been driven off the field. Once again it is a matter of being prepared to devolve power. Certainly Council tax payers must be protected against the excessive demands of some extravagant authorities, and probably we ought to rethink some of the functions and scope of local government (input from the grassroots would be useful here) but subject to that we must give more than reluctant support to local democracy. It is only when a Tory central Government is clearly seen to support the aspirations of local electorates that it can reasonably expect them to support it. Local government matters.

Another challenge to the Conservative Party is to improve the quality of the young men and women putting themselves forward as MPs. The attempt to do this by formalising the selection procedures has not been a success and the cry 'Where have all the good men gone?' articulates a feeling among the public that a significant number of young MPs are simply on the make. That must be corrected, while at the same time we must be careful not to discourage those who, like me, wanted to pursue legitimate careers in both politics and business. They, after all, are the ones who will be able to bridge the present gulf of misunderstanding between those two worlds. If the Conservative Party professes to believe in business and enterprise it should send more businessmen to Parliament. The discouragements for them may be many but their judgement and ideas are sorely needed. I hope that this account of my own experiences has made it clear what an important task that is.

My mind goes back to the time when I received the letter of invitation from so many of my colleagues in the House to stand as a candidate for the leadership. Nigel Fisher, its chief author, not himself a businessman, hearing that there might be something held against me in the City made careful enquiries at the Bank of England and elsewhere. Of course I got a good report. I should hope so. I did found the modern Unit Trust industry, and was attacked in the City and in the provinces for that; I did launch the first equity-linked life assurance contracts and was much attacked for that also; I was Chairman of Keyser Ullmann when it prospered and I was Chairman when it lost money and I was attacked for both; I became Chairman of Cannon Assurance, restored its fortunes and rescued it, and was proud to do so, and because I got stockholding control of it away from villains and into respectable hands I was criticised for the company I kept; I worked for Lonrho for twenty years and fought with pride for its interests and the interests of poor people in Africa and that certainly involved much criticism, mostly from people I have never had the pleasure of meeting and many more who know nothing about that splendid enterprise.

Well, I reflect, if you never do anything, if you live all your life in the grey area that knows neither victories nor defeats I suppose you never make an enemy, never excite a jealousy – and die miserably content. If, on the other hand, you want to tackle such an important task as bridging the gap between mutually hostile parts of our society, you may get various rewards, but they will not include an easy life. As a politician I admit to having been a member of the chattering classes; I am proud to say I have also been a member of the doing classes. God willing, I'll do more yet.

At the present time the Labour Party is making a strong bid to take over much of the Conservatives' traditional ground. After a struggle against the diehard activists of the Left it has finally agreed to change Clause 4 of its constitution, which committed the Party to an East European economy. Blair had no option but to follow Gaitskell's example: too many voters now have a vested interest in house ownership and share ownership (15 million house owners and their families in the first case, 10 million investors in the second) to tolerate an extension of municipalisation or nationalisation, especially as both stand largely discredited as methods of achieving industrial or commercial efficiency.

Blair is a politician in the Kennedy mould: find out what people want and give it to them. Never mind tradition or principle: the overriding aim is to get elected. Blair has achieved public credit as a reformer. The reality, which Conservatives have foolishly failed to expose, is that new look Labour is a phoney. One example will suffice: its attitude to corporate affairs. Labour still proposes to tamper with company boards, to allow trade union officials to dictate company policies. It intends to interfere with market forces by subjecting any change in company ownership to detailed scrutiny. It will tax short-term investments (though short-term is still undefined), thereby making it difficult for private investors to sell their shares. It says it will cap the dividends payable by companies in the utilities sector. Its taxation policies alone are fearsome: it will certainly raise taxes for business to produce an increase of almost 25 per cent in the current corporation tax yield and this, no doubt, will be in addition to a substantial increase in the citizen's higher personal tax rates, certainly to 50 per cent and perhaps to 60 per cent. None of this agenda is secret. Much of it would be unpopular with the electors if they could be brought to see clearly what it implied. It is the business of the Conservatives to make it known that they oppose these foolish intentions and that Labour proposals threatens the interests of ten million investors and their families.

The secret of political success is the careful and painstaking mobilisation of popular support. When the Conservatives were in opposition before 1979 I thought the Confederation of British Industry was lukewarm in its advocacy of business. With the full agreement of the Officers and Executive of the 1922 Committee we persuaded their leaders to adopt a more aggressive anti-Socialist and pro-business stance. This needs to be done again, in the context of Labour's anti-business proposals.

In the long-term, too, the City of London and the business community should unite to liaise with the schools and universities, as the medical profession does with the medical schools, to ensure that its needs and aspirations are better understood.

Let us be clear that the fight against Labour's proposals in the fields of business and taxation is not an attempt to cling to the past. It is part of a positive movement towards the aims that have always seemed to me important in my two lives. In business the challenge is to open up opportunities for ordinary people to participate in investment and to profit from the wealth-producing activities which it makes possible. In politics it is to allow ordinary electors, through their MPs, to scrutinise better and thereby to influence and to exercise a greater control over the actions of the Executive.

Both those aims are part of the more general strategy of creating a free and just society in which people are not subject to the power of a small elite, commercial or political. That strategy was in my mind when I first entered the House of Commons as an unfledged MP almost forty years ago. It still seems to me pre-eminently worth fighting for, not least in Europe.

Perhaps my generation was fortunate in that in my lifetime our wider political objectives were always clear. Domestically, I entered politics to ensure that Socialism was defeated in Britain. The objective is largely achieved, though not wholly. Nationally we set out first to destroy the evil dictatorship of Hitler and his National Socialists. That we accomplished by dedication and sacrifice. Our country's example to the world, based on the resolution and courage of our people, was inspiring. That accomplished, we faced the challenge of what President Reagan called the Evil Empire, the attempt by Soviet Communism to achieve world domination. Again, by an alliance of free nations among which our country was prominent, and the resolution of our people, we prevailed. It is a triumph indeed that freedom has again been successfully defended and enhanced, and without conflict.

Now there is a new and clear challenge awaiting us in Britain: the restoration of confidence in our country's destiny, that our people may believe as I did when I was a young man that ours is still far and away the best country in the world in which to live and to bring up one's children. And if in any respect, small or large, it is not, then we have the duty to make it so, each and every one of us.

Here is a political objective to which the whole nation can aspire. Perhaps the chief responsibility will devolve upon the next generation, the contemporaries of my children. They will have more energy than their elders perhaps, but we have our particular duty, to advise and to encourage. Experience has hopefully given us some judgement: allied to the enthusiasm and idealism of the young there is the power to achieve great things.

There is too much complaining, especially in the media, too little in the way of individual effort to effect improvements. Cromwell's words are relevant, praising the 'plain russet coated captain that knows what he fights for and loves what he knows.'

There is so much to love; so much that through indifference or neglect we are in danger of losing. So much to do, so little time left, even to the youngest of us, in which to do it. Time is ever in short supply.

I reflect on my own Job's progress in recent years that has seen me lose my employment, my position, my property, my reputation – such as it was – and now, unbearably, my darling wife. I cannot say there is nothing of the past I would not change, nothing that I do not regret. But I am delighted to have had my two lives, I have hugely enjoyed them both. I have learned much too; and that they were complementary I have no doubt. It was sad that they led me into personal difficulty but I now look forward to a third life and here dedicate myself again in some small measure to the ambition of helping the people of these beloved British islands regain their confidence and their sense of destiny; something that is at least as important as any of the ideals and practical policies in which I have always believed and for which I fought hard in Parliament and in the boardroom. And, God willing, I always will.

288